SUCCESS THROUGH FAILING

FINDING OUR GREATEST GIFTS IN OUR DARKEST HOURS

———————

Stories by Wendy Bunnell
And 24 Transformative Women
Edited by Evelyn Jeffries

Printed in the U.S.A.

ISBN-13:978-0692817933 (Success through Failing)

Acknowledgements

I cannot finish this book without thanking those who were instrumental in its creation. I am grateful for a family that supports me, cheers me on, and is patient with my hummingbird tendencies in life. I want to thank my husband Dan for allowing me to create, knowing that curbing my creativity would be turning my spirit to the "off button."

Of course, I want to thank all twenty-four of the other authors. My heart is full of gratitude for each of them for being willing to divulge their tender moments in an effort to help thousands of others. I want to give a special thank you to Heidi Totten for helping me see a bigger picture outside of the book. Her mentorship was invaluable.

I want to give an incredibly big thank you to my editor Evelyn Jeffries of Elegant Editing LLC. She turned the thoughts and stories into a collection of art. Without her, this book would never have been realized. I also want to thank Leslie Householder for validating the book and seeing the importance of these stories.

Last, I want to thank all of my mentors, teachers, and cheerleaders. My journey has been paved by the knowledge and inspiration you have given me. I can't list them all for fear I will forget someone. If you read this paragraph and wonder if I am referring to you, the answer is yes.

My humblest thank you goes to my Savior and Heavenly Father. The vision and creation for this project was much greater than I. I was merely the one allowed to be the "instrument in His hands."

Foreword

Nothing makes you feel better about your difficult circumstances than when you can see them from a 10,000-foot view. This perspective can reveal hidden benefits and solutions, and even disclose profound meaning contained in the hardship. Even your gifts, opportunities, and blessings can remain concealed until you step back and see a much bigger picture.

As soon as you realize you've been looking at your life through a peephole, and discover the wealth of relationships, resources, and knowledge waiting for you on the other side, the door bursts open and you can finally begin to live your life with greater purpose, strength, and fulfillment.

Individuals who suffer with broken lives can heal, and most wonderfully, they can thrive. I dare say they even have the potential to thrive more gloriously than those who do not first endure such difficulty.

As you'll soon see, Wendy Bunnell has hit the nail on the head with this groundbreaking collection of narratives, *Success Through Failing*. A captivating read, this anthology of raw and real true-life stories from twenty-five brave women provides that very perspective. It shows you where you and your life's experiences fit in this world of pain and confusion, and inspires you to take your place, so you can ultimately discover and fulfill your own unique mission.

Sixteen years ago I experienced my first major breakthrough after enduring years of chronic failure; and there are few things more life-impacting than feeling the contrast between these two poles.

My husband and I had suffered through setback after setback, disappointment after disappointment, practically to the point of wondering what was going to hit us next. Not only have we been targets of thieves and victims of fraud, but we also experienced multiple job losses, significant medical crises, car accidents, late notices, overdraft fees, and of course, more debt than we could handle. We just couldn't get in front of it.

A run of misfortune such as ours makes a person wonder if that's just the way life is supposed to be.

In our attempt to solve the problem, at one point we held multiple jobs, attended school, and tried to build a business, all while raising our young family in a tiny basement apartment. I remember being thrilled to find leftover food in trash bins at office complexes where we performed midnight janitorial services. We drove a 1969 Volkswagen Beetle in the 1990s (before it was cool), and for a time we slept on a box spring without a mattress. We reluctantly received government assistance during my pregnancies, but never let go of the belief that there had to be a way for us to support ourselves.

We just wondered why we seemed to be the only people we knew who had to fight every day just to survive.

In our longing for a way out, we searched for a shortcut or windfall, which would balance out the injustice in one fell swoop, and finally make us equal to those who lived above our version of dysfunction.

Our search led us to various mentors, books, and more than one hundred seminars. At one point, we flew across the country for training (on credit) with a can of corn in our backpack and a plan to sleep in the rental car all weekend. Unfortunately, when we got there, our credit card had no room left for the rental.

Our relationship was strained, our self-confidence waned, and our belief in better times ahead required regular resuscitation.

One thought kept us going though. It was the idea that *by our thoughts we could change our lives.*

After all, that's where everything begins. No building is ever built without first a thought. Nothing is ever said without first thinking of the words. No crime is ever committed and no glory is ever achieved without first the idea of it being planted between the ears. So if this was true, then surely there *had* to be some way of thinking that would put our lives onto a better path. Thus, our quest centered on studying people who were living happier, more successful lives, and how they thought.

And when the breakthrough finally came, I *had* to share what we learned, because it all *finally* made sense. It's what drove me to write three international best sellers and create experiences like *Genius Bootcamp* and the *Mindset Mastery™ Program* to bring others up to the 10,000-foot level. I wasn't looking for a career; I really just wanted to be a mom. But waking up showed me that I had something valuable to offer *because* of my hard experiences, and so do you.

This kind of awakening is the same reason the authors in this book came together to share *their* stories with you now. Pay attention to how they think. You'll find a common thread through each of their experiences: every single breakthrough occurred *after* a shift in their *thinking.* Watch for (and make note of) those subtle moments, as you read what is contained in the pages to follow.

I have tremendous respect for each of these women who faced and conquered insurmountable odds. These are remarkable women who were given some of the worst of the worst kinds of life challenges, and who somehow discovered within themselves that power, which likely would not have been uncovered in any other way.

The beautiful thing about this work is that it underscores and gives proof to the fact that *every one of us* has the same hidden spark, the same potential for greatness, the same access to unseen power that stands ready and eager to assist us, as soon as we're ready to put it to use.

If you stop to think about it, there is no *feeling* without a change of state to some degree. Our skin doesn't feel warmth unless it understands cold. Our face does not feel wind unless it remembers the sensation of still air. We can't feel happiness until we've also experienced misery. There is no hope unless we've first felt despair. There is no joy without first sadness; and, as this work brilliantly illustrates, there can be no success without failure.

The truth is, no matter what you're facing, there is no need to despair. Once you see what these women have seen, once you feel what these women have felt, once you awaken to what these women will reveal through their stories, and once you pause to consider the possibilities that await you, too, you will already be on your way to a life that is more happy, rich, and fulfilling than perhaps you have ever known before.

Leslie Householder, author of *The Jackrabbit Factor, Hidden Treasures, and Portal to Genius*

Preface by Wendy Bunnell

The word "success" creates many emotions and reactions. It means different things to different people, but its ultimate realization is what drives us, what propels us forward and helps us create solutions that provide meaning and purpose in our lives.

I believe if you are reading this book that you are hoping to continue your progress, learning the mindset and skillset that will help you achieve your goals. You also know that sometimes you can get in your own way. While we all want success, many of us self-sabotage our efforts, thus limiting our success. Perhaps we have "fear of dying"—of falling flat on our faces. Some of us experience "fear of trying"—of taking that first step. Finally, there's "fear of flying"—that sudden rush of momentum and subsequent panic as we start to soar toward success.

My own fear was of losing stability and security. I had a "stable" job to help with paying bills, but I always had my toe dipped into the entrepreneurial pool. After an annual review, my supervisor said, "Wendy, we love that you are involved in creating so many programs, but it kind of drives us crazy, too." I made the decision in that moment that I wasn't going to stop creating because it might make another person feel a bit uncomfortable. Six months later, I put in my two-week notice. I felt free to create the life of my dreams. The first four months were complete bliss as I woke up to a position that excited me and challenged my strengths, surrounded by people who encouraged me to live my dream.

This desire would be tested the next two years, as we experienced my husband's job loss, an unplanned move, and financial problems that led to food stamps and church assistance. The business that had skyrocketed only a year before was diving and plunging at such a fast rate it made my head spin. When others would ask me how my business was doing, I didn't even know how to respond. I was in a business that required me to find leaders who shared my vision and wanted to create their own business. How could I ask anyone to join me when I couldn't even provide for my family?

I knew I was getting in my own way. Through years of personal development, I realized I was creating my own glass ceiling through feelings of scarcity and fear. Leslie Householder states, "Solutions are only an idea away." I was determined to find ideas that would create the life I was capable of having. I hired mentors and coaches to help me change my internal dialogue. My external world started to shift and change around me. It took a long time, but through these challenges I was pointed in the right direction to create massive success in both my business and my personal life. It happened only after the struggle, the epic fail, and learning lessons from these experiences. I recognize it was all part of the "refiner's fire." Many times I wanted to go back to my life of mediocrity. I am so grateful I decided to push through the hard times, the thorny path, because I am better and stronger than I would have been had the fear of failure and the fear of success won the battle.

In September of this year, I decided to step into a role that really scared me—creating this book. I pushed through my fear. I felt as though I was the "instrument in His hands" in putting this book project together. My "why" was so strong because I knew our Creator was helping me find the right message, the right women, and the solutions to any obstacle.

Can you imagine calling a woman who had written 16 books and asking her to "join you" in this project, knowing you had no experience at all in publishing? I decided my very inexperience would validate the principles of this book. I reached out to powerful, influential women who had been in the entrepreneurial world for years, proving themselves as leaders. As I spoke to each of them, I would lean on my Higher Power to give me the strength and words to reach them. The right women heard the power of this project and chose to align themselves with this amazing movement. As I spoke to them, I told them the powerful intentions of the project.

The first was to inspire. If these 25 women can overcome great obstacles and pain in their lives as they work towards their definition of "success," then you can, too. You will read stories of "everyday fails" that most of us can relate to, but also stories of childhood abuse and poverty that many of us will never experience. These stories are not meant to create guilt, but to provide perspective and strength so that we can push through our own failures and tragedies knowing that other women have discovered their greatness in the midst of unbearable pain and tragedy.

The second was to redefine the words "success" and "failure." You will hear from women who don't necessarily have worldly riches, but they find joy in the "now" as they find peace and harmony through their relationships with themselves and their loved ones. You will hear from women who do have financial abundance, but still have obstacles and pain in their daily lives because that is what we are here for—to be refined into the diamonds we were meant to be. You will hear how the "failures" in their lives became the tender mercies that redefined them, taught them great lessons to reach the next level, and helped them find their ultimate purpose.

Why does "failure" need to be a negative word? Could it potentially be one of the greatest blessings in your life? Might you also find "your greatest gifts in your darkest hours"? Is it possible that by avoiding failure in life you could be postponing the greatness and success that is awaiting you? I believe many of us are so fearful of showing the world that we are not perfect that we choose to not fully embrace this world. We show the world only the "happy face" on Facebook, the good times on Instagram. Heaven forbid we admit we are having a bad day!

Could you also be limiting your experience in this world because of fear of success? I have worked with incredibly talented women who were "three feet from gold" and decided to give up because of the changes in their lives. Anticipating these shifts and realizing they are part of the process can help you push through them.

Preface

It's time to get vulnerable, raw, and real so we can lift each other up, instead of pretending to have a "perfect life" that is unattainable. As you read these 25 chapters, you will discover that the authors were willing to get "real." They want to show you that every book of success should have chapters on failure! You will also find there are common threads that have helped them embrace the chaos on the days they are simply a "hot mess." Among these similarities are:

These women identified their "why." Knowing what they wanted helped them identify the actions to get them there. A strong purpose always outweighed the challenges and the pain necessary to achieve their goals.

They "burned their boats." Once they made a choice they chose not to look back, and forged full ahead. Quitting was not an option. If they chose to go another direction, it was simply a chapter of the same story, not a new book.

They found their strength in a higher force outside of themselves. Almost all of these women attributed their success to something outside of themselves that helped them find solutions to their problems, ideas to create momentum, and comfort and peace during the hard times.

These women recognized that they were only one part of the puzzle and that they needed others to achieve "big things" in their lives. Isn't it wonderful that we were born with different skills and gifts? We simply cannot create without utilizing balance, help, and strength from others.

They all had mentors and teachers who helped them reach the next level of their journey.

They redefined failure. Many of the women I spoke to didn't even understand the concept of "failure"; they simply recognized it for what it is—part of the journey. They truthfully saw this as a natural part of their progression, not something to avoid or fear.

My final goal for the book was to see what 25 influential and successful women could achieve by combining their strengths, their experience, and their passion. How many people could we touch and help by combining our efforts? Could we gain momentum by allowing them to get additional training and support through our team of diverse women? Was it likely that one or more of the women would "connect" with you, the reader? Upon reading the book, if you decide that one or more of the women could be teachers or mentors to help you on your own personal journey, you will discover many ways to team up with them. Some of the choices are completely free of charge and require only time. There are many options to get involved and continue on your journey of self-discovery and improvement. Regardless of your choice, I encourage you to continue nourishing your mind and spirit.

Most of all, I hope that you will know what a gift you are to this world. I hope that you will get a small glimpse of the importance of your presence on Earth. I pray that you will find strength through these other amazing women that will lead you to have the courage, strength, and resiliency to live in your own purpose and passion.

I believe that we are living in an exciting time when women are understanding their importance to creating change in this world. As women are empowered with the knowledge and courage to stand in their purpose, the world will become more, will become better, and can ultimately heal.

Namaste,

Wendy Bunnell

Chapter One
Embracing Success Whole-Heartedly
By Wylene Benson

Chapter One
Embracing Success Whole-Heartedly
By Wylene Benson

There had been no warning of an imminent heart attack. All my life, I had great blood pressure, maintained a healthy weight, exercised daily, and ate fresh veggies. But on February 2, 2013, I learned firsthand what it feels like when the bottom part of your heart simply quits pumping.

I had arrived at work as usual that morning and printed off the orders for the snowmobile parts that would be shipped that day. This particular morning, I was working alone. After pulling the items from the warehouse and boxing them up, I experienced a strange pain in my left arm. I continued with my duties as shipping manager until the pain radiated up the left side of my neck and I felt a tightness in the center of my sternum. I went to my boss and told her I wasn't feeling well and that I was going home. By the time I arrived home, the feeling in my chest had intensified so my husband drove me to the hospital.

Lying in a curtained area in the Emergency Room, I became aware of the reality of what was happening. As I awaited results from a blood test, the pressure in my chest became almost more than I could endure. My body involuntarily squirmed trying to get away from the pain. Minutes seemed like hours and fear crept in as the pain increased. Although my husband Clint seemed to remain calm and reassuring throughout the moments of confusion and worry about the unknown, he later shared with me his concern and the heavy weight of the possible outcome.

The blood test determined that trauma to the heart had occurred, and an ultrasound showed that the bottom half of my heart had just shut down. "Takotsubo, or Broken Heart Syndrome, *caused by stress*", was the final diagnosis.

Stress? Was I stressed? That was the question I was forced to ask myself. I began pondering my recent activities and choices carefully to find some answers.

Some of the circumstances that surrounded me at the time could have been considered stressful. For 20 years prior to that pivotal day, Clint had been disabled. Although during the entire 20 years we always had enough, it seemed as though every month we were scrambling to find an additional $1800 - $2000 above our predictable income, just to cover regular monthly expenses. My job paid too little to help support our family alongside my husband's disability income, yet I was constantly amazed that coincidences and generous family and friends made it all work. Stressful? I guess you could call it that.

Three daughters living at home, transitioning into adulthood, created an environment with continual emotional, physical, and relationship adjustments. With friend and boyfriend dynamics thrown in, five adults living in a space with little privacy caused some uncomfortable moments. During this time of shifting and supporting, I was regularly having deep conversations and helping uplift someone far into the night. Getting three or four hours of sleep per night while playing mom, mediator, and mentor was not unusual. Yet my physical body had an uncanny ability to get up at 5:00 am every morning, regardless of the number of hours I spent in my bed. Stressful? Probably.

I had taken on the responsibility of provider, nurturer, leader, servant, savior, referee, all while trying to keep peace and order within a family of adults with individual desires and beliefs. Stressful? Most definitely!

These circumstances were obvious contributors to a breakdown in my body's normal function. However, they were nothing compared to the real reason my heart gave up. Yes, I said "gave up." What I discovered during my recovery was a wake-up call. As full understanding began to dawn I acquired a deep sense of gratitude for the heart attack. I discovered a gift that could not have been shown to me in a more perfect way.

Several days after being admitted to the hospital, I arrived at home, doctor's orders in hand, dictating six weeks of rest with no stress and no physical activity. My family, neighbors, and even my employer rallied around to offer everything I needed to encourage my full recovery. My days consisted of sitting in an easy chair in my living room with all the necessities and comforts of an obedient heart attack patient. I had ample time to flip through magazines, read books from my "someday" stack, visit with well-wishers, and write.

I have always enjoyed writing; I have kept journals faithfully since I was 12 years old. For the first time I was not journaling simply my surface level observations or complaining about what wasn't working for me. Rather, I was journaling my thoughts and inspiration with the express purpose of discovering me, my mission. I was 49 years old, and I knew I had been given a second chance. And although I didn't realize it at the time, I had been given the gift of an interruption in my life's patterns, an opportunity to be quiet and receive divine instruction.

One day as I was free-writing in my journal, simply putting down thoughts as fast as they came to me, the ink on the paper glared back at me, and a realization hit me with stunning clarity. The words that had spilled out of my hand—"I have been making a half-hearted attempt at discovering my purpose"—could not have been plainer. My heart was working at only half of its capacity. And now I knew why. I was putting only half of my heart into living a fulfilling, passionate life. After this discovery, I looked back over several journal entries from previous days; the word "heart" showed up multiple times. So much was explained in that singular moment of understanding. My heart had been trying to get my attention for years, and I was finally in the frame of mind to listen.

Prior to this time of deep reflection, I had experienced occasional periods of extreme emotional pain far beyond sadness. At times, I had an unexplained urge to cry out in grief. Physically retreating to my bedroom and covering my face with a pillow to muffle the sounds, I allowed the tears and anguish to pour out unrestrained. Cries of misery came from the depths of a tormented soul, yet I had no explanation of the origin. My family, home, and social life were fine by most standards. There was no reason I should feel this way, so I kept these nameless emotions to myself. I now know it was my spirit desperately begging to be heard from within the hollow darkness of a superficial life devoid of purpose.

This new glimpse into the desires of my heart was the motivation I needed to begin aligning my physical existence with the genius that would no longer remain unheard and unseen. Six weeks of quiet meditation had given me space and time and prepared me to receive instruction. My spiritual heart had been neglected. A heart attack was the perfect experience to allow me to focus on what needed changing.

Almost immediately books, mentors, and ideas began coming to me, providing insight into how to create a life of influence and joy. I discovered a gift for connecting heart to heart with people around me. I became aware of my own radiant spirit and my ability to inspire individuals and audiences. I noticed that my reason for serving others began to come from love rather than from obligation and fear of judgment. I was moved to volunteer my time and energy to causes that fulfilled *me*! As I sought the next steps and took action, I was given new insight and direction into living every moment in the most purposeful way possible for me. I discovered a gift of being guided by inspiration that I had never known before.

I learned to keep what was mine and to be the very best me. And I learned to allow and even expect others to keep what was theirs and to be the very best them. I began to see the hearts of the people I interacted with and gave them the opportunity to see themselves in their highest form.

One of my most fulfilling memories after waking up to my capacity for influence is the two years that I volunteered to facilitate a class called "Prime for Life." I was uplifted every week as I interacted with students on parole from the Utah County Jail. They were court ordered to attend my class, so probably wished to be anywhere but there. Many of my students expressed gratitude for my class, saying it was the one place they felt accepted and even loved. As I listened in class to their comments and the stories of their lives, I was the one being taught and inspired. It is easy to love an individual when you experience the greatness in him.

Becoming more aware and awakened to the extent of my influence is a miracle in itself. I am daily learning that the expanse of the human spirit is limitless. Every level of growth feels like the pinnacle, while at the same time it is but a baby step in seeking the eternal capacity and effect of every human soul upon another. This realization would have been enough; however, I received something even greater.

After six weeks of my obeying the doctor's instructions to the letter, a second echocardiogram showed no improvement to my broken heart.

I heard: "This is about all the improvement you can expect", and then, "most people lead a normal life...," "your heart is weaker...," "you have borderline high blood pressure...," and "your heart is working at about half its normal capacity."

With every word, my heart began to sink. I felt a range of emotions all the way home from the doctor's office. As I looked through tears at the top of a loved mountain peak behind my home, the somber thought came, "I will never see the top of that mountain again." I felt my heart breaking all over again.

I experienced denial, fear, and grief, and I finally settled on *anger*. For a couple of days, I was just MAD! I loved to hike and I had always been very active. With a half-working heart, my stamina was cut in half and I felt cheated!

It was at that moment that I understood what it means to be "at choice." I knew being angry wouldn't solve anything, and it certainly wouldn't create the amazing life I had anticipated for myself beyond the age of 50. So I visited my doctor again and asked her point blank for permission to do anything I felt like doing. She hesitantly said, "Yeeesss ... just contact me if you have any chest pain or shortness of breath."

I verified, "So I can work out every day if I want, I can go hiking, do anything I want, as long as I contact you if I have chest pain or shortness of breath?" She confirmed, and that day I hired two mentors: a personal trainer to help me strengthen my physical body and a mindset coach to strengthen my faith and clean up my belief system. I knew enough about the Law of Attraction to understand that if I expected a miracle, I had to believe it was possible. I threw out all the things my doctor had said that wouldn't support the miracle I was seeking. I knew the miracle existed already—all I had to do was believe it.

I am a determined person who gets things done. I believe anything is possible with God by my side and with the proper motivation and mentorship. In that moment, I believed I had all the pieces for the impossible to become possible. I had caught a glimpse of my worth and had begun to feel the joy of living a purposeful life. I had learned how to tap into inspiration and had acquired a few tools to get through any limitation or obstacle. I had a desire to serve others and was humble enough to know I still had a lot to learn. I had no evidence that a completely whole heart was even possible. All I had was the commitment to do absolutely everything I knew and rely on faith that I would be given everything else in precisely the perfect moment.

Needing a milestone to stretch toward, I made the choice to do everything possible to hike the tallest mountain peak in the Utah County area the next summer. That goal spoke to me. I felt if I was able to complete the hike, it would prove that I was back and that my heart was whole and perfect. I trained daily and continued my dedicated quiet meditation, seeking ways to align more perfectly with the beliefs that would most likely bring success.

I remember the day I stepped out of my house and walked to the end of the block. I was winded when I returned to my house that day. I was determined to increase my pace and the length of my walks. It was not long before I completed a full revolution around the block. Soon I was hiking the horse trail in Maple Canyon near my home, increasing the distance each day.

Wanting a benchmark to gauge my progress, halfway through my training I signed up to support a friend in a 25k walk/run. The distance was about the same as the round trip of my chosen mountain, just not straight up. I figured it would be a good test of my endurance to see how I was progressing toward my goal. As the day for the race drew nearer, I felt fear of failure overtake me. There was some doubt that I would be able to finish the race even if I walked the entire route. I kept pretending that I was prepared and that I was excited to test my physical stamina. In retrospect, I believe I could have finished the race. I will never know what the outcome might have been.

The day of the race dawned cold and rainy. I battled mentally for an hour before finally giving in to my doubts, rationalizing that it was the best decision to just stay safe and warm at home. I let the fear talk me out of showing up, even to support my friend as a spectator. For the first time since my faith-filled commitment to do everything in my power to rebuild my heart, I felt the inconsolable ache of regret. There is no going back and changing a choice like that. I thank God for a mentor who recognized the self-judgment and shame I was feeling and the detrimental outcome if I continued. Thanks to his wise words, I became stronger and even more determined to complete my original goal. Without this preparatory experience of regret, I know that I would not have remained committed to completion.

I am profoundly grateful for the dedication of my mentors and their unwavering belief that I could accomplish my goal. They believed in me. Their commitment to the goal was as strong as my own. I am forever in their debt for their constant integrity and for never going easy on me—for letting me set the pace and then expecting just a little more.

That moment of choice in the doctor's office was the opportunity to see what I was made of. It opened the door to a new level of energy and divine connection that I had never known before. I poured my heart out in gratitude every night and filled it up every morning with daily inspiration of the next steps to achieve the health and wholeness I had chosen. I listened for the clues of negative emotions and limiting thoughts with the sole purpose of eradicating them. I was led to books and other mentors and teachers. Daily I felt divinely tutored by a source beyond my own limited earthly knowledge. I committed to constantly adjust my beliefs to align with the highest truths that I could tune into to create my desired outcome.

I discovered that there is no end to knowledge from the divine source. I began to call my morning meditation my GPS (Grounding, Prayer and Scriptures), and they literally became my daily guidance on the road to my ultimate destination.

Scripture and other inspired writings, coupled with an openness to receive knowledge beyond mortal understanding, unlocked a space for me to receive tiny increments of wisdom that have built my road to success. At first I thought this information was for my journey alone. The more I learned, the deeper my understanding, and I now believe that what I have received is a path to success for *anyone* who has the courage to follow it.

I am a product of my mentors. Much of what I share with my clients may sound familiar because it is what I personally regard as universal truth, so it is not unique. It is merely packaged in a way that is unique to me. I have spent hundreds of thousands of dollars and countless hours with mentors, with God in prayer, and in private study and meditation, constantly challenging my current understanding of the highest truths. I do not have a degree in science or psychology. What I do have is access to a much higher and more accurate source of knowledge. Whether you believe in God or not, it is easy to believe there are undeniable powers beyond current human perception to which we all have access. These powers are part of our abundant Earth and Universe. I believe they are here for us to utilize to our benefit. All we need to do is ask and listen. It is to this source that I most readily and often turn for answers. It is strange to think that I didn't always consciously know that I could have access to such great power.

As I awoke on the appointed day to hike to the top of Mount Timpanogos, it was pouring rain, even more torrential than the rain on the day of the 25k run. Blinding lightning flashed and thunder rumbled every few minutes. I had invited several friends to do the hike with me and I was determined to follow through regardless of who chose to show up. I had experienced regret once and that was enough.

Heedless of the weather and in pitch darkness, a friend who was equally committed drove with me to the trailhead parking lot at the base of the mountain. The rain had not let up so we silently waited for 20 minutes. We later met up with a second friend who had headed up the trail earlier in rain gear. The obscurity of the downpour was so intense that we had not seen each other as he hurried past my car when we first arrived. At the first sign of a break in the weather, my friend and I bravely stepped onto the trail.

As we ascended, every step was more empowering than the last. Rather than feeling depleted of strength as the day wore on, I felt re-energized. With the rising sun, the clouds dispersed and a magnificent September day was unveiled. The autumn colors were more brilliant, the freshness of the air more pungent, the freedom of the mountain more grand than I could have ever imagined.

As I stood resting with the warmth of the noonday sun on my face near the top of the wet trail, tasting the ultimate victory, a wave of gratitude enveloped me and I saw the full measure of what I had accomplished. I sobbed openly as I descended the mountain that day, with gratitude for the physical ability to hike and experience the beauty of the earth in such a personal and private way. I felt absolute peace five months later, as I read the hand-written note my doctor had attached to my latest echocardiogram. It verified what I already knew. The note read: "This is amazing. Your heart is almost normal."

It's not always necessary to experience a life-altering event like a heart attack before you choose to make a change. It is human nature to want to grow. Change is constant. Either growth or decay is happening at all times. Choose to grow! I encourage my clients to take a moment each day to be quiet and listen. I ask questions like, "What is your inner genius eager to show you it's capable of?" I help them find their gifts and embrace their passion and answer the question "what is the next most important step to create this?" And then I teach them to be perfectly obedient by taking action on that step immediately.

At times a limiting thought or belief will creep in. Express gratitude for and acknowledge the limitation. It is a gift, showing you the precise next step necessary to complete your chosen destination. Take each one as it comes up and trade it in for an idea that will serve you in creating your ideal outcome. When these steps are followed, success is assured!

I have proven to myself that the principles and lessons I have gathered are perfect for me. I have mentored countless clients who have proven them in their lives as well. I still seek daily to upgrade my beliefs. For me, it comes mostly a tiny step at a time. I believe that what I have learned is just the beginning. I continue to learn and grow daily as I proactively search to question and trade up any thoughts or ideas that I discover are not in alignment with the absolute highest truth. By sharing what I have received, I hope to illuminate a shorter and easier way to the top of the mountain for those who follow. Every step of my own personal trail of transformation has been a preparation, and I count every step as a blessing.

About Wylene Benson

Wylene Benson is a Personal Alignment and Business Coach and has been a successful entrepreneur and business consultant for 30 years.

A Certified "Limitless" Breakthrough Coach, Wylene is a facilitator of transformation. Her gift is inspiring individuals to take the leap of faith outside of their comfort zones to create seemingly impossible results. Using the principles and techniques she has developed, Wylene has experienced countless breakthroughs in her own life, as well as inspiring others to believe something better exists for them.

During her two-year tenure serving as the Facilitator for the PS/Ankle Monitor Parole Program "Prime for Life" through Utah County Jail, she saw shifts happen, adding evidence to the belief that anything is possible when you create space for change. Wylene Benson is an Author, a sought-after Speaker, Teacher and Private Mentor.

Contact Wylene at www.wylenebenson.com.

Chapter Two
Finding Joy in the Storm
By Melissa Bone

Chapter Two
Finding Joy in the Storm
By Melissa Bone

"Success is to just doing a little better each day, striving to live your purpose, and never giving up!"

Have you ever had those times in your life when you long for joy and peace, but life keeps kicking you down? Do you ever struggle with feelings of doubt, despair, or worthlessness? Do you want to have success in your life, but you are too stuck in your "failures"?

My story of failure isn't necessarily something that I failed at "doing," although there is plenty of evidence of that, too. My story is more of a failure of "being." Ever since I was little, inner negative thoughts plagued my mind with doubt and insecurity: "You're not good enough." "It's your fault." "No one listens to you." "Nobody cares." Then life events came along and I had more and varied experiences that "proved" these thoughts, as well as other negative thoughts, to be true. I ended up incorporating these thoughts as part of my identity. Sure, I fought it the best I could. But there were many times when the fight was too much.

I'm guessing that most of us have had feelings of doubt, depression, and even questioning our worth at some point in our lives. In our highly-competitive, results-oriented world, it's tempting to look to outward sources to validate our reasons for existing. Got a massive bonus at work? "Hooray! I am a success!" Got laid off? "I'm not successful and my company doesn't see value in me." Got invited to sit with the popular kids at lunch? "I must be pretty awesome!" Sitting alone at lunch? "Nobody likes me." I'm worthless." When we make a negative decision about ourselves because of something that happens or that somebody says, our brain begins to look for more evidence that supports those thoughts and we begin to identify ourselves with labels, such as:

I'm not good enough.

I'm not worth it.

I'm too fat.

I'm not smart enough.

I don't have any support.

I am unlovable.

I don't matter.

Sound familiar?

We continue to have experiences that "prove" those negative beliefs, because we've already identified ourselves with those labels. Those first experiences during which we attach ourselves to a certain negative belief usually begin in childhood.

When I was twelve, I was molested several times by an elderly relative. I was scared and confused. He said it was our "secret." I felt powerless. I felt as though my voice didn't matter. I felt I didn't matter. Thankfully, it was pretty minor compared to what could have happened, but the damage was done. How I wish I could go back to my twelve-year-old self, give her a big hug, and tell her how loved and how valued she was. I didn't know better back then.

During my teen years, I looked to outward evidence from others to determine my value and worth. When I was about fourteen-years-old, I had planned a big birthday party and I sent invitations to several of my friends. My parents bought decorations and decked out our backyard in a luau theme. Tiki lights adorned the path to the party. It looked amazing! I couldn't wait! When the day of the party arrived, we lit the torches and waited. Nobody came. Not one of my friends showed up. I don't recall why no one came, but I do remember that intense emotion of feeling like I didn't matter. I wasn't good enough. Nobody cared. I believed the lie that my worth was determined by how others treated me.

Like most teens, my high school years were filled with emotional ups and downs. I had friends, but I continually worried about being good enough, or popular enough. Even though I wasn't overweight, I struggled with body image issues. I remember vividly one day thinking about every part of my body, trying to find something, anything, that I liked about it. I couldn't do it. I hated just about every inch of my body, which further cemented the belief that I wasn't good enough.

When I was nineteen, I married my wonderful husband, and a year-and-a-half later, we had a beautiful baby boy, the first grandchild in both our families. Even though my heart swelled with love for this precious baby, I struggled with feelings of inadequacy and worry about being good enough to be his mother, as I'm sure most mothers do. We went on to have seven delightful children. However, I received many "well-meaning' comments throughout the years about what I was doing wrong as a mother, and people were quick to let me know when one of my kids was acting up. We also got lots of suggestions about birth control. I guess people didn't realize that we actually wanted our children, and we loved every one of them. The ugly label "not good enough" was reaching out with its tentacles and taking a strong hold of my heart. I'm a fighter and I tried my best to stay happy and upbeat most of the time. But when those inner negative voices showed up, they hit hard, and it took me a while to get back up.

The problem was that I had a tendency to shrug off any positive comments, while believing and even embracing the negative ones. I wasn't in a frame of mind to receive the positive, because I believed that I wasn't good enough, and that I didn't deserve it.

There is a saying that life is like a rollercoaster. It's filled with ups, downs, and some wild and crazy turns. Sometimes it's a fun, exciting ride, and sometimes it's downright scary. But one thing is for sure—it's rarely predictable.

After my husband and I had been married for about twelve years, we were in the process of building our dream house. My husband had a good-paying job with a pharmaceutical company and I was pregnant with our sixth child. Life was looking pretty good. Then, one day my husband called me and told me he had been let go from his job. No good explanation from his boss. No severance package. Nothing.

I felt a bit of panic, but we had good savings and I thought we could make do until he got another job. I tried to stay optimistic, even when my husband was losing hope and was himself slipping into depression.

We were still able to close on our dream home, and shortly after, I gave birth to a beautiful baby girl in the comfort of our new home. My husband found temporary work as an electrician's assistant while he continued to look for a better-paying job. Our rollercoaster ride called life was twisting and bumpy, but manageable.

The ride took a terrifying nose dive when my husband had a freak accident at work and broke the condyle on his femur, which separated the lateral collateral ligament (LCL). He needed surgery and months of physical therapy. He was unable to work, we had a six-week-old baby, who was rather colicky, and five other needy children at the time. We had no insurance, and not only was our savings gone, we were tens of thousands of dollars in debt.

We ended up selling our house and moving to a small fixer-upper two hours south, away from family, friends, and support groups. My husband was deep in depression at this point. Our children were angry that they had to move away from friends, family, and home. To say that life was stressful, chaotic, and less than joyful would be an understatement. It seemed that the odds were against us. I was angry and confused that my endless prayers weren't answered. I felt abandoned by God. Wasn't I good enough to have my prayers answered? Didn't my voice matter? Did I not have any value? All of the negative beliefs that had begun in childhood, and peppered my soul throughout my teen years and adulthood, came with a vengeance. They hit me with a force that knocked me down for a long time. The dark, conniving voices whispered nearly continually that I didn't matter, I didn't have worth, and nobody cared about me. I felt I was failing my husband, my children, and God. I believed the lies. I thought they were true. There came a point when I felt such an overwhelming sense of worthlessness, that I truly believed everyone would be better off without me.

I was a failure. I believed there was simply something wrong with *me*. The inner voices were very convincing.

Fortunately, something told me not to give up yet. I had hit my rock bottom and I wanted to climb back up. I wanted to see my children grow up. I wanted to meet the grandchildren I would have someday. Even though I felt abandoned by God, I prayed for help. I prayed to know that I was loved. I prayed to know that I mattered.

On a particularly difficult day, the only thing that got me out of bed was that our dog needed to be walked. I also knew that getting outside and exercising would help lift my mood, which would help me be there for my kids. As I walked down the street, I kept a prayer in my heart. Suddenly, I had a thought sweep over me. It was a scripture:

John 15:13 "Greater love hath no man than this, that a man lay down his life for his friends."

I knew that Jesus had died for us, but had I ever really stopped to think that He died for *me*? He loved me enough to die for *me*. There's no greater love than that! Heavenly Father and Jesus Christ did love me and cared about me. I did matter to them. They saw my worth. I knew it. I also knew that one of the adversary's greatest tools is to try to take away our sense of worth and identity. If he can convince us that we don't have value and that we are failures, it can stop us from progressing and blessing the lives of others. It prevents us from living our purpose. It stops us from having joy.

I finally realized that my worth wasn't determined by my results, or by how others treated me. I had worth because I was a daughter of God and He loved me. That's all that mattered.

I put a renewed effort into my daily devotions. Meaningful scripture study every day was a must. I stopped praying that our trials would be taken from us, and prayed that I would know that Heavenly Father and Jesus Christ loved me and that I mattered to them. I prayed to know my purpose and for guidance to live that purpose fully each day. I read hundreds of books, and went to seminars, and hired mentors. However, I noticed that each time I renewed my commitment to become better and live my purpose, it wouldn't be long before I would be hit with something that would test the very thing I was trying to overcome. But now I recognized it as something that was there to make me grow stronger so that I could help others. I knew how to learn the lessons from my struggles to get maximum growth quickly. I learned different tools to shift my energy more quickly.

"Don't look at the challenges in life as failures; use them as growth opportunities." - Melissa Bone

I learned how to create an environment and routine that fostered a positive, loving energy in our home. I did an inventory on the belongings in our home and got rid of anything that didn't serve a positive purpose or contribute to the family culture that we had decided we wanted. I taught my children the skills to keep negative thoughts out, and then helped them memorize scriptures and powerful declarations that helped them feel their worth and purpose. My husband also joined us in this positive shift. He is a great example to our family in staying positive through trials, and has found a job he enjoys that provides for the family. We've also been able to move to a larger home in an area that we've always loved.

I decided to become a presenter so I could share the things I was learning with as many people as possible. I wrote books and articles as another way to help people. I became a coach and mentor so I could help people with their individual struggles and challenges. I developed classes, programs, and resources to help families have more joy and love in their homes and in their individual lives.

However, even though I am finding success in sharing my message and helping others, I am careful not to let that define me, just as I don't let my failures define me anymore. I am a success because I am a daughter of God, I know that I have a purpose on this earth, and I strive to do a little better each day in fulfilling that purpose. Sure, I still have setbacks and down days. But, I don't let those days define me as a failure, and I use the lessons I learned to make the next day a little better. That is my definition of success.

I'm excited to share with you some of the tools that have helped me and countless others to live a life of joy, purpose, and love—no matter what challenges come your way.

Joy

I'm sure we've all had those days that not only felt less than joyful, they felt downright miserable. How do we shift from miserable to joyful? It's not always easy. But, it is possible.

Honor the struggle and release the emotions. Sometimes in our busy lives we have a tendency to push our feelings and struggles aside or bury them. Yes, there are times when we need to do that—but only temporarily. Don't leave those feelings buried. Validate the fact that you are hurting, angry, or that you've had a bad day, then get those feelings out. You can do this by writing your feelings down on paper, then destroying the paper. You can shout out your feelings to your steering wheel, or other inanimate object. (I know it sounds weird, but it works.) My rule is to not dump those negative emotions onto people. Get them out another way first. Then, if you need to talk about it to someone, at least they won't get the full brunt of negativity.

Build and protect your positive energy. Begin each day with a routine that brings lots of positive energy. Connect with your higher power in prayer or meditation. Read from a book of scripture or other uplifting literature. Exercise. Listen to uplifting music. When you do these things each morning, it helps protect you from the negativity that will show up during the day. Know what your triggers are and have an action plan in place so that when something shows up, you know what to do. When something triggers me, I usually put on some music, and when possible, I go for a walk or run. This usually shifts my mood quickly.

Learn the lesson. Get out a piece of paper and write down everything you learned from your struggle or trial. Don't fall into victim mode. Learn the lesson and become a victor.

Get into a state of gratitude. If you're not in the habit of keeping a gratitude journal, start one now. Write down at least three things you are grateful for each day.

Find support. Whether that person is a friend, spouse, God, or counselor, find someone to support you on your down days, and celebrate with you on your good days.

Purpose

"A successful day isn't measured by how many things we've checked off our to-do list. It is measured by how well we lived true to our highest self." - Melissa Bone

Sometimes life seems like an endless to-do list of moving from one task or activity to the next. Sure, we've gotten some things done during the day, but did we live with purpose? Or just with busyness?

So, what can we do to live with purpose each day?

Tune into inspiration. Pray and meditate with the question, "What is the most important thing I need to do today." Then, journal any thoughts or feelings you receive.

Write down your top five priorities in life. These might include, God, spouse, family, self, work, health, service, etc.

Plan out your day so that you give specific time and focus dedicated to each of your five priorities—with more time and focus to your top priority. Be sure to include time and focus to accomplishing the inspiration you received in step one.

Review, Revise, and Report. Before you go to bed, think about your day. What went well? Did you give proper time and focus to each of your priorities? What could you do better? Make any revisions and make a plan that will help the next day go better. Record your goals and results in a journal and/or to a mentor or other accountability partner.

Love

"We can only love others to the extent we love ourselves." - Melissa Bone

When we don't love ourselves, it's difficult to love others or receive love from others. Learn to love yourself, including all of your imperfections.

Do the mirror exercise. Look in the mirror each morning and see yourself as your highest self, and in your full potential. See yourself as God sees you. Say or think at least three things you like about yourself.

See others as their highest self and in their full potential. See them as children of God who are going through their own struggles and insecurities. Think of two-three positive words for each person you meet.

Do the "What I love about you" exercise. We do this sometimes in our family before we go to bed. After our evening devotions, we sit in a circle and tell each member of our family something that we love about him or her.

My mission and my passion is to help others live with joy, purpose, and unconditional love, even when life is tough. I especially love helping families acquire these tools in their homes. It's a sad fact that even young children struggle with feelings that have them questioning their worth. I founded *Tree of Life Families* as a resource for individuals and families to create and maintain homes of joy, purpose, and unconditional love.

Feel free to check out www.treeoflifefamilies.com for resources on everything from helping children develop a strong emotional IQ, to developing a home environment that is in sync with your family culture, to learning how to live each day true to your highest self—instead of just checking off to-do lists, and more!

"Sometimes the hardest part of the journey is believing you're worthy of the trip." Glenn Beck

About Melissa Bone

Melissa is an author, mentor, trainer, and presenter who is passionate about teaching and inspiring others on how to live with joy and purpose every day.

Her struggles with depression, childhood sexual abuse, and living with family members who have battled depression, as well as anxiety, has led her on a journey to discover not only how to overcome these challenges, but how to live with joy in any circumstance.

After 25+ years of training, mentorship, and experience, she founded Tree of Life Families, which provides classes, training, mentoring, and other resources to help individuals and families create a home of joy, purpose, and unconditional love, despite life's challenges. She loves helping others take the busyness out of life and instead, live each day with purpose.

Melissa loves music, theater, running, and traveling with her family. As a wife of more than 27 years, and a homeschooling mom to seven children, she embraces each day as an exciting new adventure.

Feel free to check out www.treeoflifefamilies.com for wonderful resources on everything from helping children develop a strong emotional IQ, to developing a home environment that is in vibration with your family culture, to learning how to live each day true to your highest self--instead of just checking off to-do lists, and more.

Chapter Three
Finding Success Within
By Wendy Bunnell

Chapter Three
Finding Success Within
By Wendy Bunnell

I grew up in an incredibly loving family that supported and loved me....but let's get real....I was coddled for most of my life. I didn't even make my own bed. Everything was handed to me or done for me. As a result, I had developed no emotional resilience. The word "fitness" refers to how quickly our bodies recover after physical exertion, but it also applies to how quickly we recover from emotional stress. My emotional "fitness" was virtually zero. The first big challenge of my life happened when I was 15, when my father announced he was leaving my mother for a woman 25 years younger, and the excitement of "living on the edge." With no coping skills to handle the turmoil I felt, I turned to alcohol, recreational drugs, and boys, trying to heal the pain of seeing my family split apart.

It has been said that "your decisions determine your destiny," and I was creating future chaos. Each poor decision led to a poorer life and self-image. I came to believe I was not "good enough." At 18, I was unmarried and pregnant. Before I married the baby's father, friends and family members told me I was marrying the wrong guy, reinforcing my sense that I made only "bad choices."

Eventually, I decided if I could become a perfect mother and wife, it would wipe my tainted slate clean. Perhaps I could still "redeem" my earlier wrongdoings. I ultimately gave birth to four beautiful, healthy children, and fostered 13 others in our home. I worked for the Utah Foster Care Foundation, where I enjoyed business success and honed my marketing and networking skills while helping the children of the state. It all verified that I was doing okay.

Evidence of my success would of course be gauged by how well my family was doing. Were my children doing well in school, with peers, in life? Were our relationships strong and were we spending precious time with our family? What did others think of my family? Did we look like we had it all together?

In 2007, that view of success was shredded. I had endured numerous low points in my life that presented huge challenges. But watching my family crumble apart was the lowest point. That was where I had placed my personal value, and I felt I couldn't go on if I had failed in that part of my life. My family was in complete crisis, although no one around me would have even known. This was the point that brought me to my knees:

"Dear Heavenly Father, I am so sorry for failing you. I'm sorry I didn't succeed in taking care of the children you entrusted to me. I have failed at the biggest responsibility of my life. You trusted me, and I have let you down."

I whispered this prayer with tears streaming down my face. I couldn't sink much lower than how I felt at that moment. The quote kept running through my head over and over: "No success can compensate for failure in the home." My whole sense of identity was tied up in being a mother and wife, and I had failed them miserably.

Nick, my firstborn, was full of happiness early on. But now at 18 he hated himself. At around 11 he struggled with finding friends and decided he wasn't of value. He followed my path of turning to alcohol, followed by heroin, cocaine, and marijuana—anything to numb himself to reality. It broke my heart to see this gifted, intelligent child treat himself so poorly, with such hatred and anger.

My daughter Kelsey was 16 when she discovered she was pregnant with a special needs baby. The doctors told her that her only option was to abort the baby. It had been exposed to a drug called Accutane and would ultimately result in a baby so deformed that it wouldn't be possible for her to keep this child. She was unmarried, lacking even a high school education. The world looked pretty bleak at that point to her.

Raising Leah, my free-spirited second daughter, was like living with a human yo-yo. We could be having fun listening to the radio and dancing one second in the vehicle, and then suddenly she would have screaming rages and I couldn't help her calm down. I am pretty sure I am the only mother who ever left a parent/teacher conference bawling, as I found out my daughter was the school bully. She would target someone and organize bullying treatment with her friends. How could she do this? We took in children through foster care; she knew how it felt to be treated differently. Why did she impose this same treatment on others?

I then looked at my youngest child, four years old. I agonized over how I was going to negatively impact this one. How was I going to screw up the last one? When would it happen? It was inevitable. I ached in my heart, knowing that he was so pure but that the worst was going to happen eventually.

As I was on my knees, finishing my prayer, I heard the same word over and over: "Gratitude."

"Gratitude?" I thought. "I have poured my heart out, told you how I am a failure, and that's my answer?"

It took me a while to get over being angry at myself and at my Creator. But incredibly, this one principle would be the catalyst for my healing and my change.

I started to take note of my surroundings first. "Wow! Isn't it amazing how beautiful the mountains are around me? Thank you, thank you for mountains. Thank you for the beautiful trees, the colorful flowers, the birds in the sky, thank you."

I turned inward to my incredible body. I thought of my heart and my lungs that beat and take in air every second, every day. I thought of my mind that can absorb information and come up with solutions. My heart soared as I thought of my ears, how they can hear incredible music and hear my children's laughter. I was thankful for my eyes that can see vibrant colors in the sky, and the smile on my husband's face.

Next, I noticed the joy on my youngest child's face. He literally tells me he loves me at least 25 times a day. I hear him say, "Mom, I love you." Sigh. Oh how that touches my heart!

There is so much that I had been given, I truly am blessed.

That day was when my life truly started to turn around. This one simple step changed everything. The simple act of giving thanks created a space for my heart and my soul to heal. When you are in a place of gratitude you have to remain present. When you are present you are generally not depressed or anxious, as you are when you are preoccupied with the past or with the future. Learning to just "be" was the key to my rise to success.

I learned that gratitude is the highest frequency or vibration in which we can exist. When we are deeply grateful, we are closer to our higher power, or creative source, than at any other time. As I practiced this gratitude, I started to see myself for who I truly was, and allowed myself to start loving me—little by little, step by step. I started to feel and hear inspiration. I no longer felt I was alone in this world because I had another source who could comfort me, direct me, and guide me to my greatness and purpose.

Some of you may have heard, "It is not happy people who are thankful. It is thankful people who are happy." Many of us get this completely backwards. As a result we feel we aren't fulfilled—that we have something missing in our lives— when in fact everything we need, have, or require is all around us, every moment of every day.

Deepak Chopra states, "Gratitude opens the door to … the power, the wisdom, the creativity of the universe. You open the door through gratitude." As I placed myself in this so-called "attitude of gratitude," I found myself finding more inspiration for ways that would improve my situation, and I started dreaming again. I felt better about myself, and I began the journey of appreciating myself and some of my talents

I had been in the same line of business for many years, and while I loved my organization, the lack of forward thinking and creativity left me feeling stifled. I started to think about my purpose, and about filling my cup again after draining it for so many years through taking care of everyone's needs but my own.

The funny thing about starting to like yourself is that you begin to be attracted to others who are positive thinkers. It wasn't long after my pivotal moment that I was inspired to start working with a network marketing company that shared health and wellness products. I loved the feeling I got as I worked with positive and inspiring men and women focused on self-development, inner work, and serving others. They say that you become most like the five people with whom you spend the most time. If that is the case, it is spending time with these people that significantly changed who I was. I now choose to spend my time with those who inspire me, lift me up, and leave me a better person after I am with them.

As I climbed the ranks in this company I found that I started to plateau and got "stuck," so to speak. I worked harder, taught more classes, and made additional follow-up phone calls. Truthfully, I was a textbook network marketing professional.

It took several years to figure it out, but I discovered there were two things that kept me stuck for so long. First, I was comparing myself to everyone who had succeeded. I started the business at almost the same time as another woman, yet she passed me up after the first three months and continued to climb the ladder. I was working just as hard, but for some reason I couldn't achieve what she had. Eventually I realized that comparing is never fair. We almost always compare our weaknesses to other people's strengths. She had learned business skills, networking, and social media marketing for years prior to getting involved in the company. I didn't take into account that she had previously learned and was an expert in those areas, while I was still learning. When I viewed the situation with new eyes, I learned from her instead of envying her. They say that envy and gratitude cannot exist at the same time. Therefore, when I was in a place of envy, I couldn't receive the answers I needed to move and propel forward. It all started to make sense.

I also discovered that I had some old "beliefs" that got in my way as I tried to progress. My beliefs about money created one of those issues. It seemed as though I could make only a certain amount of money, but no more. If I did receive any additional resources, they would disappear quickly. But as I implemented personal development principles and practices each day, I discovered a program that proved to hold the missing key to my so-called "glass ceiling." The program taught a principle called "belief breakthrough."

All of us will try to make sense of our world by creating beliefs about ourselves and about our world. Some are true, but many of them are false, especially when we create these beliefs when we are young. Our limited knowledge and life experiences don't help us discern between what is true and what is not. If an adult told us something when we were three, we believed them, and held onto that belief.

One of the beliefs that I held was so strong it dictated my actions without my even knowing it. When we hold a belief in our subconscious we have something that is called "cognitive dissonance." This term means that our mind wants to have evidence that this belief is true, so it looks around for evidence. This belief actually ends up creating a self-fulfilling prophecy, because we will find reasons why we believe it to be true, and create situations that we think "prove" it. Our subconscious will resist when it hears something contradictory to this belief, so we can either continue to accept it as truth, or we can work through the discomfort to reprogram the belief.

I realized that the "tainted" past I thought I had buried long was holding me back. I had stored that intense belief about my unworthiness in my subconscious and it firmly took hold. Every time I would get to a certain level of success, my belief would show up, and I would sabotage my success. In the belief breakthrough process, you mentally go back to the event, and rewrite it in your mind. You create a new belief and then reinforce it with affirmations to ensure that it becomes permanent. And that's exactly what I did. I nourished myself with gratitude while surrounding myself with positive, uplifting people (remembering to not compare my strengths to theirs), and simultaneously purging the negative beliefs that kept me from reaching my goals. I "rewrote" my story.

Around this time, the same voice that spoke to me of gratitude inspired me to "instill hope and healing in the hearts and minds of women and youth." It took me a couple of years to learn what that meant and how that would play out, as I searched and tried to learn what my purpose was on this earth. I learned it wasn't through utilizing my network marketing career to inspire women. It was meant to go in a totally different direction. I started to give inspirational speeches wherever and whenever I could, and to coach women to break through their fears and obstacles, and to rewrite their stories just as I had.

It was a difficult decision to stop working at a business I had worked so hard to create. I shed many tears as I decided to "fail" at that business and step into a new phase. I felt I had let down my team that had worked so hard to help me. However, sometimes success means quitting, and I needed to close one door in order for another to open. My choice brought the gift of waking up excited, renewed, and energized to create programs that would help women and youth create lasting change in their lives, too.

Now my emotional fitness is strong, so I can push through my fears and challenges. When those old voices pop into my head, I push them down. I feel I am a walking testimonial to the fact that you can achieve success only after failing—perhaps even many times. I know I will continue to fail sometimes, but I look forward to the growth and insight I will gain from each "failure." I choose not to suffer anymore. I choose not to find my identity through anyone else, including my children. I feel peace and joy because I am of value, and I have gifts that only I can provide this world. This is what I have come to call "success."

Let's revisit my amazing children once again. My oldest, Nick, lives in Colorado and is starting to learn how amazing and whole he is without the need for drugs and alcohol to fill his spirit. He is finally starting to realize that he is in control of his destiny. He is a man of deep emotions, fiercely loyal to those he connects with, and probably the smartest person I have ever met.

He has been one of my greatest teachers. I have learned to love my son unconditionally, with no expectations as he goes through his story, his trials, his journey. My only job? To love him without conditions. I can love him, and I can love myself despite what he is going through. My success as a mother comes from letting him learn for himself, as my journey taught me. He gets to learn this through "failing" and picking himself up, and maybe "failing" again. That is okay— that is what life is all about.

Kelsey? Well, she chose to be courageous and strong, and decided to place that beautiful baby with a loving family that couldn't have children. The doctors were absolutely wrong, because although the baby has some special needs, she is a light and joy to everyone who knows her. Our family expanded as this couple adopted my grandbaby Olivia. We are all better people for knowing them, and having them in our lives. Olivia knows Kelsey as her "tummy mummy" and Kelsey gets together regularly with Olivia's beautiful mother. Kelsey gets to bring her two little girls in tow. All three of the girls are full blood sisters, so they get to know and love each other throughout life.

Kelsey grew so much during this time. She is a "wise soul." She touches everyone around her with light and joy. I am honored and proud to have her in my family. She is my best friend, and she has taught me strength and true courage.

Cute little Leah is still a firecracker and is living on her own, independent as ever. Probably the craziest part of this story is that she works at a care center for the elderly. I jokingly told her when she got the job that her story would end up on *Dateline,* so maybe she should choose something different, but she did what she wanted anyway (yep, still the same child), and has fallen in love with those beautiful elderly people. With them, she can let down that tough exterior and become vulnerable, loving, and beautiful. And through it all I get to watch her learn, grow, cry, struggle, and succeed. My only job? To love her through her journey. Oh boy, do I ever love her. She is one of my greatest teachers, my biggest advocate and cheerleader. I am blessed because she is a part of my life.

My youngest, Luke? Let's just say that he is the "icing" on the cake. He has a depth and understanding that is wise beyond his years. Recently my mother came into town and I wanted everything to be "perfect." I was a little frazzled and stressed when everything didn't line up when she first arrived in town. Luke picked up on this, and asked me what was wrong. I shared with him my concern, and his response? "Mom, you get to choose how you feel. You need to be happy that she is here and enjoy her while she is staying." What an amazing 12-year-old. Even if he chooses a path that brings him pain and challenges, I know that he has everything he needs to overcome those adversities. I get to watch, learn, love, and grow alongside of him. But at the end of the day, I can love myself regardless of his choices and keep cheering him on until the end.

So now, after healing my heart, I believe that I can be successful without using the definition that the world defines as "success." I have learned that true success is internal. Living in my purpose and using my strengths has allowed me to go to bed at night knowing that I have made a difference. I am excited to wake up each morning as I wake to the realization that it is another opportunity to share my gifts with the world.

About Wendy Bunnell

Wendy Bunnell is a mentor, presenter, author and confidence coach. She is CEO of Critical 2 Confidence which helps individuals learn to raise their personal value so that they can form the life, income, business, and relationships that they have always dreamt about but never knew how to create.

Wendy has the unique gift of helping find personal and professional roadblocks and reconnecting people to themselves, and their Higher Power, and as a result, her clients see a dramatic increase in personal happiness and income level.

Wendy is the driving force behind the book and movement, *Success through Failing*, recruiting 24 other powerful and inspiring women who are combining forces to change the hearts and minds of thousands of women.

She has several successful businesses including a thriving real estate career and network marketing background, as well as her busy mentoring and speaking career. Her diverse background and life experience help her to understand the unique needs of each of her clients.

Even with all of her busy endeavors, her family is foremost in her life and includes six children and eight grandchildren.

You can find more about Wendy at http://www.wendybunnell.com.

Readers: Find out first hand how powerful gratitude can be in your life, just as it was for Wendy. Would you like to access a free guided gratitude exercise that you can use each morning?

Please feel free to download this gift by visiting
http://successthroughfailing.com/downloads

Chapter Four
Success Through Failing Gracefully
By Tiffany Berg Coughran

Chapter Four
Success Through Failing Gracefully
By Tiffany Berg Coughran

I guess I've always been the one who had to touch the hot stove before I understood the concept of getting burned. I've struggled most of my life to see my own value, my own contribution, and my own courage. I've wondered what success really could mean for a girl like me—a poster child for failure.

Let me tell you what I've discovered. I discovered that no person is too broken for a new beginning. No error occurs without a healing solution, and no lost sheep is ever so lost that it loses value. If I can spend most of my life failing, and then discover wholeness and joy, so can you! You don't have to be perfect— only teachable, moldable, and humble.

Fortunately, I trust that my value in the eyes of those who matter most to me is not based on my perfection. What matters most is that I am learning how to succeed honestly, humanly, and grace-*fully*. My definition of success is a willingness to accept one's failures with grace and gratitude. Can you?

Before I share my story, let me share a pre-story—a backdrop that will come full circle with a tender call to action for you, my dear friend. You may chuckle a bit along the way, and hopefully see some part of yourself in my failings and vulnerability.

We thought we were being creative. But then, I was only 11 years old.

Downstairs at my grandparent's home, the bare, dreary walls appeared to our eyes so stale, so boring. We were simply assisting, making it look nice for Grandma and Grandpa.

After all, there was plenty of paint. Pink, green, purple—so many cans of spray paint to choose from! My sister, almost two years my junior, followed eagerly behind me, as I led the redecorating campaign. I was sure that Grandma and Grandpa would be delighted when they saw the upgrades on their pasty-white basement walls.

There was *so* much paint, we were confident there would be plenty of margin to write simply the names of cute neighborhood boys on the walls. Surely the names would be hidden by the time our redecorating efforts were complete.

"Click, click, click," went the steel bearing inside the spray can. "Shhhhhh. Click, click, click." Hmmm. Shake the can some more. "Click, click, click . . . shhhhh." Then . . . nothing. Barely even air.

It couldn't be! Picking up another can . . . nothing. Another? Nothing. No more paint. We had hit the bottom of our paint reservoir. Empty spray cans littered the cement floor. "I love Joey" and "Frankie is a babe!" screamed from the walls.

Terror gripped my 11-year-old heart. We could not cover this. It was hideous. There was no hiding what we had done. There it was—quite literally—*the writing on the wall*. All of the walls! What had begun as a truly inspired venture of love and creativity had turned into an evil magician's trick.

Have you ever found yourself in torment about what began with positive intentions, grew tentacles, and then turned on you? Maybe this has happened to you in a personal relationship or in a business, with a misinterpreted statement, or a poorly written contract? A gloomy cloud of buyer's remorse and disillusionment sets in. How do you resolve a mess like that?

We had no money to buy more paint. We had no way to even get ourselves to a paint store. Horrified at the Frankenstein we had brought to life, we sat, or should I say, "slumped," on the cold cement.

Never had I done something that would look so awful in the sight on my grandparents. I loved my grandparents in a distant, almost fearful way—my grandfather especially. He had big black shoes that always caught my eye as he knelt to pray at the breakfast table each morning. He had been a military man and a postman; both uniforms demanded respect, and as a family, he was revered as the patriarch.

What would my grandfather do when he discovered our childish damage? Would he hit me? Would he yell? Would he never allow us to come and visit? Worse, would he never again sing to us the songs of his travels? I feared his anger and his judgment. Being the oldest and the instigator of the graffiti, I knew I would take the brunt of the punishment.

We sat upstairs, my sister and I, in front of the television. We sat there as statues, hardly breathing, listening to the footsteps of my grandfather as he made sandwiches in the kitchen, whistling. Anytime his footsteps seemed to fade into the back of the house, our ears perked, waiting for the guillotine to drop.

Two hellish hours must have passed and the smell of fresh pain wafting up the stairs must have prompted my grandfather to investigate. "Here it comes," I thought to myself, panicking. I tightened my jaw, readying myself to be struck by a large hand. I had never seen my grandfather lose his temper before, and I shuddered as I pictured what was about to happen.

His big black shoes came closer. He was standing right behind us. We held our stomachs, certain wrath was headed our direction. He simply spoke. He did not strike us. He did not shame us. He simply spoke to us, and asked us what had happened downstairs. *That's all.*

Yes, he was upset, and yet I could tell just from the way he responded to our immature, misguided effort to help, that he still would sing to us.

My grandfather passed away a couple of years ago. I traveled to his side just days before he died, and I was able to kiss him on the scruffy cheek and say

"Goodbye." Maybe he never thought about the graffiti in the basement. I *always* did.

Maybe he never again thought about the boys' names in purple spray paint—or maybe he did remember the incident, and laughed about it. I don't know. We never talked about it again. And that's when I learned something amazing about my grandfather, and something redeeming about failure.

Sometimes there's not enough paint. Sometimes there is not enough paint to hide your mistakes, not enough paint to cover your tracks, not enough paint to correct your misguided attempts. Sometimes all of our best efforts cannot fix our mistakes. For those moments, there's grace.

That's what my grandfather gave me. He extended grace. He could have broken me with his anger, and shamed me with his fury. Instead, he chose grace. Not because I deserved it, but because he loved me and saw past my mistake. I had clearly overstepped, and damaged his home. Still, he was kind and merciful.

At times in my adult life I have "painted" other big, loud, and sometimes obnoxious mistakes. Some have been eyesores that offend and assault, even when my intentions were good.

Sometimes my mistakes have taken on almost a life of their own—a parasite to my passion, my heath, and my relationships. At those times I have thought of my grandfather. How I wished there could have been more paint. How I wished that I could have made it right because I loved him. And still, sometimes there was not enough paint.

Sometimes we create scenarios in our lives that become huge messes. When we see the writing on the wall, we panic and scurry, trying to hide our foolishness. We think to ourselves, if I simply work harder, work smarter, behave more perfectly in this or that area of my life, I can at some point cover up my childish destruction. So we self-medicate, borrow more money, tell white lies—hoping to cover up or rectify our greatest mistakes.

This fear of being discovered by God or man keeps us running. It keeps us awake at night, grasping at this paint can, and that. "Click, click, click" . . . nothing. "Click, click, click" . . . empty. Where can we go when the images of the truth about our failures shout out to us from the drywall?

I believe we can always go to grace. Grace has no expiration date stamped on it, and no list of exclusions. It is pure, unconditional love. It is a gift that we can receive, and a gift that we can extend.

That's one of the most powerful messages we read in the Lord's Prayer. Forgive us this day our big graffiti disasters, as we forgive those that create graffiti against us. There is beauty and wisdom in receiving and extending grace. Our spouses need it, our children need it, our coworkers need it, and certainly the slow driver in the fast lane needs it.

Not to be confused with indifference or denial, grace is active, engaging and forgiving. It is neither a doormat to be walked upon, nor a ball and chain to shackled us. It is the key that allows us closure to the most painful chapters of our lives.

Fast forward a couple of years from that 11-year-old decorating diva. I began experimenting with alcohol and smoking. I struggled with self-esteem and inability to engage in school activities. This battle would continue into my young adult life. Years later in 2000, I found myself seated on the carport of a twin home, a young mother of five, eager to take my first drink of the day. It was 8:00 am. My inner noise overwhelmed me, my inner critic destroying every hope. Alcohol was my way of taking the edge off the stress and the pressure of being a young, inexperienced mom. What had begun as a glass of wine became a gin and tonic, and then another. For any outsider, I managed to smile and repeat the expected conversations, but inside I could not wait to feel numb again.

That day on the step the house of cards fell. I didn't want to be this kind of mom. But, I didn't know how to quit drinking. Confessing to my husband, I told the truth about the depth of my addiction. Even he had no idea how often or how much I drank every day.

Again in my life I felt grace extended. I had made a mess of many areas of our lives at that time due to being asleep at the wheel of my parenting. It was awful, embarrassing, and humbling, but step by step I went to counseling appointments, classes, and church meetings. The noise would get loud, the self-condemnation, toxic. But I kept clinging to the hope that someday I would not drink again.

The healing came slowly and required me to look at ugly, painful memories and readdress decisions I had made early on about myself. It demanded that I face the internal noise and find peace. The days and months and years passed. Less drinking, then . . . no drinking. I was learning to live without drinking at all.

Ahh. To be a mom who did not drink! I was seeing freedom from alcohol open new doors to me. The stronger I felt, the more I shared my story with other moms. They too felt encouraged to make positive changes in their lives. Soon I was writing books about emotional wellness and recovery. That led to an invitation to host and produce a faith-based women's TV talk show in the Mountain West. Then an internet radio show. Then the writing of a monthly magazine column. Later an article would lead to being published in an international Personal Excellence magazine.

Me? The graffiti-painting, gin-and-tonic swigging mama of five? Yes, the very same. Each conversation with other recovering mamas gave me courage. I decided to enter the Mrs. Utah United States pageant and tell my story of failing as a mom and of a blessed grace-filled recovery. To my surprise, I won.

The title of Mrs. Utah opened even more doors to speak about addiction and recovery. My adventures allowed me to work on million-dollar charity projects and media efforts. It allowed me to speak in women's detention facilities and government conferences. I had not realized that so many women struggled with addiction and self-condemnation on so many levels.

Years had passed without alcohol. I felt the demons had been slain and my life was finally steady. Little did I know that a phone call from my husband's doctor would catapult our lives into a whole new trajectory.

Cancer. Terminal cancer. "Click, click, click. No more paint."

The news became bleaker and bleaker. Chemo, radiation, surgery, more surgeries. "Why, God? Why this? Why now?"

I watched my husband grow weaker and weaker. And in between the square tiles of the sterile hospital waiting room, I could feel a presence so very similar to that of my grandfather standing next to me. My heart was breaking with the reality of what was happening. Still, I felt grace. I knew God was not trying to hurt us, nor condemn us, nor withdraw from us.

The night my husband passed away I wondered "Did we fail? Did I fail? Did I do everything I possibly could? Did we choose the right treatments, did we try the right diet, and did I say the right things?"

Ahh, my friend. Our minds may always play these tricks on us about success and failure. When something ends we may want to sum it all up and wrap it in a bow if we think it has brought us accolades. We may want to hide our life's challenges and mountains and valleys if we feel they bring us tragedy or difficulty. But through the lens of love and grace it all comes into different focus. It blurs and then clears as we come to see new meaning and context.

Sixteen years ago I sat on that step. Twelve years ago I took my last drink. Seven years ago I stood at the graveside with our beautiful children.

And so it is. Our courage compels us to keep breathing. Our yearning for growth demands that we keep listening and stretching. Our destiny, with its divine calling, bids us take one more step into the darkness to become more than we were before. And grace, oh sweet grace, soothes the hurts and forgives even hell for the wounds that cut so deep.

I did not know that day at the graveside what would lie ahead.

I did not know I would remarry and feel blissful love and companionship. I did not know that my family would grow with more children, sons and daughters-in-law, and grandbabies. My heart would heal.

In my searching for knowledge about grief I would return to school, become a clinical chaplain, and find my way back into the ICU and ER, holding the hands of others who suffer tragic loss. Often they look at me, *"Did we fail? Did we choose the right treatment, did we drive the wrong way, did we find the right procedure?"* I understand. The inner noise clambers and the chaos crowds the stage. I sit close and hold their hands as they cry.

I know God is standing close by, quietly extending grace. No expiration date is stamped on it, and no list of exclusions. Pure, unconditional love. It is a gift that we can receive, and a gift that we can extend. *"Forgive us this day our big graffiti disasters, as we forgive those that create graffiti against us."* Grace is active, engaging, and forgiving. It is the key that allows us closure to the most painful chapters of our lives. When we feel loss and failure, and we question the meaning and value of success, God is there to quietly and confidently stand with us and for us.

What I've discovered has saved me. No person is so broken they cannot have a new beginning. No whopper mistake is without healing, and no lost sheep is ever so lost that it cannot be found.

So dear heart, when you feel you hold your life like an empty spray can, and you stare blankly at the wall of graffiti in front of you, horrified by your own failings and paralyzed by the worries of the future, please know there is grace enough to cover it all.

And that, my friend, is *ultimate success.*

About Tiffany Berg Coughran

Tiffany Berg Coughran is a recovering alcoholic celebrating 14 years of sobriety. After receiving faith- based counseling, Tiffany began empowering others battling addiction. Since 2002 Tiffany has spoken professionally and authored multiple books on emotional wellness. Her message of recovery became her statewide platform as Mrs. Utah United States 2007. Her passion led to co-founding Utah's Heart 2 Home non-profit (2004-2012), which raised more than three million dollars for needy Utah families. This work was featured in *People Magazine*, Fox 13, KSL, *Good Morning America*, and Oprah's Big Give.

During these years Tiffany's husband was diagnosed with throat and jaw cancer and commenced aggressive treatment. After the devastating loss of her husband in 2009, Tiffany returned to school and certified as a clinical corporate and hospice chaplain. Now having facilitated hundreds of case studies, in the ER, ICU, hospice care, suicide support, and determining complicated end-of-life decisions, she is a frequent presenter at hospitals, social work conferences, grief support groups and cancer awareness events for adults and children.

Tiffany also works with local and national media and understands the complexity of emotion in highly charged situations and crises. As a consultant, Tiffany has prepared individuals emotionally and intellectually for high visibility national interviews.

Passionate about life, love and healing Tiffany was reconnected to her high school sweetheart Vernon in 2013, and the two were married in 2014. Today they enjoy their eight children and are delighted to be grandparents together.

www.tiffanycoughran.com

Chapter Five
From Self-Harm to Self-Love
By Lori-Ann Cunningham

Chapter Five
From Self-Harm to Self-Love
By Lori-Ann Cunningham

There is so much pressure on and among women to be perfect. We are our own worst enemies as we attempt to do everything exactly right, the first time. To be an instant success at whatever task we take on. To look stunning, with the perfectly-toned body, perfectly-coiffed hair, perfectly-applied makeup, and to always appear "put together." To have perfectly-behaved children, because, heaven forbid, if you don't, you might be evaluated as possibly the worst mother ever. It all stems from wanting to feel "good enough." The pressure is undeniable.

I've always been an overachiever, as a result of having two siblings who were the "smart ones"—the ones who tested into specialty programs and advanced courses. I always felt I was on the outside looking in. Because of this, at an early age, I struggled with anxiety and feelings of inadequacy that followed me through decades. It didn't matter that our strengths were completely different. Their strengths were in analytical processes and problem-solving; mine were in music and performing arts. That difference didn't mean anything to me at that age; I wanted to be good at everything.

This pressure, this striving to be always perfect, finally caught up with me. The first year of creating my business was impossibly difficult. I was thrown unprepared into the world of online business and it completely blindsided me. That feeling of being on the outside looking in was magnified beyond my worst imagination. I was again the awkward one, the one who wasn't good enough, the one who didn't have everything put together, looking across the lunchroom to the cool kids' table, wishing I could be like them and with them. But this time, the cool kids were the coaches, bragging about five-thousand-dollar months, or how they had "cracked the code." In my eyes, they had created something perfect and put together.

My life was falling apart. Everywhere I turned, I confronted struggle. I felt utterly alone. My marriage was rocky and my husband and I were constantly fighting. I was losing my best friend—a woman I loved more than any other friend I had previously known. I was mother to four handsome boys, one of them a new teenager being tossed about in a mess of hormones and defiance. Our youngest was a determined and persistent toddler, at an intensity which I had never before experienced. I felt I never had enough time to work on my business. What I was trying to do with my business was completely new—no one else was doing it— so I had to figure it all out by myself while attempting to carve out my own niche. In addition, I was going to school at that time. I was burned out, and there was no end in sight.

I didn't know how to deal with, express, and release deep emotions, especially negative ones. They were pent up inside at such a high intensity, I was not a happy or pleasant person to be around. I was always yelling and flying off the handle at the smallest things. But the interesting things was, when I gave in to anger, it bred more anger, creating a snowball pattern of self-destruction. It showed up in a way I never thought I would go—in self-harm.

After a string of particularly bad fights with my soon-to-be ex-best friend and my husband, coupled with once again feeling like a failure in my business, I was filled with so much pent-up emotion, I felt as though I was going to burst! Without any rational thought, I did the only thing in the moment that helped release the immense pain. I hit myself, over and over again, punching myself in the head, until I gave myself a concussion. This soon grew to be a pattern whenever I was experiencing any intense negative emotion or in any tense situation. While it gave me release in the moment, I cannot tell you the self-loathing I felt when I fell into this pattern of inflicting self-destruction. I was in a bottomless pit. I felt completely worthless.

I reached my absolute rock bottom the day I hit myself in front of my children. As on any normal school day, I picked them up from school and headed home. Soon they were fighting with each other, as children often do, and I was trying to get them to stop. At the same time, I was trying to ask one of my sons if he had talked to his teacher about something important—something I had been asking him to do for several days. He admitted that he hadn't talked to his teacher about it. What happened next mortifies me to even describe. Furious, I totally blew up, and yelled and screamed about everything. Then, when it became too much, I took my fist and punched my head over and over again.

My boys, my beautiful, wonderful, amazing boys, were bawling, begging me to stop hurting myself. Crying and sobbing, they told me that they were sorry for everything and they would stop. They took the blame for me not having control and for punching myself. No child should EVER experience that! It wasn't their fault!

I pulled over to the side of the road, and bawled loud, ugly cries of frustration and self-loathing. I couldn't talk, I couldn't see. After I collected myself, I gave all of my boys hugs and promised them that this wasn't their fault. I promised them that I would fix what was going on with me. I told them how much I loved them and that they were so special to me.

That day, I swore I would stop—stop hitting myself for good. While I stopped hitting myself, those self-destructive patterns continued, but manifested in other ways. It took many steps, many attempts, to come from a place of self-loathing to self- love, to be completely healed and feeling successful.

I was constantly looking for the next thing to make me successful, for the next coach or mentor who would share the "secret" to success. I allowed myself to be blinded, with dollar signs in my eyes, by their over-the-top promises. I remember being drawn into the smoke and mirrors of charging thousands and thousands of dollars, just because everyone else was doing it, regardless of whether the services everyone was providing were actually worth that large price tag.

Instead, all that I acquired was a lot more grief and unhappiness. I started to hate my business and was paralyzed when I tried to share my gifts and talents. I ate my emotions away and gained a good amount of weight. This of course perpetuated the feeling of never being good enough. How ludicrous that as a health coach, I couldn't even control my own health and weight!

Spending thousands of dollars on mentors and looking outside for validation were not the correct methods for me to find success. I finally came to the realization that the only place I could find that validation—to find that success that I had been looking for—was to look inside myself. And I was guided by the perfect mentor—the mentor who has my best interests at heart and not his pocketbook—and that was God. Although I had very strong spiritual beliefs, I realized I wasn't leaning on the Lord enough. I had been putting trust in others instead of in Him. I fully recognized that He puts people in our lives to help us and to be there when we need them, but I wasn't trusting that with Him I could fully achieve what I'm supposed to do and be. When I tried to put that same kind of trust in other people, they would always fall short, and I would always end up feeling they had taken advantage of me.

I took my power back, and made God the owner of my business and my life.

I have never felt more peace, comfort, and guidance as I have since making that shift, and then acting on it. Action is an important piece of the puzzle. You have to take action to see any real changes in your life. All the knowledge in the world won't result in any changes unless you act upon the things you have learned. So I encourage you to act. Act, assess, and make necessary changes to make those actions be the best fit for you.

For me, there wasn't an immediate, miraculous fix. I'm still working on feeling good enough, feeling successful, and recognizing my successes. I'm sure I always will have to continue working on those. However, there are four cornerstones and a keystone I found that have been tremendously healing and have helped me recognize the true successes in my life. These cornerstones and keystone ground me. They are things I work on daily. When I miss them, I start wandering down the path of "not good enough" again.

It's my hope that these cornerstones and keystone will help you as well.

The first cornerstone is realizing and knowing my own divine worth as a daughter of God, a God who loves me, despite all of my imperfections. He knows my heart and knows I'm doing the best I can, even when I fall down, which I do often. He lifts me up, dusts me off, and encourages me to keep trying. I feel of His love through prayer, reading scriptures, attending church, giving service, and pondering.

Our society places too much importance on outside validation for us to appreciate our self-worth. As women, we fret and fuss about how much money we have, how many friends we have, our possessions, whether we're skinny, whether we're fat, whether our hair and makeup are perfect—the list goes on and on. When we learn how to brush all of that off and not let them affect us, our true self-worth shines through. The simple truth is, God doesn't care about any of those things.

The second cornerstone is journaling. I'm not referring to a journal of what I did in a day, although sometimes I do write about that. This is a free-writing journal, one in which I vent, ask deep, thought-provoking questions, and search for answers. Daily journaling gives me clarity and focus. It's something I've grown to love and look forward to. It helps me recognize negative patterns and thoughts, and helps me discover ways to turn them around. This is a much healthier way to release emotions than burying them or acting out in self-destructive ways.

The third cornerstone is changing my thoughts through meditation and music. I discovered that subconsciously I had numerous negative thought patterns running constantly. One thing I have found incredibly beneficial is to compose and record positive-affirmation guided meditation songs. Since I'm a recording artist, I use my own songs and record my voice, mixing it all together. I still listen to positive affirmation songs I recorded during those first few months of moving from self-harm to self-love. They have never lost their power.

Music has marvelous power to allow us to express our feelings, as well as to help us release them. I have many playlists of songs that make me cry, make me laugh, cause a warm feeling in my heart, and make me want to smile and dance. These playlists have literally turned into my life's soundtrack. A song that has had a huge impact on me is "Don't Give Up (You are Loved)", sung by Josh Groban.

Music is tied to my journaling. I write daily affirmations in my journal in the morning and reread them before bed. Sometimes they go like this, "I'm having a hard time figuring the next direction of this song, but I have trust and know it'll come." Previously, I used to think, "I'm such a failure! Why can't I figure out this song? That's more wasted time. I'm not as good as all these other amazing musicians. Why do I even try? Who I am to think I can even do this?" Can you tell the difference? Which one would help you be more creative? The first one removes all my blame and emphasizes trust that the answer is there; the second questions my character and who I am, my worthiness. Making this switch in how I'm thinking on a daily basis has had one of the biggest positive impacts in my life.

The fourth cornerstone is feeling and expressing gratitude. Research shows that feeling and expressing gratitude increases quality of life by making people happier and more optimistic. Every night I make a list of at least five things I'm grateful for that day. It could be something someone did or something I accomplished, but more often than not, I'm expressing gratitude for people in my life, for the small and simple things they do that make me feel loved and important. What you focus on, you attract more of in your life. When you're expressing things you're grateful for, more of those things will show up.

The keystone is to verbally express how I'm feeling. For so long all my emotions were pent up inside, with no escape, which is why I ended up hitting myself as a release. Having someone in my life I can talk to has been incredibly important. Sometimes it's my husband, other times it's someone who has an empathetic ear. But most of the time I find myself on my knees, pleading with my Heavenly Father and expressing everything I'm feeling.

Another technique that I've recently discovered and implemented is "Freedom Speak." Do this in an empty room where you won't worry about being overheard. You're going to be speaking to a person towards whom you're feeling negative feelings as if they're in the room with you. First, ask for their permission for you to be open and honest with them and to speak with them. Then, taking as much time as you need, express everything you're feeling towards them. And I mean EVERYTHING! Get everything out! Express forgiveness to yourself, acknowledging that you had a participating part in the situation. Then tell them that you forgive them as well.

The first time I did this, I was astounded at how much lighter I felt, how freeing it was! I didn't realize how furious I was at the person until I started talking to him! By getting those emotions out, I was able to move forward without being weighed down and holding on to emotions that were not serving me to my highest good. This technique has truly given me an outlet, a way to release pent-up emotions, in a healthier way than anything else I've ever experienced. I highly suggest you try it!

I'm happy to say that I have kept my promise and have never hit myself again, even though there are times I am tempted. Recognizing the red flags has been incredibly important. That's when I know it's time to pull out the "cornerstones" and "keystone" I've developed. I'm consciously working on recognizing my personal successes, and not by the standards the world deems as signs of success. I fully feel my self-worth and place my trust in my Lord, instead of in others.

What I've grown to know and appreciate is that I AM good enough, just the way I am! The beauty of life is we can always strive to become better, to do our best, whatever that may be. But the pressure, the need to be perfect in everything, was a false standard I had imposed on myself. I realized that I AM successful! I am still working on this every day. As long as I'm living in alignment with what's important to me and my core values, living my life with integrity and showing kindness to others, I can go to bed at night feeling grateful and fulfilled with how I lived that day and KNOW I am successful.

Now I can truly say I'm a success. I have a family who adores me and wants to be around me. I have a wonderful relationship with my Savior, and I am living my dream by creating lovely and healing music for others in my business. Music is such a big part of who I am, that the realization that I am successful in sharing my music, my talents, and my abilities with others who appreciate it, who are working on their own health and seeing results because of my work, sometimes seems too good to be true! I have thousands of clients and fans all around the world—people who are stressed, feeling low, and need a break from their hectic life, as well as other coaches and entrepreneurs who have clients who need what I can offer.

By serving so many, I can further expand the much needed message of healing and motivating music and sound, like a ripple effect in a pond or lake. That ripple effect is spreading this message much faster than I can do by myself! I'm the creator of the music health coach brand, "Health Sounds Music," and the host of "The Health Sounds Revolution Podcast." Without having experienced the trials and struggles I have gone through, I wouldn't be able to help and serve in this capacity. It's my pleasure and honor to serve people from all around the world in so many and varied ways, by owning my true success!

If I can be successful, even through my myriad failures, then there's no doubt that you are successful too! You are a success, right now, just the way you are!

About Lori-Ann Cunningham

Lori-ann Cunningham is THE Music Health Coach, Certified Holistic Health Coach, award-winning musician extraordinaire, creator of Health Sounds Music, and sought-after motivational speaker and performer.

After discovering through her own health and mental challenges how the powerful tools of music and sound can be used to help heal and change physical and mental states, Lori-ann is now on a mission to help people fine tune their personal symphonies of health and well-being so they can experience health, love, and deep joy as they fulfill their missions here on the earth, and ultimately, change the world. She teaches the impact sound has on our health and well-being, and creates healing and relaxing music and meditations using revolutionary technologies, mixed with a lot of love, intuition, and a sprinkling of playful fun!

Lori-ann sneaks away to create music every chance she gets, working around her four handsome and CRAZY boys and a husband who's obsessed with her—obsessed in a good way!

You can find more at www.MusicHealthCoach.com

Chapter Six
Trial by Failure
By Wendy Cunningham

Chapter Six
Trial by Failure
By Wendy Cunningham

As he screamed an inch from my face and squeezed my biceps, I felt his thumbs digging into my skin. I could almost feel the bruise forming where his thumb pressed into my muscle. I'm sure I was crying; but I couldn't really focus on what he was screaming. It wasn't the words that were hurting me. And frankly, it wasn't even the thumbs. I could tell he was getting ready to hit something, and I just prayed that it wasn't me. But I didn't want him to punch the wall either. I wasn't sure which would be worse. This was my mom's house. She was asleep downstairs—at least I hoped she was still asleep downstairs. How would I explain a hole in the wall? But wait, how would I explain a bruise on my face?

I'm a cliché. It's my college graduation party, I've brought my boyfriend home to meet my friends and family, and now he's drunk and about to hit me. This is a new low, even for me. I wonder if my friends can hear us. I wonder if they're going to come try to break us up. I wonder if I want them to. How humiliating! This is what I deserve. I put myself in this spot, in these hands that are violently shaking me. They say you're likely to marry your father. Well, I've managed to walk right into the addiction cycle here. Try as I might, I just can't escape this. It's my destiny. It's in my blood. I'll be an addict or marry an addict or hey, maybe I'll be killed by an addict if he doesn't calm down soon!

It wasn't always this way. I used to have a chance. I wasn't always such an epic failure.

My name is Wendy, and this story starts in the small town of Woodland, about thirty minutes northwest of Sacramento. It's where my mom was born and raised. It's where she still lives today. In so many ways it will always be my home base.

I have a few great memories of my father. He was hilarious, and occasionally would read my little sister and me a bedtime story, and we would giggle. He would laugh until he started that hacking cough that made me wonder if he had something wrong with his lungs. The book was about animals; it's the only one we would ever read. I only remember reading it maybe a dozen times. I also have a few bad memories of my father. He was a severe alcoholic, and struggled with many forms of addiction. I remember sitting in the back seat of his silver van and it was dark outside. The car came to a stop, but I continued to stare out my window, unaware that a police officer had approached my dad's window. We had to follow the police car back to the station. I'm not sure why, or what happened when I got there. I was afraid, though. I still can't piece together what happened that night.

My young life with my dad was filled with a lot of yelling, an exorbitant amount of drinking, and an occasional laugh. That was the good part—the laughing. My family situation wasn't great, but it wasn't out of the ordinary for me. That's just what I knew. That's what I thought marriage and a family were all about. From the outside, we were your typical middle-class family. Nothing too dramatic, nothing too crazy. Just another case of some closet daddy issues, but no one would have guessed that we were falling apart. That is, until we became a statistic—a "broken home."

Mom found some maxed-out credit cards in the garage one night when my dad was out of town, and he never came back. I was twelve. I was so mad at my dad for hurting my mom and breaking up our family that I didn't care if I ever saw him again. But I didn't have to make that choice, because he didn't make much of an effort to see us anyway. That was when I first learned what it felt like to have a parent not choose you. It was a soft blow then, but it laid the groundwork for the blow that would later break me.

After my dad left, my mom and my sister and I became like three best friends. My grandma—my mom's mom—came in and saved the day. She gave us a car, watched and transported my sister and me, and had us over for dinner regularly. She had stepped right into the role of co-parent with my mom, and everything was quite wonderful. Mom also didn't miss a beat. She kept all the balls in the air and made it feel as though nothing had changed. The house was quiet. It was happy. Mom didn't seem to be as stressed. I was in no need of a dad or a father figure. I didn't feel like anything was missing, and I felt like there could be a different version of a family—one that knew peace. My sister and I felt like the center of my mom's universe. There were no other distractions. But this oasis was unfortunately short-lived.

Within a year of the divorce, we met the man who would become our stepfather. It was New Year's Eve, and my sister, my cousin, and I were at my grandma's for a sleepover, just as we were every year. We camped out in the motorhome in front of her house and played checkers, built drum sets and other noise-making concoctions, and ate candy while waiting to make an obnoxious amount of noise at the New Year. Mom met a man out on the street as we three Peeping Toms watched their interaction. He wore a Christmas sweater stretched over his enormous potbelly, tight Wranglers and cowboy boots, and he kissed my mom. I didn't like him.

He might not have been drunk that first night that I met him. But from that point on, there were not many nights or days when he wasn't. They didn't move in together right away, but the three of us did go stay at his house several times. His walls were covered with dead animal heads, and his furniture with dead animal skins. I would lie in my designated bedroom and cry all night every night I had to stay there. It felt like I was slipping further and further away from my mom, and further away from the family I loved. It wasn't long before he moved in and things started to go downhill. For the first year, it was easier for him to disguise his alcohol addiction, when they didn't live together. But once we were all living under the same roof, there was nowhere for him to hide.

By the time I was sixteen, I hated Jim. He drunkenly flirted with my friends — even smacking their butts. He called my mom a "cunt" and a "bitch" and a myriad of other colorful names, while she remained silent. I found myself stepping in to defend her. I found myself regularly engaged in full blown, adult-caliber arguments with this man. He would claim to be sober while unable to stand up. He would drive all of us at times when he was intoxicated. No one said a word. Except me. I felt I had to save my family from him. He was ruining our lives. But I was failing to pull us out.

Then they got engaged. I couldn't believe it. I remember sitting in the living room as they sat my sister and me down and told us, the same way you would tell someone that their puppy had died. They knew what our reaction would be. We were devastated.

All I could think was, "My mom didn't choose me. She chose him."

And suddenly, the wound my dad had made when he left started to bleed again just a little. Just enough.

Around this same time, my grandma—the woman who had become my rock and my anchor through this crisis—was diagnosed with ALS, known as Lou Gehrig's disease. It was a devastating blow, and it allowed the focus to be drawn away from Jim. He had the space and the distractions to push himself deeper into our family, as we were forced deeper into his lies and addiction. We moved into a house they bought together. The wedge was pushed ever deeper. He was winning. I was failing.

My grandma died two weeks before I left for college, and by that time I felt there was nothing left of my family worth fighting for. My mom was lost to this man, my sister was only a few years from breaking free herself, and I was out of there. I moved to the farthest part of the state that I could. I wanted space. I needed to redefine my life. I had spent almost all of it fighting my mom's battles, and hoping things would change. They weren't going to change. This was my life. So I left it.

Unfortunately, not even 524 miles could keep the hauntings at bay. Mom's boyfriend got a DUI. He claimed it was the officer's mistake, of course. My mom called me crying just before I was due home for Thanksgiving, telling me she wanted to kick him out, but he wouldn't leave. So I left midterms and got in my car and drove home. He was gone when I got there, but returned as soon as I left. He said he was sorry, of course. The story continued, the drama never stopped. I couldn't fix it. I was failing.

In a parallel world, nearly forgotten in my day-to-day life, lived my dad. Since the divorce years before, he had had a massive heart attack and had almost died because of his drinking. His heart had stopped four separate times, and he was in a coma for several days. But he pulled through. He was given another chance. And I had thought that he had turned things around. For several years, he tried to make up for some serious lost time with my sister and me. He took us on an amazing vacation to Disneyworld. We spent Christmas Eve with him. He started dating a wonderful woman, whom we loved. Things really seemed to be going well for him, or at least that's what I allowed myself to believe. I was desperate for him to do better because of us—his kids. I wanted him to choose me. I wanted to believe he would.

In the months leading up to my mom's wedding, my dad fell off the wagon. As a matter of fact, he never really got on it. That was just my wishful thinking, mixed with his incredible ability to pretend. My stepmom—although she never officially held that title—told me the truth once I finally got the courage to ask. She had kicked him out. He was pretty bad off. Back to square one again.

Things started to unravel for me at the convergence of my dad and mom making awful choices. It started to become painfully obvious that no one was going to choose me. I remember thinking, "If my own dad—the only man who has a biological predisposition to choose me—has never chosen me ... who will?"

Who, indeed.

This realization caused me so much pain, I wondered if I would ever have the strength to recover. I knew I would never trust a man again. And it wasn't even about trust—it was about not believing I was worthy of love, that I would never be successful in love. I was a hard-core romantic. I wanted the whole thing! I wanted the love thing, the married-until-we're-80 thing, and the have-a-bunch-of-kids thing. In an instant, all that was just gone. I had failed at that dream before I had even had the chance to pursue it.

In my desperation, I decided to make a power move. There had to be a different way this could go. I decided to try to prove myself wrong. It occurred to me that I had never told my dad how much he had hurt me. I had never asked him to change. I had never been open and vulnerable with him, so perhaps he just didn't realize what he was doing. Maybe he didn't mean it. Maybe he didn't know I cared. So I told him. I told him everything—on paper, handwritten—and I put it in the mail. I confirmed the address with my stepmom so I knew he would get it. And I know he did.

He never responded. Nothing. Not one word.

This was the only card I had left to play. This was the daughter card. This was the ultimatum card. This was the one wake-up call you answer. It hadn't occurred to me that he wouldn't change, or at least go to rehab. The very last thing I could have imagined was no response at all. That felt too final. It was too hard to consider. But that's exactly what I got. He had said nothing. And everything.

I. was. broken.

A few months later, after my drunk stepfather-to-be had crashed the car with my mom and me in it, she decided to marry this man. They got a date, a dress, and invited 200 people. I tried to tell her I wouldn't be at the wedding, I begged her not to go through with it. But alas, I stood there in a bridesmaid's dress, sobbing, as my mom didn't choose me.

I hardly remember that night. I decided that if I couldn't beat him, I should join him. He could hardly stand by dinner time, so I set out to race him into oblivion. There have been only a few times that I've had so much to drink that I didn't remember what happened. That night was one of them. It's not something I'm proud of. No wonder having an alcoholic parent leads to alcoholism. It suddenly made so much sense.

I woke up the next morning at the tipping point of a very steep slide into depression. It started, ironically, with a hangover, and moved quickly into a soul-sucking sadness. Returning to college and getting back into the swing of things was different now. I was numb. I spent a lot of time drinking. I sat in my room a lot. I was mostly writing, or that's what I wanted my roommates to think, but I was withdrawing.

Within a month of my mom's wedding, I found myself the victim of date rape. I had had sex with only one other person in my entire life before that, and he had been a boyfriend of three years. This guy was someone I knew, but barely. I had definitely not wanted it. But I had also never allowed myself to be vulnerable in that way before. It wasn't me. But then, who was I?

At the time, being taken advantage of in that way was just one more blow to my crumbling self-worth, but then I quickly decided—as victims often mistakenly do—that it was my fault. This was totally on me. I had put myself in this situation. I had said no, of course, but if no one else respected what I wanted, why should he? Why should I hold this particular man to a higher standard than any other man who had stomped all over my life? It wasn't his fault. And then there was this other weird thing: somehow, in allowing (I use this word loosely) him to take my body, a small part of me felt chosen.

I lay there, wanting to crawl out of my skin and yet barely able to keep from passing out. I wondered if this was where my worth was going to be found from now on. Maybe it was just in sex. Maybe that was all I had to offer. Everything else felt like failing. This felt like something.

In that moment, I accepted my fate as a victim. I took on the role. I donned the cloak. It felt easier somehow to be a victim—even freeing. After all, it wasn't my fault that everything got so screwed up. Life was clearly just going to happen. I didn't have any control or influence over it. The people who mattered most weren't valuing me; why should I value me?

And so began my descent from depression—to sheer worthlessness.

Being a victim was easy. If I had no control, surely I couldn't be held responsible for any consequences of my actions. Nothing mattered anymore. Trivial moments strung themselves together into hours and days and weeks. I went to class in my pajamas without makeup, and came home and went back to bed. I struggled with terrible insomnia and felt like a zombie. When you're numb on the inside, you can hide it on the outside. You know how you're supposed to act, you know what you're supposed to do and say. You fake it. I became a professional faker. I knew that this wasn't the type of thing that you unload on someone else. This is the crap you bury. This is the heavy stuff that later in life you just call "baggage."

After about a year and several more sexual partners, I found that the little piece of me that felt chosen after each encounter was fading away. My tolerance to that "drug" was getting higher. I needed more.

Looking back now, I can see very clearly that I was just desperate to be loved. It wasn't enough to feel "kind of" chosen. I needed love. I wanted to give it, and I wanted to receive it, and so I found myself head-over-heels in it the summer before my senior year of college. He was a boy from back home, one I had known most of my life. He was bad news from the moment I knew I was going to love him. I knew he was going to break me into pieces, but I was just so desperate to be loved that when he told me he loved me, I just went all in. He was controlling, but hilarious. He was incredibly jealous, but flattering. He was demanding, but immeasurably charming. The relationship ended when he proposed to the girl he was sleeping with while I was in college. I found out when I went home for Christmas. I sat crying between two cars in the parking lot of a bar. It was raining.

I. was. failing.

I was single for about five minutes before I found myself madly in love with the man who would end up leaving bruises on my arms the night of my graduation party. He was the worst. I was afraid of him—not only of what he would do to me physically and emotionally, but afraid he would leave me. I was afraid of what I knew about his alcohol and drug abuse, but afraid he would leave me. I was afraid of his anger issues and his manic outbursts. I had seen him beat up people at bars and in parking lots for no reason at all. He broke his hand on someone's face and fell asleep, bleeding onto my feather bed. But I was afraid he would leave me.

And of course he did. For the other girlfriend. I'd like to say that I left him, and for the record, I was the one who moved out and left over a heated, dramatic, screaming match in the front yard at 3 a.m., but he had made the choice. And he hadn't chosen me.

If this is you, if you relate to this, to any part of my story, I want you to know that I see you, and I hear you, and my heart breaks for you. But I also want you to know that this is where my story takes a dramatic turn, and I pray that the same becomes true for you. Because there is a different end to your story. I promise you that. And each and every day, I want you to know that you're holding the pen.

You get to write the ending. As Glenda the Good Witch says to Dorothy, "You've always had the power."

You've already got the ruby slippers, my friend. So how's it going to go?

Because here is the thing: I know now—I surely did not know then—that God has a very specific plan for my life (and for yours), and it included all of this pain, hardship and struggle. His plan for me included every last bit of suffering I had to walk through. I had to learn that in the same way I had made a choice to be a victim, I could un-choose it. I could choose to break the cycle. I could choose to take the reins. I know that sounds simple, and it is not at all simple, but it's there. It's just a choice. We are where we are in this life for no reason other than that we chose to be here. Every decision takes us another step down the path. I just finally got sick of the damn path and decided to try another!

After I mourned the loss of yet another piece of myself in that shameful relationship, I decided to take stock of what I still had left of me. Wouldn't you know it, I still had ALL of me. I was still all there, just a little worn and torn in areas. But I was just waiting to be reclaimed, rebuilt, and renewed. So I did that.

It started with simple reflection: What did I still have? What did I want more of? And what was I done with? I knew with utmost certainty that I wanted to be a mom someday. It was a part of my heart that burned brightly and wasn't going to be ignored. And as I was now in my early twenties, I started to think about these future children and what I wanted their lives to be like. Let me tell you, it didn't include any of the crap in my life up to that point. I had no healthy boundaries with my mom. I had a terrible rage-filled anger towards my stepfather. I had not spoken to my father in several years. I had resentment. I had pain. I had boatloads of shame. I had guilt. I had stress. I had numbness, and I had nothing to offer these beautiful future children as a woman or as a person. That sounded pretty damn pathetic to me, so I proactively chose to change the story.

I. chose. me.

For God's sake, someone had to do it. Why not me? And why not you?

What does your future look like? What do you want to make different? What small shifts can you make today to step in the right direction? This is not about perfection, this is about progress, tiny baby steps. But intentional baby steps.

The first thing I did was give myself boundaries. No dating. Not at all. I couldn't trust myself. I knew I had slipped into a cycle of co-dependence, and that if I did not seriously pump the brakes on that freight train, I would end up married to my father. I would have rinsed and repeated the cycle of my childhood. There are bad guys in this world. But they weren't just ending up in my life by random happenstance. I was choosing them. I played a role. And if I was playing a role, I could decide to play a different role.

The second thing I did was find healthy outlets for my emotional turmoil. I had been an actress for as long as I could remember, so I threw myself into the roles I had been cast in. I used that as an avenue to get out all that was within me. That was the easy and obvious thing for me. I'm sure there is an easy and obvious thing for you, but if there is not, writing is a wonderful tool. It's so amazingly powerful to journal. Only in a journal do you tell yourself the real crap you're struggling with. And then you're faced with it, and you have to deal with it. Or at least you've now purged it. And sometimes even that is enough. So I wrote.

I also stopped withdrawing. I clung to the friends I could be open and honest with—because we need people in this life. We need good people, and it's okay to lean on the good ones when we're struggling. I knew I could be myself with them. Being my imperfect self was an important part of the process back to feeling successful. Success starts—and ends—with imperfection. I needed to embrace that big time.

When you feel like a failure, you don't just think you're not successful. You feel like you CANNOT BE successful. I was telling myself some amazingly harmful stories about what had happened to me. But the fact is, it's not the things that happened to me that mattered. Lots of bad things happen to people—much worse than what happened to me. It's not the events of life that shape us, it's what we tell ourselves about these events that makes all the difference.

I have shared some of the ways I was disabling myself, but the truth is, if I hadn't been able to stop that self-sabotage, it was absolutely going to seal my fate as a failure. I wouldn't have gone on to accomplish anything at all—I'm sure of it—if I hadn't learned how to breathe life into myself. Positive self-talk is an incredibly important tool in bringing yourself back to life, let alone achieving any kind of success.

In the last seven-and-a-half years I've spent building a successful business, I've learned that most of what we face in life is 98% mental. The war is waged between your ears. And the old saying we heard back in kindergarten is 100% true: "Whether you think you can or think you can't, you're right." I went from thinking I couldn't, to thinking I could. Notice the key: Thinking. The entirety of my life shifted just because I shifted my thinking and my self-talk.

I recognized that I was not on the path I wanted. So I stopped walking on that path. I did a hard stop and looked around to gain perspective. I took responsibility for getting off track. Then, I cleared my head of the emotional clutter that was making it hard for me to see where I was going. Last, I made the decision to change, and did. I told myself different stories about what had happened, and those things started meaning different things.

It sounds so simple. But that's the trick: It IS simple. It's possible. And that's all that you need to know.

I had been afraid of winding up in a marriage like my mom's. I was so focused on not being co-dependent that I had become cripplingly co-dependent. I had become so enslaved to the FEAR that I would marry my father that I almost did!

I was walking that dangerous path simply because I had become obsessed with the idea. Scary how that works!

I had also told myself that my worth was in sex. That was an easy victim mentality— and a valid one at that, given my history—but it didn't have to be my truth. It didn't have to define me. So I told myself a different story about my experiences with men and how that was going to influence my future relationships with men. Instead of the mindset that I was doomed in love, I knew exactly what I was looking for, and that my next relationship would be wonderful.

After about two years of my working diligently to remain independent and focused on me, God brought me an amazing man who would become my husband. During that time, I realized that I had all of the control as to what relationship I chose. I raised my standards and decided to avoid—instead of ignore—all personality red flags, or addictive and aggressive tendencies. In addition to knowing what to avoid, I also started to pinpoint what I DID want in a relationship. I determined the values I wanted to share with a significant other, and I began to look for those things right away. As soon as I met my husband, I knew that I had finally figured out how to love correctly, for all the right reasons. When he said the most important thing to him was to become a father, I knew I had met my perfect match

My husband and I have been together for nine-and-a half-years and married for eight-and-a-half. We have three beautiful children. Our five-year-old daughter is incredibly kind and thoughtful, calm and maternal, and whimsical. We have a three-year-old son, who lives life at full speed, laughs with his whole heart, and is inquisitive and bright. And last, we have a one- year-old son. He's my "joy boy." He's easygoing, filled with love, incredibly engaged, and desperate to keep up.

Although our family is not perfect, I feel the success of having built it. I had to work through some serious failures—failures that continue to reemerge and reappear and re-threaten me to this very day—to achieve the blessing of my marriage and my family. But I had these three sweet babies in mind when I stood at the darkest moment of my life and DECIDED that they were worth whatever it took. I will forever be grateful that I took the steps I needed to take to become their mommy.

Happily, as soon as I started to value myself, my mom followed suit. She divorced my stepdad and broke the cycle for herself. She came to the same place I had come to, realizing she had to change course. I like to think that in some small way, I showed her what was possible. Each positive choice we make sends a positive ripple of influence out into the world. The world is in need of your ripple.

After about four years of clearing the emotional clutter and trauma, I was introduced to a business opportunity with a direct sales company in the health and wellness industry. The former version of me would have immediately written it off. I would have THOUGHT that it wasn't even worth the attempt. But a broken person DID build a COMPLETE success story. I am broken. I am cracked. I am scarred. I am altered. And I am all the better for it. I am a work in progress, which is how I was, and am, able to build this business piece by piece, from the ground up. After all, that's how I built me.

Within six years, I had reached the top of the company. I continue today to build a remarkable business, one that I wouldn't even have guessed I was capable of building. One that allows my husband and me to be present with our kids every single day, and allows us to travel the world and bless others. I help women and men all over the world stop on their broken road, reflect, envision their future, and start to make that reality their own.

Looking back, I honestly wouldn't change one part of the road I've walked. I don't believe in regrets. To me, regrets come from missed opportunities to learn. It's through failure—and not avoiding it—that I have learned so much that has been essential to my success.

I recently keynoted a retreat in Colorado where I spoke about how life prepares you for success by sending you through the ringer. God doesn't call the equipped; He equips the called. He calls you to your position in life and equips you as you walk the path. Everything we walk through conditions us and prepares us to be the exact game changer we've been put on this earth to become. It's all part of the plan and part of the process.

I believe that we all have a story and it's not meant to be private. We are here to be influential. My dear friend recently said, "It's our collective responsibility to leave this earth and the people on it different—better—than how we found them." I couldn't agree more. You're so completely a part of that. And you're more than capable of being that game-changing influence on someone else. You just have to be brave and push through.

Brene Brown, teaches us that as humans, we don't want to be vulnerable. It feels yucky and we avoid it at all costs. I get it. This chapter, and the rawness of my life, was hard for me to write. But here is the deal—it helps people. People become empowered by your vulnerability. People connect when you let your guard down. So don't be afraid to be imperfect. Imperfection is a blessing and a part of being on this earth. So embrace it. Just decide that it's absolutely okay. And then tell your story—however you can, in whatever way you find meaningful.

I'm so grateful for the opportunity to share mine here, and I pray that it serves you, whoever you are. But my bigger prayer is that YOU realize how truly powerful YOU are. You have the chance and the responsibility to begin to change many, many lives, by deciding to change your own. Embrace your journey. You're exactly where you're supposed to be. And if you're willing, the greatest success you'll ever know is awaiting you on the other side of whatever you THINK is your biggest failure.

Walk through. Be bold. Someone is desperate for you to do so.

About Wendy Cunningham

Wendy Cunningham is a wife, mother, entrepreneur, friend, coach, mentor, writer, and speaker. She is an Independent Consultant with an extraordinary health and wellness company, and has built an exceptional business. She's also an aspiring blogger and game changer!

After spending more than 15 years pursuing her passion for theatre performance, Wendy has found success in taking the road less traveled—the one she never thought would lead her to her life's passion of helping others step into their God-given purpose. Wendy helps people gain perspective in their lives and on their journey, and hopes to continue to inspire people to live their very best life despite their circumstances or setbacks.

Contact Wendy directly at WendyRickaye@gmail.com

Gainingmyperspective.com

Chapter Seven
Afraid You'll Fail? Do It Anyway.
By Amanda Earnest

Chapter Seven
Afraid You'll Fail? Do It Anyway.
By Amanda Earnest

"Anyone else. Anyone but me. I can't. I'm not good enough. I don't have anything relevant to teach anyone."

These were my first impressions when I was invited to share my story here. The words "I can't," "I'm not," and "I don't" flooded my mind. Doubt set in, followed by fear and anxiety. Once again, I found myself out of my comfort zone, wanting to flee. But I didn't. Because after experiencing these same feelings innumerable times before, I have finally—FINALLY—started to understand how to deal with them. I've learned how to acknowledge them, to set them aside, and to eventually move past them. I'm not ready, but I'm going to share my story with you anyway. Because I've learned that doing things even when you feel you aren't ready is one of the best ways a person can achieve success through failure.

In 2004, I was expecting our first baby. I was as thrilled as I was sick—which was a lot! I struggled through a nausea-filled pregnancy while finishing my bachelor's degree at Brigham Young University. I had earned a four-year degree from a top university in only three years.

Summertime came and my husband Mark and I moved into my parents' home for three months. While we were there, my mom threw a baby shower for me. It was at that shower that I experienced my first entrepreneurial ah-ha moment.

My mom, a very creative person, wasn't the type to just go buy a gift from the store. Her gift was large, homemade, heavy, and fluffy. The bag it was in bulged on all sides. I pulled out what appeared to be a blanket, and I opened it to show an inquisitive crowd. But the blanket didn't "open." It was sewn shut—but just on one side.

"Wait, what is this?" I wondered. It was soft and beautiful but I wasn't sure what it was. "It's a baby sleep sack!" Mom exclaimed from the kitchen. She was fussing with refilling the lemonade beverage dispensers and cookie platters, or doing some other "hostessy" thing across the room.

I loved her gift, and so did everyone else. It was the perfect thing to take with us on our big move to frigid upstate New York, where Mark would be starting law school just one month later. Madelyn was born and we moved to Ithaca. Our new home and new city were accompanied by something else that was new: student loans. Big ones.

Having just one baby and a husband who spent 12 hours a day at school, I decided to do something from home to help us earn money. I loved Mom's baby sleep sack, and so did baby Madelyn. I thought, "Maybe we could sell these!" So we did. Mom and I became business partners.

Starting a traditional business is costly, so we obtained a loan. We already had a student loan debt at this time, and adding a business debt to it made me very nervous. But we believed in ourselves and in our product, so we moved forward.

Our first shipment arrived and baby Madelyn crawled around the boxes full of blankets. I felt great excitement, but also an overwhelming feeling of "now what!?" The "now what" moment, I think, is when many people just stop. They don't know what to do or how to do it, so they just don't do anything. Have you ever felt that way? I was scared, but I knew there was no turning back.

At first, we sold our blankets directly to the consumer right out of my living room. But eventually, the real excitement and serious profits came through wholesaling. I still remember the day an email came in that literally caused me to jump out of my chair cheering. It was from a lady named Kate. Her email address extension was that of a swanky big-box department store. It was an order! I couldn't believe it. I printed the official purchase order. I remember just staring at it, smiling and taking it all in. Had I ever fulfilled an order from a national retailer? No. Had I ever had to read a "compliance" manual? No. I didn't even know what that was. Had I ever done a presentation on my product to a group of strangers whose job was to sell it? No. But I took on all those things anyway, learning as I went. Because I believed I could.

Now what about this story encompasses any facet of "failure," you might ask? Well, it happened about four years in—in 2008. After we had enjoyed a long, happy, and continual relationship with the big-box store, the economy began to shift. Unfortunately, we didn't realize it nearly soon enough.

The biggest order yet was sitting in my email inbox. The buyer let me know she'd be sending the official purchase order in July for their fall lineup. I was so excited. I had the items made, invested a lot of money, but July came and went with no purchase order. August came. And finally, an email: "Oh yes! Hi. I am so sorry I didn't have a chance to reach out to you sooner. We have actually decided to scale back our layette department. We hope you understand and look forward to doing business in the future."

I probably read that a dozen times before it actually sunk in. No order. *There would be no order!* There I sat with a substantial investment of thousands of pieces, and no one to buy them. I felt like a complete and total failure. "How could I be so stupid? Why did I get ahead of myself and have all these blankets made before I had an official purchase order in my hand? I should have known. I am not good enough to achieve success. I'm not a business person; I'm just a mom. I can't do this."

Those were the words that filled my head. Feelings of defeat and failure, confusion and fear took over. I was devastated. And there we were, with a mountain of product and no one to buy it.

It was then, after baby #3, that I decided to "move on." Mom didn't really need the money, and I told myself I didn't have the time. Looking back, I realize now that "no time" is an easy excuse we allow ourselves. Because for me, "no time" really meant "no desire." I no longer wanted to sell baby blankets. I had gotten discouraged and felt overwhelmed, and those feelings were all the excuse I needed to quit.

The negative, primitive mind in each of us will affirm feelings like this. It would take several years before I would start learning how to combat those feelings. I decided to close down the business at that point, feeling that I had failed.

We eventually earned our investment back, and then brought in some nice side income for a few years. But once I lost the desire, it was extremely difficult to stay motivated as an entrepreneur. I decided to focus 100% on being Mom to our three little girls, and I took some time off.

Having my first business was a great experience, overall. I realized that I can learn how to do anything. Everything I did for that business, I had never done before. And in traditional business, you really are on your own. I didn't have any mentors showing me what to do. But I didn't care—I figured it out, and I did it anyway.

Life truly is one giant learning curve—entrepreneurship, motherhood, serving in your church or community, your marriage—everything. It's all a vehicle for self-growth and learning. And it's a vehicle for failure.

Let's fast forward a few more years, and two more babies.

I was pregnant with #5. Once you get to that number of kids you start to just assign numbers to them. As usual, I was sick. Again. It was at that point in the pregnancy when you wonder to yourself, "Why did I do this? I can never do this ever again. For SURE this is our last one." I spent most days on the couch, not able to move around too much. On one of those days my phone rang.

"What can I do for ya?" I asked my friend. He was super jazzed about something. He told me he always thought I was a sharp person, and that he remembered that I had once owned my own business.

"I've got a little work-from-home business opportunity for you," he said. I smiled and rolled my eyes. "What?! Sounds like multi-level marketing, Jimmy!" I darn near laughed him right off the phone. Then I told him all the reasons why I couldn't.

"I can't have a job right now. I can't even drink a glass of water and keep it down." I told him "no" several more times and offered a plethora of other excuses, but I thanked him for thinking of me.

Jimmy insisted that at least I try the product—a face cream called Nerium. Although he didn't say so, he has probably noticed the mess my face was in because of my pregnancy. The cream was a botanically-based skincare product formulated for not only lines and wrinkles, but also dark spots, splotchiness, scarring, uneven skin tone, and uneven skin texture and large pores. I actually had been really self-conscious of my skin after having been through so many pregnancies and I was open to trying out a new product. If it did what it said it would do, I'd at least be glad to have found it. So I agreed to try a sample.

He dropped it off, but in my pregnancy woes I found myself forgetting to even brush my teeth, let alone wash my face each night. So I never used it. But, with my permission, Jimmy kept me posted on the company in the months that followed.

It was during this time that I started to have a more open mind to the network marketing industry. I started to realize that there were actually quite a few people whom I knew who had achieved incredible success, across all different types of companies. The more I educated myself on the opportunity that the industry can provide for an average person—a busy mom like me, for example—the more interested in it I became. I realized that before, when I laughed at my friend Jimmy, "I didn't know what I didn't know." I started to feel bad for teasing my friend so many months before—for laughing at him because he was in "one of those things."

I quickly realized that Nerium International* could provide me a way to have my own business again – without all the risk of a large investment, and without the pressure of being everything for everyone, the way I used to be. I wouldn't have to be customer service, the accounting department, fulfill orders, or do anything else I used to hate doing as a traditional business owner, because the company would do all those things for me. And I was so excited to have a team of mentors and a world-class system and training in place to help me achieve the success I wanted.

Six months later, after the baby was born, I decided not only to become a customer but to also become a "Brand Partner" with Nerium International. I wanted to get the products for free and I figured I could recommend it to a couple of friends and make a little money on the side, so I joined. I had never done network marketing before, but I took it on anyway because I believed that I could. I was right!

The months that followed would become a great part of my story. Starting a business with Nerium was one of the best decisions I ever made for myself and even for my family. My friend Jimmy became one of my many mentors. Thank goodness we don't do network marketing alone. I had serious insecurity and fear around my business. I had owned my own business before but for some reason, in the beginning, this business felt different, even though it really wasn't. For example, if you opened a restaurant in town, would you be afraid to invite your friends and family to try it out? No! Absolutely not. And so I began my great journey to finding a shift in mindset, and a path of personal growth, realizing success through failure in this, my second business.

Earlier I mentioned that life gives us the opportunity to fail. Well, entrepreneurship is one of the things in life that I would call the "failure fast track." Do you want to fail fast and hard and over and over and over again? Then start a business. Because you WILL do it wrong. You will fall down. You will also get up. And over time you will learn how to get back up faster and stronger than the time before.

One thing that I've learned to do since starting my Nerium business is to set realistic goals. I learned I had been doing "goal-setting" wrong for years. Call them goal-fails. My goals evolved as I evolved as a person and as a leader in my business. Before, I just had ideas in my head—things I wanted to get done. Every once in a while I'd write them out on some sort of to-do list, but a few months into my journey, I realized I probably should make a more conscientious effort. I went from not even really having goals, to jotting them down on a sticky note, to writing them on a large piece of paper, to typing them out, to putting them in a paper planner, and finally even making a dream board for myself.

Now, I don't always hit my goals. That's for sure. On one occasion I was particularly downtrodden in my business. An amazing woman on the other side of the world wanted to get started with me. She was going to be one of our leaders as we launched a country in Asia. But as quickly as she decided to get started, she changed her mind. I was heartbroken; I lost her. It brought back the feelings I had when reading the email from the big-box buyer that said, "Thanks, but no thanks, enjoy your million extra blankets with no one to buy them."

The following morning I woke up early, before everyone else in the house, and I worked through the pain. I did a little yoga, some early-morning prayer and scripture reading, and I wrote in my journal. I even went into our walk-in closet (so I wouldn't wake up the whole house), turned on the light, and did a live broadcast on social media to all my followers about how I had been defeated. I went on to assure them that I was currently in that moment working hard to acknowledge my disappointment, own it for what it was, and then set it aside and move forward so I could learn from it.

There are many more stories of ups and downs of life, motherhood, marriage, and entrepreneurship, but all of them have a similar lesson to offer—an underlying theme relating to success and failure. My own personal journey across several different businesses and many other experiences in life have helped me to redefine failure. I have made so many mistakes. Those mistakes are the tests—they provide the "what now?" moments. That's when negativity sets in. It's when your primitive mind wants to protect you. It wants to prevent you from getting hurt so it tells you not to try anything new, and certainly not to go "back for more" if you get burned. A fearful mindset will prevent you from progressing.

Part of achieving success through failure is learning how to push that fear and doubt aside. Push the negativity out, replace it with focus and desire to succeed. Believe in yourself and in your ability to be YOU—who you truly are inside—an amazing person capable of great things, with talents and gifts that only YOU have.

Do what you have never done before, so you can not only have what you have never had, but so you can BE the person you have never been. Take risks. Fall down. Get comfortable being uncomfortable. Believe in yourself and become the best version of you that you possibly can be. Realize that success is not what the world defines for you. Rather, it is what you define for yourself. Sit down and write out your goals for your life—your business, your family, your marriage, your journey—whatever it may be. Decide what makes *your* journey special and define what success means to you.

If, to you, success is just getting dinner on the table at the end of the day, then good job. If it's making a million dollars, then that's just as good, too. The key is, YOU define it. And you achieve it. Don't know how to do something? Do it anyway. I did. And I still am, every day. I'm doing it right now, as I write this book.

Visualize your dreams, your success; write down a plan and execute it. Pursue your goals in a way that is vulnerable and accepting of the fact that you are not perfect, and you're not supposed to be. You will make mistakes, and that's okay. Acknowledge them, celebrate them, and get back up. Don't say the words "I can't," "I'm not," and "I don't." Believe you can be more; believe you can do more; and believe you can become more. Because you can.

This chapter was not paid for or published by Nerium International, and is my own personal story.

About Amanda Earnest

Amanda Earnest is from Orange County, California, and has been married to her best friend, Mark, for 15 years. She is honored and proud to be a stay-at-home mother to their five children.

Her bachelor's degree in child development benefits her daily as she enjoys sharing parenting successes—and failures!—on her blog, ocbeautymom.com.

Amanda's passion for the beauty industry also serves as the inspiration for sharing live beauty tips and makeup tutorials with viewers on various social media channels. She loves makeup artistry and teaching women how to feel as beautiful on the outside as they are on the inside!

Having always had an interest in entrepreneurship, Amanda has owned several businesses, from traditional to non-traditional. Recently, she started a business in the skincare and anti-aging industry. She is an Independent Brand Partner with Nerium International and was recently featured both on the cover and inside *Beautiful You* magazine.

You can learn more or get in touch with Amanda by visiting amandaearnest.successtoday.com.

Chapter Eight
Shame as a Mountain
By Naomi Fox

Chapter Eight
Shame as a Mountain
By Naomi Fox

"My brokenness is a far greater bridge than my pretend wholeness ever was."
~Sheila Walsh

We all have our weaknesses. The things in us that are not perfected. We are human and that is ok. But we also have in us a mission—a purpose and a reason why we are here on earth. In fact, we have many. The combination of our callings and our imperfections is what creates the need for failure. Indeed, it is the most powerful way that we learn. The unique lessons we gather as we travel the trail of shattered attempts are actually the very gems that we have to offer to others. They are our bits of joy, hope, clarity and peace. Without them, without our brokenness, we cannot fully serve others.

I am very open and public about my life. I have been married twice, and divorced twice. I have had a miscarriage at 12 weeks and a stillbirth at 22 weeks. I have had some powerful and unique birth experiences. My blog post about giving unassisted birth at home at 43 weeks and 4 days (that's 25 days past the due date if you're counting) has been viewed and passed around tens of thousands of times. I am happy to share what I've learned as I feel prompted.

I have had many failures in my life, at least the kinds of things others would consider to be "failures." I see them as powerful lessons for which I am forever grateful, and I would not change any part of them. Not one. Some are easier to talk about than others. Some come with shame, some do not, and all come with sorrow. I feel some anxiety as I share one of my biggest failures in a way that I never have before. It is a powerful and deeply painful story, one that has caused me more sustained trauma and heartache than anything else I've endured.

In 2010, at the ripe age of 29, I was a co-founder of an international childbirth education organization. We certified and trained birth educators to teach a method developed by a team of phenomenal people. It was awe-inspiring to be a part of the program. More than 320 educators signed up to become certified in this method in six different countries across four continents; we were the fastest growing company in our industry in history. We also made over $150,000 in the first six weeks of business. But more than that, I believed I was filling my life purpose through this mighty organization. I felt part of the reason I was on this earth was to change the world through birth education.

I believe that a great deal of unnecessary trauma happens before, during, and shortly after labor and delivery, and that with better education, much of it can be minimized or totally avoided. I have seen great damage to families, couples, and children as a direct result of a lack of information and an overabundance of fear. There are 4.2 million babies born in the US every year and we had aims and desires to touch nearly one quarter of those at one million birthing mothers, annually, who would have more grounded, balanced information to make the best choice for themselves, their babies, and their families. Simple as that. The workbook that was developed and intended for every expectant mother taking these courses is still unrivaled in the industry, with 200 full-color pages packed with phenomenal information. We printed thousands of them. They have dwindled down to just a few boxes left gathering dust, stacked in my front hall closet, never to complete the measure of their creation.

With all of this momentum and so much passion and clarity, it is hard to imagine what could have possibly gone wrong. I have yet to see another business come together with such unity, drive and purpose.

Three weeks after we started, and on my 30th birthday, there was a ring of the doorbell and a giant stack of papers left by a long-gone process server. We were being sued in Federal Court for trademark infringement. The complaint was riddled with both outrageous lies and plenty of truth intentionally phrased to make us look bad. The lies were laughable at first, and the truths were mortifying. I also learned that if you put something in a complaint, no matter how untrue it may be, that you cannot be charged with libel or slander.

The stack of papers must have been four inches thick. There was a copy for each of us named in the lawsuit. The merits of the case had little substance. It was clear that our main competition, which had been in business for decades, did not like the fact that their people were stampeding away in droves to join our company, because we offered what they had all been begging and pleading for. Still, they had enough traction to get a TRO, a temporary restraining order, against our business. We immediately changed the allegedly offending name, but the lawsuit proceeded. It lasted only six months and ended in a settlement, but it cost the company $300,000 in legal fees and costs. It completely crippled us financially. Mission accomplished.

The funny but sad thing is, we likely would have been able to pull through, since everyone loves an underdog, especially in the world of natural birth. The big problem was that just before the lawsuit hit, a full-on "hate blog" had cropped up, started by my closest friend of six years. She was furious and was hell bent on showing it. To this day I am still not sure why she was so angry, as there was never a confrontation or an expression of strong disagreement before the blog was born. Nevertheless, the once-laughable claims in the original lawsuit started to be repeated and exaggerated so many times that those who initially laughed with us not only started to believe them, they were actively spreading them.

I watched in horror as my life slowly and steadily crumbled. Every close friend faded out of my life, save one, due to that blog. I had previously experienced what it felt like to essentially be a celebrity, to be praised for my work, to have people want to take their picture with me and just have a brief conversation with me as the co-founder of this phenomenal movement. This was sharply contrasted by the whispers, isolation, and even private messages asking me how I could sleep at night.

I had wanted to be praised and admired for my efforts when we started the business. The idea of being granted such a status was intoxicating and the allure of fame was calling. Those desires turned into dust and burned me hard. I not only had to let go of those and stay focused on my true "WHY" for getting started, but had to operate in a place of total humility to even be able to get out of bed in the morning.

The lawsuit alone was difficult, but the blog cut us off at the knees. It raged for a good year and a half with regular postings, and continued intermittently for years even after that. I could not make a move without it being twisted and blogged about. I had a pregnancy during that time that was incredibly difficult. I struggled a great deal with my mental health and suffered extreme ante-partum depression. (That's depression *during* the pregnancy.) The bloggers would say how it was tragic that we were having more children and curse my unborn baby.

After my son was born and my blog post about his labor and delivery went viral, I saw one person post "I throw up in my mouth every time I see someone share Naomi's birth story. SHE IS NOT A BIRTHING GODDESS and I wish people would stop celebrating her." They did not pull any punches. Nothing was sacred. Even years later, when I had my stillbirth at 22 weeks, they commented on a blog post I wrote 11 days after he was gone. I had to have surgery to remove my son because I was not going into labor on my own. I lost 40% of my blood as a result of some complications from the surgery. When I was still so weak from the blood loss I was fainting as I got up to use the bathroom, one of them said that God took my baby from me because we were such awful people and didn't deserve to have another child.

I scoured the internet looking for anything I could find on how to deal with a situation like this. There was precious little. The closest I could find were posts about how to deal with "haters," so I devoured everything I came across. But I eventually came to see that "haters" and the cancer that I was dealing with were not very similar at all. Haters will comment on your YouTube video and criticize the way you talk or the less-than-flattering things you wear. Still hurtful, no doubt, but these attacks I was receiving were on another level—they were personal, even intimate, and meant for the jugular. It was a unique kind of trial and the loneliness I felt in this shame-riddled struggle was truly unbearable.

They spewed their favorite accusations: that we were scam artists and just out for taking people's money. That my husband had physically assaulted the president of our company during a meeting. That he had threatened physical violence to others as well. They would harp on these things as if they were fact. They were simply not true.

Sadly, one of the things they merely *speculated* about being true—saying that my husband was being physically violent with me—well, that one *was* true. A few months after we started the business, he threw me across the room one night when I unknowingly triggered his PTSD after he unknowingly triggered mine. Then a month later he had slapped me one night so many times he gave me two black eyes. I remember feeling like such a cliché, putting on purple eyeshadow to perfectly balance out the bruising as it was healing so that I could finally leave the house. But I couldn't tell anyone. We had built this business together, and we had a new baby, and shortly after had another one on the way.

The mountain of shame that had piled on top of me, just waiting to crush me, was too much to bear. If I admitted what was happening at home, that I was a victim of domestic violence, I thought the things that they did lie about would "become truth," and I simply could not allow that to happen. It is hard enough to get out of a physically violent marriage, let alone when you have children with the man. It was made harder by a high level of psychological abuse.

Things got so difficult I wanted to abandon my dream business shortly after the lawsuit was settled. But he wouldn't have it. To me, it felt like having a child die. He wanted to see it through to success, to prove them all wrong. So I went along with it, thinking that we could "rise above" all of the ultra-haters, and our success would speak for itself. So I was going to take to my grave the fact that he had ever been violent with me. If I reported it to the authorities I could kiss goodbye my chances of ever seeing this business succeed, or so I thought.

I felt as though I had chains around me that were preventing me from moving forward. Any move I made to grow the business only created more motivation for this angry mob to generate more blocks to my progress. I cherished and clung to the idea that the harder it got was a reflection of it being what we were meant to do. I felt as though I was pushing a boulder up a hill. I just wanted so badly not to be misinterpreted in my actions. Even though I've had two abusive husbands, I have never been more repeatedly violated and betrayed than by this group of women that once called me friend. I felt as though my failures would never be overcome. But I lacked the skills to know how to diplomatically respond to the criticisms, so I just stayed quiet. I never publicly responded to anything that was said about me. In fact, this is the first official story I've shared about that whole experience.

My husband and I even started other businesses together, but the "haters" followed us and would actively reach out to our new customers and clients, warning them of how deceitful we were, and directing them to their blog. Their goal seemed to be to ruin our lives and our marriage.

We moved out of state and were able to get some semblance of separation from them. But I was slowly dying. The more oppressive things got, the more supportive and adoring of my husband I became. I called my husband "the Hubbalicious" on social media and painted our lives out to be that of a near-fairy tale. I did not think I could handle the shame of being divorced twice. I wanted so much for us to just "grow out of this phase" and have all of it just be the typical trials of the first few years of marriage.

But things became worse and worse. My stillbirth in 2014 was a catalyst for things coming to light. My husband decided to reach out to some old girlfriends while I was rebuilding my blood supply and was too weak to manage his emotions. I discovered he had a couple of emotional affairs, back to back, before I even hit my original due date. One I found out about from finding a string of intimate text messages; the other I learned about because the "lady" sent me a long, detailed email outlining all that they had done together and was so ashamed she had to unburden herself. I received that message the day after we became homeless. Failure after failure after failure.

And yet, even as my world seemed to keep crumbling, as I truly did not know how much more I could bear, there was a light that was guiding me. I was led to spend some time nearly 500 miles away with my one dear friend who had survived the "friend apocalypse." While spending a week with her, I received some powerful and painful experiences that showed me unquestionably how broken that marriage was. Miracle after miracle got me out of that situation, and more miracles came at a steady rate the more that I emotionally, physically, and legally separated myself from his narcissistic abuse.

I began to experience miracles on a daily basis. One of them came in the form of a woman I greatly looked up to and admired, as her book changed my life: Leslie Householder had reached out to me for a random request and I was able to get on the phone with her. It was only a couple of weeks after deciding to leave him, and we talked for just a brief ten minutes. I explained my situation and she responded with two things I will never forget. First, she told me that I inspired her, which I knew could have come only because the Lord was directing my life. Second, she asked me how I got out "so quick." Dumbfounded, I replied that it took me five years to leave him. She reaffirmed that it was fast and that most women married to men like him, with our situation being so complex, take decades to leave, if ever. Her statements echoed through the following months as I started to detox from the brainwashing and see more clearly than ever before in my life.

As I wrestled with what to do to provide for myself and my three boys as a single mom, I could not ignore my passion for building businesses. I felt that I had been specifically groomed by a divine and loving God to prepare myself to help others through branding and website design. It wasn't until I looked back after watching it all unfold that I could see the perfection in the careful guidance I had been receiving all along the way.

I had been branding and managing my businesses since 2005 and had even learned how to do website design as a way to bootstrap our way through all of those lean years. I had learned a great deal about intellectual property, the hard way, and even had learned out of necessity how to design in programs like Photoshop. From having so many failures in business I knew full well how important trust, consistency, and overall business integrity are. I have adopted a policy that is rooted in lessons that are written on my heart of always being honest no matter what.

These insights, along with my social media savvy, have created a potent combination. I have also learned through my healing process how powerful my intuition is and has always been, and have developed an intentional confidence in the impressions I receive. And all of that energy and talent at making things *appear* to be perfect is now channeled into generating a beautiful look and feel for my clients' brands through their logo, social media, and website.

In learning about group dynamics, company culture, and business chemistry I have become quite skilled at coordinating and managing people and projects. I have grown my company, Branding Intuitive, from a one-woman show to having a dozen people working for me to create high-end packages for my inspired and amazing clients. I have been able to connect and get to know some of the most incredible people on this journey and have been able to channel my deep passion for fulfilling my life purpose into helping hundreds, so they can go out to help hundreds of thousands.

I believe that when we feel called to do something professionally, it is because it is part of our purpose and mission here on earth, and that we are entitled to divine help. I am able to uniquely and intuitively connect with my clients and their businesses through branding and website design to help them grow and develop to become all that they need to be to fill the purpose of their creation. I am humbled and honored to step into this role and help them see what makes them unique, and show them in real, tangible form all that they can and need to be.

I continue to experience failures, but more often I witness success after success after success as I grow and progress at an amazing rate. I am continually directed and guided to specific people and organizations where I can be of direct benefit and share the good things that I have been given. It is all because of my Father in Heaven, for I would truly be nothing without Him.

My three boys are thriving and happy and connected. We are still learning every day, which means we are not yet perfect, but that is also where the beauty is to be found.

About Naomi Fox

Naomi Fox is a serial entrepreneur with a deep passion for the creation and early growth stages of businesses. She believes that when we feel called to do something professionally it is because it is part of our purpose and mission here on this Earth and that we are entitled to divine help. Naomi intuitively connects with her clients and their businesses through branding and website design with Branding Intuitive to help them grow and develop to become all that they need to be to fill the purpose of their creation.

She lives in St. George, Utah with her three boys. She home schools and has a deep passion for motherhood, parenting, and vulnerability. She believes that we are at our strongest when we lean into vulnerability and that this is a difficult and acquired skill. Naomi also believes that vulnerability is the birthplace of creativity, love, and connection.

Chapter Nine
Turning Pain Into Purpose
By Wendy Starling Gardiner

Chapter Nine
Turning Pain Into Purpose
By Wendy Starling Gardiner

I'll never forget the day I died. Inside, anyway. The day I lost custody of my infant son marked some of the darkest hours of my life. Yet, looking back—because I know the outcome of my story—that day also marked the beginning of a life-changing journey for me. It was a journey that would bring my son back to me, and eventually bring me back to life.

For most people, that day back in 2000 was a get up and go to work day. Much of the planet was busy speculating about the Y2K computer crash that never happened, while my world was crashing in around me. For several years, I'd been living in the grips of a vicious addiction to methamphetamine. At the time, I thought it was all about weight loss. But looking back, I now realize there were other issues. As a child I was diagnosed with Oppositional Defiant Disorder (ODD) and Conduct Disorder (CD), and even as a young adult had emotional and behavioral issues. Basically, I spent my entire life since I was six years old angry, alone, depressed, and confused, with difficulty connecting with anyone, especially my own parents. My whole life I felt like an outsider looking in, a stranger in my own family. I knew I was broken, I just didn't understand why. Five days after I turned 19, I married a much older man who turned abusive the day after our wedding. He took an already broken girl and crushed her even further. After a year and a half with him I had "eaten my feelings" and gained a lot of weight. I was even more shattered inside from my experiences with him. When I was introduced to the drug it made the lifetime of turmoil inside me melt away. I finally felt good inside, and needed more. The rapid weight loss sealed the deal for me. I was hooked.

Day after day I would wake up groggy after a late night of getting high, if I ever went to sleep at all which I often wouldn't for days at a time. Then I would try hard to act like sober person, all the while chasing the high again. Miraculously, when I found out I was pregnant I sobered up, and I managed to stay sober while I breast fed. I remember holding my son close and feeling a sense of love and true connection I had longed to feel, but had always escaped me. Seeing his blue eyes stare into mine made me feel as though I was his whole world. I'd cuddle him and feel a sense of purpose. I was his mother. And I loved being a mother.

However, back then I knew nothing about of the lifesaving and life-changing principles of recovery, so sadly even though I'd managed to stay clean that long through shear will, as soon as I had weaned my baby the addiction beast inside me rationalized my using meth again. I had no internal sense of self-worth, so my desire to shed the 80 pounds gained during pregnancy outweighed any logical or rational reason why I shouldn't use "just enough each day to lose weight." The day came when I fell over that edge into full-blown use—my addiction was too strong.

I gave in. And I gave up.

After I'd been using meth again for a few weeks I could tell my brain had switched fully over to addict mode, because I started thinking only of myself. With my addiction in full swing, I struggled to manage my need to fuel my insatiable hunger for meth with the constant need of feeding and taking care of my infant son. Addiction and motherhood do not mix. But when you are in that situation, you convince yourself you can do both.

Then THAT day came. First I lost my job. It hadn't taken much for my boss to catch on that I was using, and I got the call that I'd been fired. Then I learned I'd lost my car. At that time, my car had been in the shop getting repaired. It had taken me several weeks to come up with the money to pay the deductible. Once I had enough money, I called the shop to see when I could pick it up. The manager told me that my parents had already picked up my car a few days earlier. It was then I learned that although the vehicle was registered in my name, and I made the payments, that because the loan was in their name they could take the car from me. Needless to say, I was upset. So I called them.

That's when the last pieces of my world crumbled. My parents had been babysitting my son for a few days. My grandparents had been in town visiting, and they wanted some time to see my baby. I had agreed to that, somewhat hopeful that my willpower would be strong enough so I could sober up enough to be a good mother. Willpower lasts for only so long. I needed more help, but didn't know how to ask and was probably too proud to anyways.

I remember demanding my car back and my baby. They responded by saying they would not give me the car back because they believed I was using again. Then I heard the words that would sear my mind for years to come.

"The judge signed the papers giving us temporary custody. You'll have to wait until we go to court. The judge will decide if you get visitation."

Their words cut into my soul like millions of tiny shards of broken glass.

I don't remember intending to scream. I just opened my mouth and the sounds that escaped from my lips were like thunder that had been pent up for millennia. I felt myself die inside. Gasping for air, I dropped the phone, tears pouring from my eyes—surely enough to drain my body of every ounce of fluid.

My soul cried out as I sobbed.

I felt as though I was in a narrow space, becoming narrower by the second. Everything felt dark. I fell to the floor, curled up in fetal position, while wave after wave of sharp pain racked my entire body. I remember feeling a physical manifestation of emotional pain so intense every part of me ached. I'd been through my share of hurts and disappointments. But this pain was different. My sobbing would ease enough for me to wonder if the pain would subside, but then I'd think of my son. His fresh, baby smell. His tiny fingers. His curious eyes. I had to experience the reality that he would no longer be with me. Over and over rolled the horror that my baby was gone, taken by own family, those who claimed to love me and cherish me. Later in my journey to sobriety I would come to understand things from their perspective and why they felt removing my baby from my care was necessary, but in that moment I could only feel pain, betrayal, loss, and sorrow. It consumed me completely.

In the space of just two hours I'd lost everything, but everything else I had lost paled in comparison to losing my precious child.

I have no idea how long I lay there screaming. At some point, I resigned myself to the only solution to my pain that I knew. I could numb it. And, of course, because I was living in addict mode, I convinced myself one fix would be just enough to allow me to breathe again—to survive. So I took the money I had planned to pay the auto shop to get my car, and I went to the first so-called "friend" I knew would have a stash. I bought as much meth as I could. There are still parts of the addiction story I can't wrap my head around. Like how an addict caught in the depths of the disease somehow views the substance that could lead her to destruction as the solution to her current pain. And yet, that was the reality I saw before me.

I would learn several months later that there are wonderful addiction treatment programs for mothers with children. Sadly, in the beginning of my recovery, I had no idea that such a thing existed, or how to go about getting into one. My Division of Children and Family Services social worker, who was assigned to me by the courts, just stated that I had six months before they would decide on permanent custody. I was determined to follow the court's requirements and try to stay clean so I could get my baby back.

I would learn later that DCFS had the ability to provide resources like drug treatment programs, job seeking assistance, housing and the like. But when I first landed in a court of law these programs were not offered to me. They simply told me to "figure it out,"— to get a job, an apartment, and "get treatment somewhere."

I had no clue what treatment was or where I could find it.

I struggled. I struggled to find a job. To find a place to live. And to get help. I was young, alone, all my friends used drugs, I had no idea where to even start, but I was going to figure it out.

In retrospect it's much easier to see the "defining moments" – the moments where if only I'd made a different decision the entire course of my future could have been altered for the better. One of those moments came soon after. It was preceded by one day in particular that shoved the depths of my despair even deeper. I discovered that I had head lice. Dear friends and loved ones who know me today know I wear my hair long, and I love styling it. I shudder as I remember the shame I felt the day I had to ask my mom to help me treat head lice. On one of the visits with my son, I mustered up enough courage to be vulnerable, and I asked my mother if she could please help me treat the lice. She said she would, and told me to bring a medicated shampoo called RID to our next visit and that she would help me.

An hour after I left that visit, I received a call from my DCFS worker informing me I was not allowed back to my parents' home for visitation until CNS (Community Nursing Services) treated me and declared me lice free. My heart broke when the worker explained that since they were booked out three weeks, I couldn't see my son and would be denied visitation.

I felt rejected by my mother. I felt ashamed. Not able to stand having them, I treated the lice with some over-the-counter product, thinking I was doing the best thing. But when the CNS nurse finally visited me she let me know that because I'd used those products too recently she could not do another treatment for several more days. Only, she was booked out another three weeks.

My arms ached! My soul ached! Seeing him, holding him, feeling his sweet kisses was the only thing that kept me going! Another three weeks without the feel of my baby in my arms felt like a death sentence. Again, that beast inside my mind reared up and reasoned with me: "You're in pain, and I know how to help."

And my addict brain worked like this: The penalty for a dirty UA (urine analysis) is no visitation for a week.

My thought was, "You can't see your baby anyway, so why not numb the pain?" Remember, I was still lacking any real recovery principles, so I listened to that voice. And so, in that defining moment, I picked up the pipe again. After that, I relapsed several times. I was still determined to "beat this thing somehow," but I just didn't have the tools. The "treatment" I had found was meeting with a counselor once a week. That just wasn't enough to overcome the hold that the addiction had over me. And so the battle inside my soul raged on.

The date of the final custody hearing came. I remember thinking I at least had a chance to get my son back, because I had made some strides to do what the judge had said. I was fooling myself. I had a lot more work to do. But I wanted to believe it. I walked into the courthouse that day feeling as though my body was literally vibrating because of the fear and anxiety. It took every ounce of courage I could muster to walk in that courthouse and face the outcome.

"Please God," I silently cried. "Give me another chance to be the mommy that my baby needs and deserves."

I can still remember walking down the hallway, taking a deep breath, holding my chin high, turning a corner, and ... the entire wing was dark. I rushed back downstairs and was told there were no hearings in that section of the courthouse that day. I was advised to call my attorney.

I called my court appointed lawyer and to my astonishment, she told me the hearing happened two days earlier!!!

"Wendy," she paused. "I sent you a letter so you should have known, and because you didn't show up the judge automatically awarded permanent custody to your parents. It's over; there's nothing you can do."

I wish I could say this is where I conquered the evil beast inside of me and charged forward into a successful life of sobriety, growth, and transformation. And that in only a short period of time, because I worked hard to learn sobriety tools and apply them, I was given custody of my son back. But that's not how my story goes.

In that moment when I learned I'd lost custody of my son, for good this time, my soul just....just withered and died. The shame. The loss. The pain and suffering of disappointing myself, my family, and my child overcame me. I crossed over that line going from a struggling addict to a committed junkie. The last lingering glimpse of hope I felt faded away. I felt like my reason to overcome my addiction was gone. I felt I had nothing, and that I was nothing. So why not love nothing?

I did then what even as an addict I had once thought was unthinkable. I picked up the needle. Something I'd resisted and even detested. Shooting up? That meant you had crossed a line. That you'd given up. Descended to the lowest of low points. And for many that was the point of no return. A point that until that day I'd stayed away from.

The day I first shot up I made a decision to embrace the darkness. I put as much meth up my arm as I possibly could, not caring if I lived or died. If I'm honest I think I hoped that I would indeed die. Thankfully, instead the day came when police found me in a car full of drugs, guns, stolen checks, needles, and drugs. They handcuffed me and hauled me to jail.

I mark February 12, 2001 as the day God said "No, my child. Wendy this is NOT where your story ends," and pushed me out of the darkness towards the light. It was the start of my new journey to long-term recovery. It included incarceration for a year, treatment for 9 months, and recovery for a lifetime. I was placed in a treatment program for mothers and children. Although I didn't have my child there, I learned that I had courage, strength, hope, and possibility. I learned life skills that to this day are like precious jewels, and I wear them with pride! I experienced setbacks, triumphs, and life lessons, but piece by piece God put me back together. He showed me the only way to get my baby back was to believe I could become the mother he deserved.

Those that know me, know that I absolutely love all things sparkly. So when I tell people about my journey I say that God used glitter glue to piece me back together. There were pieces in treatment I struggled to glue into place. At graduation my counselor Anne told me that in the beginning she was convinced I was one of the ones who would not make it. I had a lifetime of pain and issues that had led me to the start of my addiction, and each piece had to be exposed and examined and properly repaired. Uncovering these issues, at times, petrified me. But I combined the counsel of those there to guide me with sheer determination, and I applied the recovery principles I was learning in treatment. I found strength inside me that I didn't know existed. Each day, a new light emerged. A new woman. A new me.

This life transformation didn't happen overnight. But it did happen! I can't identify just one moment of change, but rather hundreds of thousands of tiny moments. There were also many moments when I wanted to run where no one could find me, because facing the hurt and forcing myself to grow seemed so much harder than forgiving, loving, accepting, and blossoming. But eventually I had made the decision that even if I never got custody of my son back, I would be the kind of mother he deserved. I wanted to be a mother he could be proud of, even if I only ever saw him one day a week. So I pressed on in this journey.

God placed some wonderful agents of change along my path. They helped me believe in me when I didn't believe in myself. I'm living, walking, breathing proof that anyone can overcome the grips of addiction, and can create an amazing and wonderful life, if they are persistent.

Today, as I write these words, I not only have custody of that little boy, who just turned 17, but I also have another amazing son. And I have a wonderful, devoted, family man of a husband who treats me like his equal and his queen. I'm also blessed to have three terrific bonus kids— my stepchildren.

I have attended college and become a certified substance abuse counselor. I then went on to a career in real estate. I began it ten years ago, and today I own a brokerage firm with my mother. I have a home, a mortgage, nice car—all the material things to make my life comfortable and content. But most important to me are the meaningful relationships I have with my husband, my children, dear friends, and yes, even my family. I also started a non-profit group with my sister, and for six years we've been feeding the homeless in our local community. I even speak to other women who are at the beginning of their journeys, hoping to inspire in them the possibilities that await them!

Here's the real miracle. All that pain, that for so long I tried to hide from, numb out, run away from....I can't change how it hurt back then. I can't change the choices I made that catapulted my life into despair and destruction. I can't erase the pain. I can't even say that it doesn't drive me anymore, because it does. But today, all that pain, all those lessons, drive me to do something good with those experiences. It's given me a purpose! I mentor those who struggle and long to triumph in their life, to find their light again and see it shine. I see the confident, grateful, energetic, creative, giving, and loving woman I am today. And, in my mind, I go back in time and I hug the woman I once was. I hug her with warm, comforting arms, just like I would hold my baby. I feel empathy for her, knowing how hopeless she felt trying to fight a losing battle.

When women doubt they have what it takes to overcome the impossible, I'm honest in telling them that I have plenty of faults, and that my path to recovery had a lot of bumps and turns along the way. For example, it took me ten years to get custody back of that baby boy. TEN YEARS! Even when I had an apartment with his very own room, furnished with toys and a bed, I had to be patient. He didn't sleep a single night in that bed for more than two years. But, I refused to give up! I refused to stop believing that one day everything would be right again. Even when an attorney told me it couldn't be done.

It took much longer than I wanted to bring home my son. He wouldn't fit in my arms by the time I'd get custody of him again. But that day did come.

Once again I walked into that courthouse. Getting off the elevator, I took a deep breath and held my chin high. This time when I turned that corner...... the lights were on. The hallway was filled with people. I stood with confidence in front of the judge who would say to me, "Ms. Starling, I want you to know something. We don't do this. Returning custody after Permanent Custody and Guardianship has been granted, especially this long after the fact—we just don't do that. Pretty much ever. I want you to understand that. To know how incredibly unusual this is. But as you stand here before me I can see that you have obviously made great strides in your life, and I believe this is the right thing. I'm choosing to grant your motion for custody."

Those words mended my broken heart with one final dab of glitter glue. And oh, how it sparkles now!

Today, I'm no longer broken. I can tell you that I know I am an amazing woman! I believe it! I found a way to rise up, like a phoenix from the ashes of my pain and addiction, and I believe every single person is capable of transforming painful, broken pieces into light and happiness. I believe, I know, that whether your story is one of addiction, abuse, eating disorders, mental illness, or loss—no matter the source of your pain or the depth of your despair—there is hope! All those years ago, the day I lost custody of my son I lost everything. But my journey to recover what I'd lost brought my son back, and along the way I found myself. And so much more!

About Wendy Starling Gardiner

Wendy Starling Gardiner is about as diverse as they come. She's been a Realtor for over 10 years and is co-owner of Starling Real Estate. She's also co-founder of Soul Food USA, feeding the bodies and souls of the homeless for the last 6 years. But her real passion lies in her work as an author, speaker and mentor/coach to those who struggle with the challenges that she herself has been able to overcome, despite insurmountable odds.

Through her company The Phoenix Group, she helps women to stop letting the pain & struggle of addiction, abuse, weight and emotional baggage prevent them from living a life of joy and purpose.

You can find out more about Wendy at: www.ThePhoenixGroup.info

Chapter Ten
Going From the Pit to the Promised Land
By Stacy Harmer

Chapter Ten
Going From the Pit to the Promised Land
By Stacy Harmer

I'm passionate about living a vibrant life and finding joy now! Why? Because I know what it feels like not to have a happy, whole, healthy, and vibrant life, and to be stuck in a pit of darkness. It has become my mission to share and teach others the tools I have discovered during my own healing journey through the sadness and grief of unexpectedly losing a beloved daughter. My journey took me further down as I spiraled into a deep clinical depression a couple of years after her passing. After years of learning and healing, I feel I have discovered a formula to help others find joy in the present, despite the challenges they may be facing. I describe my experience as going from the Pit to the Promised Land.

Every healing journey is personal, but as my path unfolded before me, the journey I went on was one of discovery, trial and error, progress and growth. As I began changing and healing personally, I began to teach small groups of women these principles. That has grown and evolved as I created a worldwide organization–Vibrant Living Academy, in which we focus on healing our bodies, hearts, minds and souls, discovering our purpose and passion and sharing those gifts with the world.

Adopting Olivia

We had been blessed with four wonderful children. I loved being a mom and found great satisfaction in raising and playing with my children. But something seemed to be missing. I felt as though our family wasn't complete and deeply wanted another child.

I'm a deeply spiritual person. One morning as I was pouring out my heart to my Father in Heaven in prayer, trying to understand His will as well as expressing my desire for another child, I had a simple but profound experience. As I was reading in my scriptures in the Book of Esther, I had the clear and distinct impression that we had another daughter, but that she wouldn't come to us in the traditional way. I felt impressed that we would adopt her and she would be of a different nationality. Like Esther, she would be beautiful, chosen by the King, and be instrumental in saving her people. I wasn't sure what all this meant, but since I'm an intuitive and spiritual person, I trusted that this would be the case.

I wondered how my husband would react to this. We both knew we had been abundantly blessed, and he had a good heart. When I approached him about adopting, his heart was open to that possibility because he felt that was something we could do to also bless a child who needed a home.

It wasn't quite quick or easy, but we did get the process started. Participating in an international adoption is quite an ordeal. It involved months of paperwork, fingerprinting, interviews, and patience. The day finally arrived when we received our referral. She was a darling little Korean girl with tons of hair. We were able to meet her in the Seattle airport two months later. This was in 2000, before all of the airport security, so we were able to meet her at the gate when she was carried off the plane. I can't begin to describe the absolute joy, tears, and happiness I felt as this tiny four-month-old baby was placed in my arms. She was only 13 pounds, and felt like a newborn baby.

The feeling I had when she was placed in my arms was absolutely no different than what I felt when each of my birth children were placed in my arms. The instant bond and outflow of love were incredible to experience. She was calm and content. I couldn't contain my tears, and knew that God had immensely blessed us with a sweet angel baby.

When we arrived at the Salt Lake City airport, we probably had 40 people gathered at the gate to welcome us home. Our four children, ages five to thirteen, were ecstatic and jumping for joy, each eager to hold their new precious sister. This was just days before Christmas, so our home was overflowing with love and joy for our long-anticipated "gift."

The years that Olivia graced our family were "Heaven on Earth." Little did we know that our time with this angel would be limited. She became the center of our family and existence. She had each of our hearts tied around her little finger. She could get anything she wanted because she had that much charm and influence over us! Olivia's siblings, family and friends adored.

One afternoon in 2005, I was mentoring a group of women in my home. We were studying the classics and would read, write, and discuss different books and themes. We met every week. As usually happens with women in that type of setting, we all grew to love and support each other. I remember thinking that all of these women had gone through significant challenges in their lives—divorce, serious illness, difficult children, raising siblings because a mother had passed away, a serious accident that had left one bedridden for many years, etc. I deeply loved and appreciated each of them.

After they left my home one afternoon and after hearing of some of their challenges, I went upstairs to my bedroom and leaned against my door. I said a little prayer, telling my Father in Heaven that I wanted to assist Him in helping others who were going through hard times. My life had been relatively speaking a "piece of cake" compared to others. I said I would be His servant, but I did include one caveat—I just didn't want to go through any of their hard stuff. I would devote my life to love and serve others, but only if I didn't have to go through the hard stuff myself. I didn't think much more about that little prayer until around two weeks later when my life was completely shattered and would change its course forever.

Losing Olivia

Never did I imagine the heart-wrenching experience awaiting us. Olivia was our everything. She was the center of our family. The children all wanted to be her "best buddy," a coveted position. Everyone wanted to be her favorite! It was almost like she was the glue that held us together. Finding her that morning was almost more than we could bear. She passed away unexpectedly in her sleep following a brief illness. The shock and trauma of that experience still instantly stirs up painful feelings of grief that cut to the core.

We couldn't imagine our lives without our little angel. How could we possibly carry on? It was five years to the day after she was first placed in our arms that we had to lay her body to rest. We immediately felt an outpouring of love and support. We had never been surrounded by so much love. It was palpable. Between receiving loving notes, gifts, flowers, acts of kindness, listening ears, food, etc., our hearts were being held in a safe and protected place.

I had been given some sweet spiritual assurances that all would be well. I knew that Olivia was in a beautiful place welcomed by all of our loved ones. I turned to my Savior and Source, Jesus Christ, like I never had before. I had always believed in the Atonement, and knew He was the only one who could carry our pain and burden. As I began pouring my heart out to Him and pleading for help, beautiful things began happening in my life. I was blessed with great light and understanding. I would wake up early in the morning and spend hours in prayer, meditation, and journaling. All these things strengthened me, and I held on to them with all of my might.

But there was one problem. Our minds are powerful forces and our thoughts can take us to places that can bring us down pretty quickly. When I would start dwelling on "if only" or "what if," I would spiral downward, feeling like a failure to my family and to God. It hurt my heart so deeply that I didn't know if I could go on. Then I would receive His sweet spiritual assurances, and I would hold on.

I came to understand the power of the Light of Christ. But as there is opposition in all things, resulting in darkness as well as light, I would fall into negative thinking. After a couple of years, my body, mind, spirit, and heart simply broke down, and I spiraled into clinical depression. Those are days I don't like to dwell on; it was a painful time in all of our lives. Not only had we lost our beloved Olivia, but now my family was losing me as well.

Fortunately, I was surrounded by people who loved me and were concerned about what was happening to me. My husband stepped in after painfully watching me spiral downward. He got me the medical help that was necessary to put me on the track of recovery. I will forever be grateful to him as my hero who literally saved my life, but I had a long healing journey ahead of me.

The Healing Journey

I would wake up in the mornings and begin writing. I was reading the book *The Artist's Way* by Julia Cameron in which she described "Morning Notes." These are a way to declutter your mind and thoughts, putting them down on paper. Through this process of getting the whirling thoughts down, you open up space for your creativity, insight, and inspiration to flow. I would engage in this process nearly every morning before anyone else woke up, pouring out my heart to God to help me know the steps I needed to take to heal my life.

The Tree Analogy

Roots

One morning, thoughts and ideas started coming to me as I was writing my Morning Notes. I started sketching out a tree with the roots running deeply into the soil. Four distinct roots emerged. We are multi-dimensional beings, and the four roots seemed to represent our **body, heart, mind, and soul**. Just as a tree needs to get constant nourishment from the rich soil and water reaching its roots to sustain growth, we need to nourish our body, heart, mind and soul on a daily basis. I now put it on my daily "To Do" list and strive to nourish those roots daily by incorporating specific practices in each area.

Trunk

The trunk of a tree represents form or structure—holding things together and helping to sustain growth. In our personal lives, we also need structure, forms, or systems to keep our lives running smoothly. As a busy mother and health coach, I need systems in all areas of my life in order for things to run more smoothly. S.Y.S.T.E.M stands for Save Your Self, Time, Energy, and Money. Once we identify the roles that we have in our lives and implement systems, we find greater balance and streamline many of the daily and weekly tasks we do.

Branches

The branches of the tree represent finding our Purpose and Passion. This is really the fun part of life! When we are living our purpose and passion, everything is brighter and more vibrant and we find joy in all that we do. We find our purpose by utilizing our strengths, abilities, and talents. Often it is the difficult things in life that point us in the direction where we are meant to be of the most service. When we find our voice, a new zest for life and energy just flows!

Fruit

Finally, the fruit of the tree represents sharing our unique gifts with others. Often if a fruit tree is not producing fruit, it is because it is not receiving the proper nourishment to the roots—the body, heart, mind, and soul. It may be diseased or sick. And if a healthy tree is producing fruit, but that fruit is not harvested and picked from the tree, what happens? We've all seen trees with ripened fruit that has fallen to the ground without being harvested. The fruit begins to rot and make a mess! In our own lives, the fruit represents our gifts and talents. If we are not sharing these gifts to fulfill our purpose and passion, those gifts and talents lie dormant and we begin making a mess in our own lives. It is only by giving and receiving that the flow of life occurs. Why is the Dead Sea called the Dead Sea? Because there is no outflow. The air in a room without ventilation becomes stale. A wet sponge in a sink soon becomes stinky.

All of these images began flowing into my mind, and I realized the importance of sharing the fruit in our lives if our personal trees are producing fruit. At the time I was discovering all of this and creating the analogy on paper, I personally was not producing fruit. I needed a great deal of daily nourishment to my roots—my body, heart, mind, and soul—on a regular basis. That is where I began focusing.

Body

Our body is the first root we need to address. It is a gift we must protect and nurture. If we were given one car to last us our lifetime, how would we care for it? We would be proactive in making sure that we did all of the scheduled maintenance, got the oil changed regularly, and fed it the best fuel possible. Our bodies are no different. We get one body to last our lifetime, and how we care for it or what we put into our bodies makes a huge difference in our quality of life.

During my healing journey, after turning to food for comfort and gaining 25 pounds and feeling awful, I decided to transform my health and studied to become a holistic health coach. I began working with clients and developed a Vibrant Living Holistic Health Coaching program that encompasses all of the principles I share here.

Heart

Our hearts are beautiful and tender things! Our emotions are stored in them. They are meant to be soft and open. But depending on our life experiences, we tend to bandage up our hearts or create walls. We don't consciously do this, but we may have been hurt deeply and want to protect our hearts, so we put up barriers.

Each of us needs to do what it takes to peel back the protective layers on our hearts so they can be more open and soft. When we have an open and loving heart, we are able to connect deeply with others, creating meaningful and loving relationships.

As mortals we experience a wide degree of negative emotions—fear, frustration, anger, sadness, grief, jealousy. But we don't want to hold on to those emotions. When we stuff our emotions deep within our hearts, they are still alive and festering. One of my favorite books on this subject is *Feelings Buried Alive Never Die* by Karol Truman. The message is that if we don't properly release and heal our emotions, eventually they will manifest in our lives in one form or another. Often it is in the form of an illness or disease—physical, mental, emotional, or spiritual. We can come back to a place of peace, healing, forgiveness, joy, and even gratitude for our experiences once we know how to properly release and replace these negative emotions.

Whether we like it or not, we will go through difficult trials that will not be easy to handle. We will feel the gamut of emotions, and unless we know how to let them go or release them in a healthy way, we will probably stuff them and let them fester and smolder until they become unbearable. We actually may forget about them for years and even decades. But when something comes up and triggers us, we know there is something going on inside that needs healing. Our lives become unbearable, and we know that it's time to change.

Through my healing journey, I became an Emotional Release Facilitator and now assist others in this process, which is priceless in helping you move forward in your life and replace any negative emotions and beliefs into new positive changes.

Mind -

Do you know that we have around 60,000 thoughts daily? Our mind can be our best friend or our worst enemy, and it is within our power to decide which one it will be. One of the great challenges of this life is to be able to control the mind, because it can really have a life of its own if we let it go uncontrolled. If you don't like where your life is now, just take a look at where your thoughts have been. It takes personal control and discipline to be able to master your thoughts, but believe me, it is worth learning the tools and skills to do this. If you feel stuck or discouraged, this one principle will transform your life if you can master it. A simple technique is to say daily affirmations—words that describe the person that you want to become. Engage visualization and feel what that would be like. As you use this technique, you will create powerful neural pathways in your brain— your subconscious, which starts creating your reality.

Soul -

From my experience, nourishing your spirit is the best way to aid in that personal transformation. When we can let go of our egos and strive to live in our true essence, we begin to discover who we are and who we've always been.

I admire C.S. Lewis' insights and writings. He struggled to understand how an omnipotent Being could allow such suffering in the world. Lewis suffered much pain in his life. But, with the change of his worldview from atheism to Christianity, he looked at God as a good, conscientious surgeon: "The kinder and more conscientious he is, the more inexorably he will go on cutting. If he yielded to your entreaties, if he stopped before the operation was complete, all the pain up to that point would have been useless."

At this time that I was in great need of comfort, I began meditating. This is something I had never done before, but I had a great desire to connect with my daughter spiritually. The best way I could think of doing this was to go to a quiet place. I would lie down, empty out all of my thoughts, and breathe deeply. I had a great desire to connect with her and the Lord. I would imagine myself as an empty vessel that was open to receiving all that the Lord would give me. After doing this on a regular basis every morning and evening, beautiful experiences began happening to me. It was as if I was able to transcend this mortal experience and connect spiritually beyond the veil. The Lord started pouring out beautiful blessings to me, and I was hungry for it, grateful for any spiritual connection I would receive. It taught me in a very personal way how important it is to quiet our minds and deeply connect with the Divine. It truly transformed my life and understanding.

According to the law of the harvest, there is a gestational period during which time must pass before the fruit is produced. I learned that I needed to be patient during this time in my life. As much as I wanted to be out there making a difference in the lives of others, I knew that my focus at this time had to be getting myself healthy and whole again. That is when I started learning and implementing the practices of nourishing my body, heart, mind, and soul on a regular basis.

Over the past 10 years of my healing journey, I've not only been able to learn the lessons that have transformed my life, but I've had the opportunity to create the *7 Steps to Vibrant Living* course, a mentoring program, and the *Vibrant Living Holistic Health* coaching program that implements all of the tools I've learned along the way. I've developed a world-wide organization to help share these tools with others and provide a platform of healing, community, and mentoring within the Vibrant Living Academy. Doing this has helped me in my own healing journey as well as being a catalyst for me to discover my own purpose and passion.

Whenever we go through difficult experiences, there is always a silver lining. Ask yourself these questions: "Whom have you become because of your experiences? What positive character traits have you developed because you've gone through your own particular challenges?" As I ask these questions to my clients, they usually tell me they would not trade their life experiences because of the lessons learned and because of the person they have become. It is through our challenges and painful experiences that we then can turn those around to be a light and blessing to others.

You can learn more about Stacy and Vibrant Living Academy at www.vibrantlivingacademy.org or www.vibrantlivinghealthcoach.com

Readers: Stacy has compiled over 150 healthful recipes from health coaches around the world. Want access to these amazing dishes?

Go to http://successthroughfailing.com/downloads to get these free recipes instantly as our gift to you.

About Stacy Harmer

Stacy is on a mission! Her personal path of loss and depression took her on a journey of healing from the Pit of Darkness to the Promised Land! Through her personal experiences, she's discovered a formula to live a full, healthy, whole, vibrant life and is passionate about empowering others with these tools! She is the founder of the Vibrant Living Academy, a world-wide community of women whose purpose is to help others heal their body, heart, mind and soul, discover their purpose and passion, and share their unique gifts with the world. She is a busy mother, Certified Holistic Health Coach, Raw Food Chef, Emotional Release Facilitator and Co-Creator of the Vibrant Living Holistic Health Coach Certification Program. She is speaker, trainer and the author of *7 Steps to Vibrant Living–You Deserve to Find Joy Now* and has a mission to spread these principles to the world!

www.vibrantlivinghealthcoach.com

www.vibrantlivingacademy.org

www.stacyharmer.com

Chapter Eleven
Wholeness Through the Pain
By Alycia Huston

Chapter Eleven
Wholeness Through the Pain
By Alycia Huston

I always thought I would grow up to be a doctor or a lawyer and live a fairytale life. Never did I anticipate crawling through deep valleys of pain and sorrow in my relatively young life.

I grew up in an affluent home with highly educated parents. There was no question that I would go to college and "make" something of myself. Both of my parents had multiple graduate degrees, and my father had his doctorate. As African-Americans born in 1937 and 1940, they had witnessed and experienced their fair share of segregation and roadblocks. They were adamant that their children take advantage of each opportunity afforded. I too believed this would be the path I would take. Boy, was I wrong!

I left home for the University of California at San Diego in 1991 (yes, you can deduce my age). I was excited to finally be away from home and on my own. College provided me a sense of adulthood, and my parents had been a bit strict. So I was happy to get out of my childhood home and have freedom. I had always envied my childhood friends for the freedom I had witnessed in their lives.

In the process of leaving home and seeking out freedom, I lost my way. I began focusing less on my school activities and much more on my social life. I became sidetracked and disillusioned, so much so that my grades suffered year after year. I had been stellar in my high school academics and I kept telling myself I would study harder and raise my grades. I soon painfully learned that college doesn't work the same as high school when it comes to grades. To compound this painful realization, I was on the trimester system, which moves much more rapidly.

In my fourth year of college, things got so bad I received a letter "inviting" me to take some time off. I was being kindly ushered out. I was in shock, but I also knew I hadn't been performing up to the required standards. It was one of those situations in which I knew this could happen, but I just didn't think it would happen to me. In my naïve thinking, I believed that because I had always risen to the occasion previously, this time would be no different. Boy, did I fool myself! To make things worse, my response was one of an utterly immature child. I recall making the audible comment, "FINE!" I went into complete victim mode as a defense tactic. I knew deep down that I was not only disappointed in myself, I had let my parents down. I also knew they were going to flip out. That was when an utter state of panic began to set in.

What hadn't yet been exposed as the root cause of my suspension was that my grades had been gradually slipping because I was too busy spending time with a young man. Not that he was a bad person, but as I reflect with more wisdom, my focus should have been on my studies—not a relationship. I was too busy living in the fairytale confidence that we were perfect for each other. In my mind, this was a great connection—two highly motivated individuals striving toward successful positions in life.

Fast forward a few years. We had married and produced a beautiful son, and four years later, a gorgeous daughter. I was 24 years old when I got married and thought I knew it all. I was so naïve! The sad thing is that my parents saw it all from the beginning, but I was too young and blind to see that anything was wrong.

Of course, when you have babies, that's a whole new set of responsibilities. You begin to see very quickly the character of the person with whom you have chosen to spend the rest of your life. It became painfully clear that we had different views on life, marriage, and family. For the first time I began to think about divorce. I almost had to look around the room to see if anyone could read my thoughts, I was so ashamed. How could my parents have been married for more than thirty years when I could barely make it five years? What would people at church think? What would others say about me? What would my parents say? All of these thoughts were running rampant in my head.

How was I going to do this? As a result of my sense of helplessness, I decided to stay for a couple of more years until it simply became unbearable. There's a point in your desperation when you begin to question your own sanity and ability to make rational decisions. I was in that stage when I began to blame myself for all that had transpired and wondered how I had gotten myself into this mess. It was just too much. I told my family and friends I was getting a divorce. The time had come for me to release the shame and judgment that I had attached to that word.

When I had the very difficult conversation with my parents, it was extremely hard on them as well, because they were thinking about my children and how this would affect them moving forward. I made it very clear that they were the ones I had been thinking about the past few years, but the time had come to think about me. I had already stayed in that marriage longer than I should have, and I was through putting others before what I knew to be true for me.

Was it difficult? Absolutely, but I knew this was still the right path for me. It was also quite interesting—after I made the final decision to "break free," I felt peace within. That doesn't mean that everything was easy as I went through the process, but there was a deep assurance that what I was doing was absolutely the right thing for me and my family moving forward. What I found ironic was that the financial struggles that I had previously experienced while being married just seemed to disappear. Mysteriously, there was more money to meet my living requirements than before. All of these various experiences combined were powerful indicators that I was honoring myself and moving forward in the right direction.

The time I spent being single was absolutely divine. It allowed me an opportunity to connect more deeply with my then young children (ages two and six), with my friends, and most importantly, with myself! It was during this time that I also made the choice to become a full-fledged entrepreneur. I left my 9-to-5 job and dove whole-heartedly into a business venture with a couple of partners. It was a very scary and exciting time in my life.

About four months later, in early 2005, my mother informed me of a tumor discovered in her uterus. Her doctors had decided it was best for her to go ahead and undergo a full hysterectomy. The doctors were very confident, since she had caught it early, that they would through this procedure alleviate further issues. They also wanted her to undergo chemotherapy and radiation as a precaution after the procedure was completed. My mother had lost her sister the year before, and had seen what chemotherapy does to the body. She opted to have only radiation. The doctors once again agreed this was an acceptable solution, because she caught it early and they had done a full hysterectomy.

In December 2005, my parents decided to sell the home we grew up in and have a home built in San Diego where both my sister and I and their grandchildren lived. It was also at this time that my mom began to feel very weak. She had developed a deep bronchial cough that she just could not shake.

This was nothing new, as she had developed these same deep coughs when she would overdo it and not listen to her body. However, we suggested she see the doctor. That was a day I will never forget. It was the day we learned her cancer had spread and her life expectancy was 100% in question.

The doctor stated very matter-of-factly that chemotherapy was imperative, as this was a very aggressive form of uterine cancer that had spread. We were all perplexed because we were so sure the hysterectomy had taken care of it. From our previous information, we believed the radiation was just an extra precaution to be "safe." My mother was adamant about not undergoing chemotherapy and decided to trust whatever God's will was for her life. In all honesty, I was angry with her for choosing that route. I wanted her to employ all of the available choices she had, but she had a different vision.

As I sit back, now 10 years later, I realize the choice my mother made was a very personal and fitting one for her. We each have to individually look at our lives and choose how we want to live. I can't say how I would have chosen to proceed, as I was not the one sitting there with my life flashing before my eyes. Unfortunately, the cancer grew more poisonous in her body. Her various organs began to shut down and I saw my mother losing her battle right in front of my eyes. There was one thing that Mom never wanted, and that was to have a machine keep her alive. As it became painfully clear that her physical body temple was shutting down, we knew it was time to honor her wishes. My immediate family (my brother could not get here in time) gathered around her bed while the nurse quietly turned off her assisted breathing machine. We sat around her bed praying and speaking to her—I vividly remember touching her hand that was lying by her side and telling her it was okay to let go. We would take care of dad and everything here. Then she quietly let go.

As you can imagine, this was a very difficult time for my family. My parents had been married for 40 years and now my dad was a widower. I was only 33 years old at this point, and my children were also very young. My parents had spent an enormous amount of time with their grandchildren. They also took their grandkids on vacations all over the United States, so this was a huge hole that had also been left in their lives. I felt that I needed to step in and step up to take care of everyone. So I did just that. I put my house up for rent and we moved in with my dad into the custom-built home my mom had lived in for approximately two months prior to passing. I believed this would be the best way for each of us to begin healing.

During this time, I was also preparing for my wedding the following year. Needless to say, there was quite a bit going on. From running a business (with employees), to being an engaged mom, to making sure my dad's needs were taken care of, to making sure my fiancé didn't feel neglected—there really was NO time for me. I kept this up for months, non-stop.

I then received news that my best friend's breast cancer had returned and was back with a vengeance. I prayed that she would beat the ugly cancer; I knew there was no way I could be losing someone that I loved so much, especially so close to the death of my mother. Ten months later, she too was taken from me.

I was numb. I began to gain weight, not honoring my body in the manner that I should have. Ironically, I still couldn't see what I was doing to myself. I just continued to push.

My wedding day finally arrived in April 2007. In all honesty, it whizzed by. I was so busy ensuring all of the pieces were in place, I didn't have time to enjoy the day or my guests as I would've liked. Don't get me wrong—the day was full of joy and fun—but there was also an emptiness.

When we got married it was time to purchase our own home, so we did just that. We purchased a beautiful home, with a gorgeous backyard and pool! We bid my dad adieu and moved to settle in as a new family. Once again, I was going through the motions and somehow putting one foot in front of the other.

As I look back, I realize I was a mere shell of a person. Losing my mother and best friend within ten months of one another generated feelings that I am still unable to put into words. I can't even explain how I was able to get up daily and function, moving in and out of my daily responsibilities like clockwork. In that period, I did what needed to be done to ensure everyone was taken care of. However, I was operating at about 50%.

A couple of years later, I had stepped into the role of CEO in my company. It was at that time that I also learned I was pregnant with my beautiful daughter. I had no clue at that time, but I still had not dealt with all the feelings of loss from the previous years. To add to my stress, the housing market balloon burst and the slump in the economy directly hit my business. I continued to mask and fake and pretend that everything great. I was so good, I even fooled myself. My weight had become even more out of control— I tipped the scale at 220 pounds! I proved true the theory that what's going on inside shows up on the outside.

Of course this dip in the economy directly affected our household finances— we could no longer afford the mortgage on our beautiful home. I knew many friends who had undergone loan modifications, so I was sure we would apply and get one, too. Wrong! We were denied for a modification three times during the next two years, and eventually the bank told us they were going to foreclose. Thank goodness, we were able to get approved for a short sale, and we moved forward with that option.

I still owned my first home that was now being used as a rental property. Unfortunately, this home was also affected, because our tenant could no longer afford his rent—he too had lost his wife the year before. Talk about feeling like your world was crumbling right around you! As a result, this home also had to be sold on a short sale.

While all of this was going on, there was something in me that stirred, and I was jolted into the realization that it was time to take action. I was tired of feeling sluggish, out of control, fat, and completely unhealthy. I made the choice in that moment that I was going to take charge of my life in every aspect. I began to research eating healthy and started watching what I was eating. I ordered a workout program that came with a meal plan so that I could be supported. I invested in a coach to help keep me accountable. It was time to make a change for a better me and I KNEW I was worth it.

After we sold our home, we moved back into my parents' custom home. It was also during this time that my husband became very resentful of me and what had transpired with our having to sell our home and move. He blamed me for the loss, believing I should have done something different. I tried explaining to him that this was a business decision and a new home could be purchased down the line. He made it very clear he didn't really care what my reasoning was. There came a time when we were unable to see eye to eye and made the decision to separate in hopes of allowing time and space to heal both of us.

Even though we separated, I continued to work on myself. It was imperative that I keep my promise to myself and continue on my path of seeking self-mastery and personal growth. I became the fittest and healthiest I had been in my life, losing 55 pounds and feeling amazing. It was during this time that I began to make my spiritual practices non-negotiable, and to honor myself and my boundaries. This is when life shifted drastically for the better.

My business began to experience exponential seven-figure growth. In 2014, my business partners and I were approached out of the blue with a request to purchase our business; we had not sought any of this out. Our business was an

Independent Review Board (IRB), an entity that oversees the research to protect the rights and welfare of the individuals who choose to participate in various research studies. When we met with the potential buyers (two gentleman), they told us they had been watching our business for the past two years. We were blown away, as we had no idea! They were impressed with the consistent growth we had been showing in the research industry and were also pleased that this was a business owned and run by women. I vividly recall thinking "This is what happens when you honor your dream and take action".

After many more discussions, we were offered a generous sum for the purchase of our business, and we accepted. It was at the very moment when I saw those funds actually IN my account that I recalled the words my mom so adamantly stated, "Owning your own business is NOT a good idea. You have two small children and a mortgage; I suggest you stay in your safe job." I just smiled in my heart and sent her love and gratitude. I was able to purchase an even larger and more gorgeous home for my family with a pool and spacious backyard for us to enjoy, as well as to entertain my friends and family.

My husband and I were able to come back together; it's a never ending dynamic of being willing to be flexible and patient, as no perfect person exists. What I learned is that we are always evolving and it's important to connect yourself with other like-minded individuals who believe in you and your success. It's about being honest with yourself and your willingness to put in the work that is required to create the change you're seeking. Without the ability to self-reflect in humility, the struggle will remain; and you will find yourself repeating the same self-sabotaging behaviors over and over again.

It was also in this time of separation when I was able to honestly reflect not just about my relationship, but also about my next steps in life. As one chapter was closing soon, what was next for me? It came to me almost immediately — *Women's Leadership*. It made perfect sense. The journey I continue to travel has provided me with insight and wisdom which could only be garnered from my own experiences. These same experiences have richly added not only to my professional life, but to my personal life as well. I'm happier, as are my children and my husband. I'm able to honor myself on a deeper level as I enjoy helping other women integrate business into their own lives. It is my greatest honor to help women of influence "Locate, Lock in, and Lead" from their true inner brilliance. There is really no other way to live.

Although my road was painful and downright heartbreaking in its darkest moments, I wouldn't change a thing. My experiences have contributed greatly to the woman I have become today and continue to develop. I'm equipped with the ability to be a beacon of light for others and a living testimony that you CAN overcome, but you must have the will and desire, followed by ACTION. Divine flow exists around each of us daily and when we sit back in non-resistance, we see the beauty of this vast universe we live in and are able to appreciate what God has created. For this lesson, I'm so very grateful.

About Alicia Huston

Alycia Huston is a Certified Life Coach, Business Mentor, and Speaker specializing in women's empowerment and leadership. Her mission and passion in life is teaching strong women leaders how to step up, be fierce, and play bigger in their business and personal lives so that they can live the lifestyle they always desired.

In November of 2004, Alycia decided she was ready to go full throttle into the world of entrepreneurship. She co-founded Aspire Independent Review Board, LLC, and found herself stepping into the role of CEO in 2008. Within three years at the helm, the company soared into multi-million dollar status and remained there until its sale in late 2014.

She is a busy wife to Andre and mother to Bryce (19), Asiyah (15) and Adanya (7); plus two bonus children DJ (18) and Adrian (16).

Alycia absolutely believes and operates on the premise that one should live a Soul-Full life!

You can connect with Alycia at www.MajesticSoulWoman.com

Chapter Twelve
God Had a Purpose for Me
By Christine Sakali Khamasi

Chapter Twelve
God Had a Purpose for Me
By Christine Sakali Khamasi

In the last moment before I was going to give birth, I had no choice but to have sex with a man, because I did not have anything to even buy water to wash, and I cried. I asked a man if he could give me even 50 shillings ($0.50) to take care of my needs. Even that had to be in exchange for something, and what else was there to exchange? I really cried. I still remember that day.

My dream as a child was to become a doctor. I wanted to become a doctor until my dreams were shattered because I could not stay at school every time my period came. I became pregnant at the very early age of 14 as a result of having sex in exchange for money to buy a pad. This is my story.

I grew up as a girl in Kenya. My mom left me when I was only five years old. When I started menstruating, I started very young, before the school could teach me about how to manage my blood and before anybody at home could teach me. It was very hard for me because I did not have a pad. I only had one panty, and it was just a wash-and-wear. I washed it and wore it. Because I had no way to take care of my menstruation, I would go deep into the maize plantation, and I would stay there for days. I would just sit down and let it go. It was a lonely time when I was menstruating. It was not a happy moment, not like now when I can tell girls that it is beautiful. It wasn't sad just because I had to stay there alone. I could not go to school because I did not have a suitable panty. Even if I used a rag, the panty had many holes in it, and it would have just fallen. The only comfort I had was to go hide somewhere in the bananas until I could go back into the house. It was not good, and I felt the pain that girls go through in school. I do not want girls to go through that experience that I went through.

I did not know anything about my calendar, so every time my period would come and I was at school, my clothes would get stained. It was very embarrassing, and I had to go home. The school uniform I was wearing had many holes around my buttocks, so it was bad. It was REALLY bad. My classmates were young girls running around saying, "Christine is running around putting blood all over." It was so embarrassing that I would just go home. My stepmom was not supporting of me, and she did not explain things to me, so I had to stop going to school. I stayed home for those days, and I got behind in class; then no one wanted me in school. I was always messy. I would wash my one panty that was wash-and-wear, but without time to dry, it would get smelly. I dropped out of school because it was too embarrassing, and every month I just hid in the bananas.

After I dropped out of school I worked as a housemaid. The man of the house would take advantage of me, but I had to work there or sleep on the streets. I wanted to commit suicide, but every time I wanted to kill myself, I would see Jesus coming. He would hold me and tell me it was going to be well. I would see that image, and then I felt strength, and I didn't do it.

I became pregnant. Not even knowing the father of the baby, I felt bad having to carry a pregnancy at that early age while my age-mates were in school. I tried many times to kill the baby or do an abortion, but it did not work. Having to see other people wear their uniforms and go to school while I was at home washing clothes and taking care of other things was really discouraging. I was having to prepare kids to go to school while I was taking care of the house, and it was not good. It was bad. I would feel it.

Slums of Nairobi

I went to Nairobi in search of my mother who had abandoned me, and that is how I ended up in the slums. Life in the slums was not easy. This was where my life collapsed, because prostitution happens at a very high rate. In the slums you have to buy water. You have to buy everything, and so you exchange your body for 10 shillings ($0.10). The houses are very small and made of a piece of iron, or sometimes a box or piece of wood. When it rains, the water just comes in. You have to buy everything. There is no electricity and no water, and some places do not even have toilets, so you have to pay for the toilet, too. In the slums, if you live somewhere but you leave to go elsewhere, when you come back your place is often burned. I used to have a box where I kept my things. All I kept was just a comb in the box because in the evening, I slept on the box like a pillow. In the morning, I took the comb to my hair and put it back in the box. You do not know what is going to happen at night, so it was very risky. Life in the slums was not easy.

This was where my first baby was born, at the lowest point of my life, the time when there was no hope of having any kind of life for the two of us. Something happened when I had the baby. I looked at the baby, and she was so precious. There was a kind of connection, and I just loved her, so the baby became my reason to go on. Whatever I did, I did for the baby. I got my inspiration from her. She had an energy of love that kept me going, and was the reason I had to go back to the street with her to beg and to sleep with men to get something for us to eat.

Turning Point

At one point, I realized we had no future if I did not do something different. By that time, my eyes were opened and I saw that this was not the kind of life I wanted to live, because now I was aware. That was when I decided to do something. I knew how to plait hair, so I would do that or wash somebody's dress, and they would pay me. With that money, I paid someone to teach me how to do the sewing, and that is how it began. I knew I had to make a choice. If I did not work very hard, I was going to be infected with HIV, and I did not want that to happen, so I chose to do something different. I would go somewhere and ask if they wanted any help. I would wash people's houses and their clothes, and they would give me some money, and then I would go pay my school fees to learn how to sew.

I learned to speak English because the church I attended had many white people coming and sometimes they wanted to speak to me. I really did not know how to do it, but that also inspired me to learn English.

I learned how to sew and when I finished the first dress-making course, I was able now to get paid when I made a dress. I was still very hungry for more education! I wanted a degree or a certificate, so I went for a certificate class in theology. I attended for one year and earned the certificate, but the director wanted me to earn the diploma. I told him my education did not allow me to, but he said I had earned the certificate and I was the best student, so I could get the diploma, which I worked toward for two years. After that, some people from the US came and heard about my story. They suggested I get a degree, which was too much for me because I didn't know how to use the Internet. For a degree, you have to do a lot of research, so I did not think it was going to be possible. With their encouragement and support, I learned that nothing is impossible, and I studied for three years.

LIFEstory Transformation

As I was building my tailoring business, I acquired a lot of debt. I would borrow money and buy materials, but then the clothes I made wouldn't sell. I still had to pay the person who loaned me the money. Everything was a struggle. Then I was blessed with mentors who taught me about LIFEstory Transformation, and how I could write down what I wanted in my life, and it would happen. Your LIFEstory is a description of the person you want to become. I learned that everything begins in the mind. If you are willing to change your mind, then there are no limits. I began studying the *Science of Mind* by Ernest Holmes to learn my purpose in life, and began focusing on the good and focusing on the customer. I learned to see things in a different way. If someone asked me to make something but then didn't take it, I knew it was not meant for them.

I wrote in my LIFEstory that I wanted my business to become international. I wanted to do sewing for my friends in America and all over the world, and that is what has happened. When I wrote it, I did not think it was possible, but now when the humanitarian groups are coming to Kenya, they tell their people in advance that they are going to meet me, and people are excited to make orders for clothing. My business is changing and doing well since I described it in my LIFEstory. It has changed completely because anything I write down in my LIFEstory is manifested.

I wrote that I want to move around to different schools teaching Days for Girls, and I am now going to really big schools, finding that they have very high expectations. I have been to Mombasa, to remote schools, and to the biggest schools, and the girls are very receptive. Along with giving them their Days for Girls kits, I tell them that their lives can only change if they write their LIFEstories. Do you want to become a doctor? Write it in a journal. As you are writing, it changes your perspective. You will listen to the science and the math teachers, and your perspective about them will change because you have already written it in your LIFEstory. You start loving the sciences teachers, you get connections, and things start unfolding. The girls are finding it is very easy, and lives are changing with LIFEstory Transformation.

My brothers and sisters look at me as someone who didn't go to school. When I travel internationally, they wonder how it is possible. I recently had an opportunity to visit Ghana with Days for Girls and LIFEstory Transformation, and my brother said, "We have the degrees. We have the certificates. We have everything it takes to fly out of the country, and we haven't done it. This is our sister who has never had any school." By the grace of God and through writing my LIFEstory, it is so.

Because LIFEstory Transformation has made such an incredible difference in my life, I love to share it with others. People are excited to know what LIFEstory is, and I teach them that if they write it, things are going to shift. When I teach them about LIFEstory, they get so excited! They get passionate about life. They can see their future. It is so easy, even for the person who has never been to school. It does not have any complications.

Nothing is impossible with LIFESTORY because I have seen it in schools, and I have seen it with women I work with. I have seen it with everybody. My pastor bought land that she wanted to build a really nice house on, and I told her to just write it down. The how and the when are not a problem. Just plant the seed. When we went to the church the next Sunday, the church headquarters published that every church should give the pastor 200,000 ksh for their project. She looked at me and sent a message on my phone that said, "LIFEstory." I told her to not worry about the money. The pieces will come. So it happened.

I met a lady who saw me pregnant at my old age, and asked me how it was possible. She was unable to become pregnant. She had tried many things and had thought it was impossible. I told her about LIFEstory. She said, "I have nothing to lose, so I will write it." Right now, she has a baby who is about three months old.

My eldest daughter wanted a salon, and I told her to just write it in her LIFESTORY, which she did. After two months, her husband gave her 60,000 ksh for whenever she found a shop that was comfortable for her so she could just pay for it and buy the things she needs. It has happened. So everything she writes down happens. She knows the secret is to write it down. Do you want to be healthy? Write it down. Do you want to achieve something? Write it down.

Her husband wanted a job as a banker because he was teaching in the university, which was not his passion. His passion was to work in the bank. I told him that with LIFEstory Transformation it could change. I asked if he would write it, and he said he would try anything. Soon he had three banking positions in different locations, but not Nairobi. He came back and said he was getting results but not in Nairobi. I told him to write down "in Nairobi" and see himself working in Nairobi. He said it was impossible, and I told him nothing is impossible. He went and wrote it and visualized himself working, and it happened.

LIFEstory is really life-changing, and I am loving it. Right now, people who knew me in the market look unto me, and they say, "What happened?" And I say, "It is LIFEstory. You can write yours, and your life can change." It is empowering. They are looking at me as the example. If you ask my husband, he will say it is LIFEstory that is changing me in an amazing way. It has changed me from the person I was into the person that I am now.

Days for Girls

As my sewing business began to grow, I was offered an opportunity to become involved with Days for Girls, train as an ambassador, and begin a Days for Girls enterprise. Girls are given a kit that contains washable, reusable pads and two pairs of panties. It sounds so simple, but by giving a girl two panties, now she can wash one and, while it dries, she has the other. I wish I had grown up in this time! I could have become a doctor. If someone had visited our school and had given me the Days for Girls kit, life would have been much better.

This was very important to me because it is about the journey I have walked myself. Through Days for Girls, I know a girl somewhere is going to stay in school and become a doctor. She is going to change the community and the nation. Girls are very bright, but they leave school when they become pregnant or become HIV positive because they do not have the Days for Girls kit or something to manage their menstruation.

In Kenya, most of the areas where I've been, they do not talk about menstruation in the family. It is taboo to talk about blood issues with your parents or with the immediate family. Many end up becoming pregnant at a very early age because they are exchanging their body to receive the money for their feminine hygiene. In many families that are struggling to even get a breakfast, the daughters feel guilty about asking for money for their hygiene. They prefer exchanging sex for money. With Days for Girls, we are empowering them to stay in school and not have to risk their lives through HIV or early teenage pregnancy. We are keeping girls in school. This is my passion, because I know what it means not to have it. I have been there.

Whenever I give a kit to a girl, I imagine she is me! I am helping her to live her dreams! I know that girl is going to bring about a great change. If this girl understands the meaning of this kit, it is going to change the entire nation. It is going to help that girl stay in school, write her LIFEstory, and become a doctor or whatever she wants. I see the great changes that are happening in very remote areas because a girl persevered, went to school, went to college or university, and started a rescue center or a school. You will always find the person who is the administrator is a girl. She will tell you she did not want to see what was happening to girls, like female genital mutilation (FGM) or marrying off the girls very early. You see, it is a girl who is fighting for them. You can see the great changes the girls can bring in the nation, even in the village, in the city, and in the country. The change coming is from the women!

The Future is Bright

I used to think that if I could find that man in the slums, I would just strangle him to death, but that was part of life. Life in the slums was very, very hard, but when I go back and think about it, I think, "God, you really had a great purpose in my life." Now when I am teaching Days for Girls, I can look back and realize God was making me pass through things so I could know. It was my life purpose, and God had a reason for me to walk through this journey so I could help other people.

In every situation, you need mentors, people who are going to guide you. My mentors taught me about LIFEstory, and everything started unfolding in a different way. I don't see life the way I used to see it. Back then I used to see struggles and everything seemed impossible, but now I see God unfolding and answering prayers. Every time I write something I want in my LIFEstory, it just manifests. Now I see a blessing. I see transformation. I see great things happening in my life and even in my children's lives. I tell people that when they write their LIFEstory, everything is going to change.

My friends and family can see the change in me. So, I look at them, and I look at other people, and I say, "It is not impossible. Everything is possible." Right now, I see EVERYTHING is POSSIBLE! There is nothing that can't change. Everything can change. It is so amazing!!

About Christine Sakali Khamasi

Christine Sakali Khamasi grew up in Kenya with dreams of becoming a doctor. Abandoned by her mother at age 5, she was subsequently forced to drop out of school because of the unavailability of feminine hygiene products and her own lack of knowledge about how to care for herself. She suffered great abuse by men, became pregnant at 14, and ended up in the slums of Nairobi where she was forced into prostitution just to feed herself and her baby. Her story of transformation and personal development is an inspiring example of achieving success no matter how difficult the trials.

Christine eventually learned English, went to school to learn sewing skills, and is now the proud owner of a successful tailoring business. In addition, she is an ambassador and trainer for Days for Girls, devoted to bringing young girls out of lives of poverty and servitude. As a LIFEstory Transformation coach, she teaches her people how to achieve their dreams and goals. A film titled "Rescue" about her life is shortly to be released.

Chapter Thirteen
Perfectly Unpredictable. Perfectly Unique. Perfectly Perfect.
By Becky Mackintosh

Chapter Thirteen
Perfectly Unpredictable. Perfectly Unique. Perfectly Perfect.
By Becky Mackintosh

What happens when what you hoped and dreamed for all your life and envisioned as your plan for yourself and for your family is thrown off course? Someone in your family gets divorced. Are you now a failed family? NO, you are just a family with a different situation and perhaps more complex relationships.

Do you turn into a dysfunctional family because your unwed daughter gets pregnant? What if your child is enslaved by drugs, alcohol, pornography, or some other addiction? No one planned for that, right? Are you now a failed family? NO, you have not failed; you just become a family with a particular set of circumstances that needs special attention.

What if your child tells you he is gay? Are you now a failed family? NO, you have not failed; you are a family with a member who needs special love and understanding and who has love and understanding to give back.

If any of these scenarios are actually indications of failure, then I have a failed family. But, wait: my husband Scott and I have not failed because of our focus on staying in the right place—a place of love. I have never thought of myself as an expert, but I can share some of my life lessons learned from a difficult past that I now call success.

My Story

Growing up, my greatest hope was to become a mother. In fact, I wanted *ten* kids! How hard could raising ten children be? After all, my great grandmother, Mary Jane Thomas Jones raised sixteen children.

As I teenager I made a list of qualities I wanted in a future husband. Some of those qualities were integrity, compassion, and a desire to raise a family with strong religious values. I was certain that if I married an honest, loving man and we attended church, had personal and family prayers, weekly family activities, and read our scriptures *a lot*, our children would grow up without a hitch.

Well, everything started out as planned. I married a man who had all the qualities on my "must have" list. Yep! That handsome, fun-filled guy—Scott Mackintosh—passed the test with flying colors. He also happened to steal my heart. We were married September 22, 1983.

Remember, I wanted ten children; therefore we wasted no time in starting our family. We began welcoming children one by one into our home. I have to admit, it was not easy. Unfortunately, I discovered I was one of those nauseated, throwing-up-all-day-every-day-for-nine-months kind of gals. Still, I loved my children with all my heart and had made up my mind that it was worth it to go through whatever it took to get them here. When child number seven was born I told my husband it *felt* like *ten* and I was calling it good. Our family felt complete, so we named our last son, "Skye" 'cause "Skye's the limit!" (That is not really why we named him Skye, but he was our caboose and it makes for a really good story.)

I had my first five children in six and a half years. That alone accounted for some crazy times at the Mackintosh house. I would tell myself that as soon as I was down to having only one child in diapers things would be easier, or as soon as they were all in school life would be easier. I hadn't taken into account that the prayers, family activity night, scripture reading, attending church, and volunteering in the community were all to be fit in between piano lessons, soccer practice, football practice, t-ball, 4H, scouts, wrestling, dance, gymnastics, chores, meal time, laundry and dishes. Not to mention trying to squeeze in a few hours of sleep! Zzzzz!

Then one day it hit me! I had not done the math!

The five children who were all born within six years had all grown into teenagers at the same time, and three of them were teen-age girls—and beautiful ones to boot! I think you get the picture. There is a reason I color my hair, have bags under my eyes and have calluses on my knees. Ha! Don't get me wrong— Scott and I have been blessed with good kids, normal kids, and in fact, *perfect* kids:

Perfectly rambunctious,

Perfectly unique,

Perfectly stubborn,

Perfectly moody,

Perfectly unpredictable,

Perfectly "I'll do things my own way,"

Perfectly ours!

I will tell you that they were not perfectly perfect. I cannot count the sheer number of hours worrying, and on my knees praying, and often even pleading with God over my concerns with one of our children. His answer was often the same: "Be patient and love unconditionally."

Most days the loving part came easy. It was the "be patient" part I often struggled with. Don't ask me why, but I wanted things fixed right then! Some parenting skills I learned a little late for my children's liking. But I did the best I could each day with what I knew, and each time I learned a better way to parent, I would then commit to do better.

I think parents' fondest wish and greatest desire is that their children discover the divine potential within them, right? To know just how simply special they truly are. How do we as parents help our children do this? How do we encourage, praise, and build up our children? How do we help our children feel appreciated, accepted, and that they are worthwhile?

I believe the process begins the minute our children are born and continues until the day they leave this earth. Whether your children are toddlers, teens, or adults, as a parent, you never stop worrying and loving them. Have you ever stopped to think that from the day your child is born, you have only 18 summers with them? Then they are gone! And let me tell you it goes by *fast*! Take a moment and remember your last summer—how fast it came and went! That's exactly what I'm talking about. Cherish every minute. Enjoy every stage.

The best advice I could give you as a parent is not to miss an opportunity to be with your children, because there's so little time. Attend school events. Go to teacher's conferences, cheer them on at sporting events, read to them, help them with homework, take them on business trips with you and never miss a birthday or graduation day. Why? Because someday your kids will pick out the nursing home they are going to send you to! Funny, but true. Still, in the meantime will be all the years for you to have an adult relationship with them—an adult relationship primarily built on those 18 fleeting years.

We don't want to shackle ourselves to our children and oversee every decision they make. Okay, yes we do, but we know we can't and shouldn't. Agreed?

"At the end of the day people won't remember what you said or did; they will remember how you made them feel." ~ Maya Angelou

How do *you* make others feel? What if everything you did and said came from a place of love? *Then* would they remember what you did and said? Or at least in the way you would want them to remember? When we deal with people in tough situations such as family disagreements, professional conflict, or political controversy, we have a tendency to line up the facts like little tin soldiers in our minds to make sure that we are right. We check our facts and information and make sure we are coming from the right place.

That's pretty good. We should come from the right place. But what is the right place? Perhaps the bigger question is, are we coming from a place of love?

As I have traveled the world, I have found that people are the same. No matter your profession, demographic, location, social status, educational degree, or what your religious beliefs are; no matter whether you are rich, poor, brown, black, white, pink or green—we all have the same basic needs. We all want to feel loved, safe, appreciated, trusted, respected, accepted, and valued for who we are and the diversity we bring. Right? Our children want the same things, but for some reason we sometimes forget that they are people, too.

It has been my experience that treating people the way you want to be treated keeps customers coming back, employees giving a 100%, and a puts a smile not only on your face, but on others' faces, too.

Have you ever stopped to think that regardless of what type of particular family you come from, whether it is a traditional nuclear family, a stepfamily, a single-parent family, an adopted family, or a single-person-with-a-pet family, it consists of those who care about each other? And that's what it really boils down to—caring about one another and feeling you belong and are valued—and loved!

If you are irritated with someone—or just don't like them much—everything they do or say is going to bother you. But when you really care about a person they could spill an entire plate of food onto your lap and you'd probably laugh—and make sure *they* were okay. It's true. Why is that? When something like that happens will you act kindly or react harshly? It's a choice. Wayne Dyer is right: Change the way you look at things and the things you look at change. You see situations, circumstances, and people in a different perspective. Coming from a place of being right is reasonable. Coming from a place of love has nothing to do with reason or being right, but it works. Try it. Feel it. You'll see how it really is more "right" than being right!

Of course, no one is perfect at everything; but you can be perfect at some things. You can be perfect at trying to be perfectly kind, perfectly loving, and always coming from a place of love. And your personal payback is wonderful; you feel better—you even look better! Did you know that a simple act of kindness benefits your health by boosting your immune system and reducing your heart rate? Yes, a *simple act of kindness* actually triggers the brain's pleasure center releasing endorphins, and others *feel good happy chemicals*. It also reduces wrinkles! Can't beat that! An act of kindness costs you nothing, and saves you much.

Your mother said it, your grandmother too, *"'Do unto others as you would have them do unto you.'* That's the golden rule!" But what happens when the golden rule is challenged—*really* challenged? How do you respond then? Does the rule become obsolete because you are certain it was *not* intended for you in *this* situation?

Remember all the scenarios I mentioned at the beginning of this chapter regarding family challenges such as divorce, addiction, an unwed pregnancy or a child coming out and if that makes you a failed family? The answer is still NO, you are not a failed family. Success is taking on life's challenges in the best way you know how, and when you learn a better way, commit to do better.

I know what it is like to be the mother of an unwed pregnant daughter. I know what it feels like to be a mother of a gay son. And as difficult as those things were when they presented themselves, approaching them from a place of love created beauty and wonder instead of disaster. I wouldn't trade my set of circumstances for anything in the world. No, these things were not on my vision board, and I could not have prepared myself for these events, except to focus on the positive and try always to approach difficult situations—every situation— from a place of love.

Jesus' counsel in John 13:34 to "Love one another as I have loved you," means what it says. Love *everyone,* even those among our families and friends who may make different choices from those we would make. Intolerance creates hate, war, bullying, sadness, and pain. Seeking to understand cultivates trust and respect. This was personally put to a test when my belief system was challenged and my world turned upside down.

It was January 9, 2012, when my twenty-four-year-old son Sean told his father Scott and me that he was gay. Sean is one of the millennial generation, so he told us the best way he knew how—in a Facebook private message!

Precisely at 11:11 pm, he sent us this:

"Hey so I'm not gonna beat around the bush too much, I'm just going to tell you something that I'm sure you already know or it has at least crossed your mind plenty of times. I'm gay. I'm sure this isn't the best news a parent could hear, but I feel like it's not right for me to not talk to you about something very real to me. I want you to know I'm very much the same weird Sean. Ha! I love you and dad so much and you're the best parents a kid could ask for. This is why it's taken me so long to tell you, I'm fine with the pain it can bring me at times; but I just didn't want to hurt you 'cause you don't deserve it. Once again I love you very much, but I want to keep this brief because I am sure you'd rather talk in person and I am one hundred percent fine with that. I haven't told anyone ever, I wanted you and Dad to be the first to know."

The sting of reading the words "I'm gay," was soothed by his last sentence:

"I haven't told anyone, ever. I wanted you and dad to be the first to know."

That validated how awesome, amazing, and considerate my son is—and let me know that we could deal with this if we approached it from the only place possible—a place of love. We loved our son. He loved us. Therefore, somehow, it would all work out. What concerned me, and caused me to realize that I still needed to work on love and acceptance, was the fact that my son had hidden deep in a closet, and secured them with lock and key, his most conflicted and torn feelings, and had dealt with them all alone, by himself, for years.

That, I was not proud of.

Sean was correct in his assumption that this had "at least crossed my mind." I had often wondered about my strikingly good-looking son who only dated when girls took the initiative and asked *him* out. It was something I kept quiet and secret, hardly daring to think even to myself. I hoped it was not true, but I had wondered. And there it was in black and white on my computer view screen—my son's courageous announcement that he was gay.

His father had no clue. Scott was blind-sided by the news. It shook him to his core. Those words "I'm gay" coming from his son were not on Scott's Family Vision Board either. Scott had no clue as to how to acknowledge his son and reply to this heartfelt, vulnerable message—except he knew he loved his son; and that, as it turned out, was enough.

Immediately upon reading Sean's message, I responded by asking him to hurry home so we could talk, face-to-face. I am not proud of everything I said in that very first conversation. I said some things completely out of ignorance. I had never researched the subject, naively thinking that it was something other families had to deal with—not mine.

First, I told Sean I loved him, and that my love would *never* change. I felt very strongly that he needed to know of my unconditional love for him. That was good. Then I said some really ignorant stuff like: "What are you going to do about it?" and "You are a fighter, Sean—you can fight this." "Hang in there. This is your test—your challenge." As these phrases spilled off my lips, I honestly thought I was giving words of comfort; not knowing each phrase was a dagger in my son's heart. Why? Because I was busy "fixing" the "problem" in my son rather than simply hearing him from a place of love.

The words weren't new to my son. He had grown up hearing them everywhere. And he had spent a lifetime trying to digest and understand why he felt the way he felt and what kind of life that meant for him. As I listened to my son tell us what it was like growing up "fighting that inward battle" and trying to "fit in" into a world that frowns upon gays, my heart broke at the thought of *my own flesh and blood* growing up feeling like a misfit right in my home, in our schools, and in our community. I realized that the pain and loneliness would have completely dissolved if people would simply treat another as they want to be treated.

While growing up, Sean never revealed the sadness or the confusion going on inside. He wore the mask very well since we saw him as a very happy, active, fun-loving boy and teenager. We didn't know. His friends didn't know. No one knew. But Sean knew. He acted as if he was just like everyone else—never revealing his inner turmoil and conflicts. If an Oscar could be awarded for such acting, he would have won. My heart felt pierced with daggers when I replayed Sean's words telling me of how many times during his tender years he contemplated ending his life so no one would ever find out he was gay. I am saddened that he, and so many millions like him, ever felt that level of despair. *I am so thankful Sean never acted upon those dark feelings. Today he is happy with who he is and with the person he is becoming.*

This isn't just about being gay. It's about being different—unique. It's about every person on the planet wanting to fit in—to feel loved, safe, respected, accepted and valued for who they are. It's about responding to people and situations from a place of love, compassion, and willingness to walk in another's shoes. As I began to look at people and situations in a new perspective, I felt a deep desire to come out of my *own* closet, to speak openly about *real* family issues—*my* family issues—in hopes that individuals and families will know they are not alone and they have not failed. Success is never giving up. Success is in cultivating loving healthy relationships that come in all shapes and sizes, beginning with family. My husband Scott and I have spoken to hundreds of groups at every conceivable venue on this subject. We often stay up late into the night talking to someone on-line who is contemplating ending their life, feeling misunderstood, mistreated, and unloved. Don't let this be your son, daughter, co-worker or neighbor. Love. Listen. Learn.

Life's not fair. In fact, it's perfectly unpredictable, and for that I am grateful. I have come to recognize that every challenge is actually a perfectly planned education that we often can't see at the time. Life's a roller coaster ride with twist and turns and loop-de-loops. When we love people unconditionally, and see them as perfectly unique, we create a positive, profound ripple effect that gets them safely through the ride. Hearts are healed, families are reunited, and lives are saved.

Remember, your family is perfect—perfectly unique and perfectly yours!

Love. Love unconditionally. It - is - a - choice. It is *the* perfectly perfect choice.

About Becky Mackintosh

Becky Mackintosh is a mentor, speaker, author, life-coach and mother of seven, but her favorite hat to wear is that of grandmother. She serves as a board member of the Mountain-West National Speakers Association Chapter, and North Star International. Becky and her husband Scott co-host a weekly podcast radio show called "Life in 22 Minutes" during which they share stories that inspire, give hope, and bring a smile to your face in only 22 minutes.

Becky is dedicated to helping people accomplish their goals and feel better about themselves and life. She is a champion of humanity and a whole-hearted people lover. She and her husband Scott have been featured on: *Good Morning America*, *TODAY* show, *Rachael Ray*, CNN, *Inside Edition*, *Fox and Friends*, and many more.

To connect with Becky visit http://lifesshortlessons.com

To follow Becky's Podcast Radio show click here: http://www.lifein22minutes.com

Chapter Fourteen
Learning to Shine
By Julie May

Chapter Fourteen
Learning to Shine
By Julie May

As an elementary school music teacher, I work with more than 500 students each week. Among my students, childhood insecurity seems to be a rampant problem. We spend the first few weeks of the school year working on their insecurities, so that when it comes time to play music, they are confident enough to perform. We do little things like having the students turn to their neighbor and tell them how incredible they are. I also teach them little chants and cheers about how awesome and hardworking they are. Then I show them how working hard and giving your best effort makes you feel amazing. After that, the students will sing or play instrumental music to the best of their abilities. They know the other students in class support them and that their teacher thinks they are amazing no matter how they sound.

The other big thing we talk about those first few weeks is failure. In music, the first time you try anything new, you're probably going to make some mistakes. Life is a lot like that. Albert Einstein said "A person who never made a mistake, never tried anything new." Elementary school students are in general completely afraid of failing. They've been taught that every time they do something wrong, they are going to get a bad grade, or get sent to the principal's office, or won't get to go out to recess. That doesn't work for music class. If a student isn't willing to try hard enough to make a few mistakes, then he'll never be good at music. Some of these students are so afraid to fail that they won't try at all. What is important is being able to notice the mistakes (or failures) so that you can do a little bit better next time and keep making progress as you go. If you can make a mistake, acknowledge it, and work on fixing it the next time, you'll do well at whatever it is you are trying to do. In my case, I let my fears and insecurities lead to mistake after mistake, until I felt as though I was trapped in a world of pain with no way out.

It all started with fear. Fear leads to far more failures than being courageous and sure of yourself ever could. Insecurity stems from fear. It's a fear of who you are and of what other people will think of you. It changes you. It changed me. I never felt as good as the other kids at school. I saw them as prettier, or more popular, or smarter, or more whatever! I went to very large junior and high schools on the wealthy side of town. My family was middle class, but we were by no means wealthy. I felt I wasn't as good as those kids who went boating every weekend in the summer and skiing in the winter. Boys didn't pay attention to me, and I wasn't particularly good at anything. It felt that way at the time, anyway. When other kids at school had their 16th birthdays, they got cars, or a big trip somewhere, or a huge party at their mansion with a live DJ. None of that was in the cards for me.

I realize now I had no reason to be insecure. I was a good student. I didn't have straight As, but my grades were pretty close. I was very self-conscious of the way I looked, but as I look back at my pictures, I realize I was very pretty. I wasn't overweight, didn't have horrible acne, and was fairly talented in some areas. Everything I was insecure about was made up in my head. But in my little teenage mind, I couldn't see that.

In my religion, we are advised not to date until we are 16 years old. So that's when you can finally start saying "yes" to all the boys who ask you out. Or in my case, pray that someone finally notice me. So when a boy finally did ask me out right on my 16th birthday, of course I said yes. It made that fear of being alone on my 16th birthday go away. I may not have had all those other things, but at least I had a date. I wasn't a complete failure. I knew the boy. We had grown up down the street from each other. I knew he had made some bad choices in the last few years and ended up in a bit of trouble. But I didn't care about that. I had a date for my 16th birthday, and despite warning from my parents, we went out.

This date was meant to be a one-time thing, just so I could say that I had a date on my 16th birthday and wasn't a complete loser. Well, Corey and I went on lots of dates after that, and pretty soon we were a couple. The bad things my parents had warned me about were true, but I didn't care because he could also be really fun to hang out with. I had only one or two friends in high school, so dating him meant I always had someone to do things with. Unfortunately, the things we did weren't good things. We got into trouble, sluffed school, and ended up in the principal's office pretty frequently. I made some bad choices during those years, but I did make it through high school and graduated. However, on the same day as my high school graduation, I found out I was pregnant. So we ran off and got married.

We got a tiny, 350-square feet studio apartment and began our life together. That pregnancy was rough and I ended up on bed rest for almost half of it. I was allowed out of bed only to use the bathroom. For months I lay on an old mattress on the floor by myself, because Corey was either working or off doing something stupid.

When we got married, I wanted to start being more responsible and make better choices for the precious life that was coming into our home. Corey wanted to continue down the path of irresponsibility. This caused a lot of conflict between us and he started to get physically violent with me. He would have affairs or go out drinking and come home to fight with me about it. I was terrified.

We stayed together for seven long years, during which we had two more children. I kept thinking, "He'll change when this happens or when that happens." "If only I would be better and kinder, he wouldn't have to go out and have an affair or get so mad at me." That last year, he started to take his anger out on the kids. Up until then, the violence had only been taken out on me. He would yell at the kids, but he never got physically violent with them. I was so depressed by then, I could hardly function. I felt like I was living in *The Jerry Springer Show*.

I had three young children. We were living in a trailer park. My husband was physically and emotionally abusive. He was drinking and going out with other women. I wasn't working because I was home with the three kids. I couldn't afford daycare for them while I worked. How was I supposed to get out of this situation and create safety for me and my kids?

When you close your mind to possibilities, none come to you. When you live your life in fear and scarcity, it promotes more fearfulness. I was so depressed and fearful at this time that I felt as though there weren't any options. I had also not kept my connection with God open so that I could receive the inspiration to do what I knew needed to be done. I was going to church and going through the motions of being spiritual. But I didn't have the faith that my Heavenly Father could help me through what looked to me like an impossible situation. I did pray for a way to get out, though. And that prayer was answered in a really strange way.

Thankfully, I had a friend at that time who was open to inspiration. During my time on bed rest, I had gained quite a lot of weight and it bothered me. Those of you who are into nutrition also know that what we feed our bodies really affects our minds. I was eating a lot of junk food at the time and my depression was out of control. My friend was inspired one day to hang out with me and the kids. She mentioned an eating plan she was using to help her lose weight. She thought I should try it. I honestly didn't feel up to trying anything, but a few days later it kept nagging at the back of my mind and I decided to start the plan the coming Monday (you can't start a diet on any day but Monday, right?)

After two weeks of eating better, not only had I lost weight, my depression seemed to disappear! It was a miracle. I could think clearly and my faith started to come back. If Heavenly Father could help me with something small like my weight, perhaps He could help me with something bigger, like saving my family. I prayed every day for inspiration to know what to do. This time I was open to any answers He gave me and had faith that no matter what the answer was, I would be able to accomplish the task. Honestly, the answer I got wasn't what I wanted. I wanted to save my whole family. I never really wanted to leave. But the answer I got was, "Leave him. He's never going to change."

In actuality, I kicked him out. Why should I leave our home when he was the one making bad choices? But I was stuck with a house payment, a car payment, credit card debt, three children who weren't in school yet, and no job. It's at times like this when you have to do more than just have faith. You have to WORK and do absolutely everything you can to be in tune with your higher power.

I'm good with kids, so the inspiration came to me to open my own in-home day care. That way I could stay home with my children and still get some money coming in. Within a year, I had paid off the car and every credit card. Lack of money had been one of the biggest reasons I had stayed all those years. Within a year of acquiring the faith to leave, I had more money than we ever had during our married years.

I learned a lot during those years of failed marriage. I learned what I wanted in life and what I didn't want. I learned about the dangers of fear, insecurity, and doubt. I also learned that God loves me and is trying to communicate with me all the time. It's up to me to open the door to receive His inspiration and guidance. Once I learned that, a world of joy opened up to me and to the thousands of people I teach in the classroom and from the stage.

Later on, I met and fell in love with my wonderful husband Joe. We've had some amazing years, and we've had some hard years just like any marriage has. But I am so grateful for everything that I learned through the seven hard years of my first marriage. I would not be who I am today if I had not learned how to get through the pain and despair I felt back then.

About three years ago, Joe and I hit rock bottom. We had had a pretty good life up until that point, but then all of a sudden everything completely fell apart. We both lost good jobs within a couple of months of each other, and my daughter Brittany, who has bipolar disorder, had been put on the wrong medication by her doctor and was spiraling out of control. Suddenly we had feelings of distrust toward each other. Things got so bad that Joe and I separated. I moved to Cedar City with the kids, six hours away, and Joe stayed in Vernal and looked for work there.

This all sounds like it was really bad, and in some ways, it was. But it was also through this time that everything got better and the inspiration came to start my business. It took me a couple of months to find work. While I was in Cedar City figuring out how to support my family on my own, I made the decision to go back to school and work on getting my degree. I don't think I would have ever gone back to school if I hadn't lost my job. Going back to school has been a huge blessing to me. At the same time, Joe and I started to work on healing our relationship. We started praying together over Skype and learned how to forgive each other and really connect. It was through this process that our relationship went from "good" to "fantastic."

After six months of living apart, I moved back up to Vernal with the kids, which meant another round of trying to find a job. Through going back to school, I was able to start teaching music at the elementary school here. I adored my students and couldn't wait to go to work each day. However, it still didn't feel like it was enough. There was something more for me and I couldn't quite put my finger on it. Right after I moved back to Vernal, I went to a couple of seminars to start figuring out what I wanted to do with my life. I prayed about how to move on and support our family in a way that would be meaningful. I wanted to make a difference in the world and help people.

One day after I had been praying, I got the inspiration to create a women's conference. We would have great speakers and musical numbers to uplift and support the women in Vernal. Our area had just gone through a huge economic crash during which thousands of people lost their jobs. It was starting to affect the health and well-being of everyone. Domestic violence and suicide rates were at all-time highs. When the wife and mother of the home suffers with depression, the whole home suffers. So I created the Joyful Living Women's Conference to uplift the wives and mothers of the home and by doing so, uplift the whole family.

When I made the choice to move forward with that inspiration, it almost took on a life of its own. Every time I would receive inspiration to do something for the event, and actually followed through with it, everything just worked out. I learned the value of acting on that guidance. The event turned out to be a huge success. We had great attendance, people loved it, and I was able to help support my family. The Joyful Living Women's Conference is now expanding out of our little town to big cities where it is receiving wonderful support.

There were many lessons I had to learn to move from those dark days with my first husband to experiencing the joy that I have in my life now. I have looked up to many people throughout my life who have had a certain quality about them. I started to notice them first back in my days of despair in the trailer park. The people who were most in tune with who they were and with the inspiration coming to them had sort of a shiny glow around them. It was something I could see and feel. I knew I wanted to have that glow and to be a person who was helping others by my own example. My life was changed when I learned how to open the door of inspiration and guidance from a loving Heavenly Father who knows everything I need to become my best self and help those around me. I named my company "Shine Events," because the greatest joys in my life have come from my desire to become a light in the darkness for others.

The first thing that I learned was to forgive. First, I needed to forgive myself for my mistakes. Then I needed to forgive those I felt had harmed me. I came up with a quick self-test for knowing if I had really forgiven that person. If I could honestly, in my heart, say that I was grateful for learning from that situation and not feel the need to talk about it anymore, then I knew I had forgiven them. When we hold onto hate, anger, bitterness, and resentment, we are not harming the person we feel has wronged us! We are only hurting ourselves.

Forgiving people, especially ourselves, can be difficult at times. A few techniques have helped me release these negative feelings when they occasionally come up. The first one is exercise. I'm not saying that you have to go out and run for 10 miles in order to forgive someone. I'm saying that moving your body in any way that you find enjoyable for about 20 minutes releases endorphins and physically helps you release that pain. It's as though the good things flowing through your body are helping to push out the bad. You can also ask God to see the other person and their struggles through His eyes. He loves all of His children regardless of their struggles. When you can start to see them with that love, you can start the path to forgiveness. Forgiveness does not mean that you allow that person to repeatedly harm you. You can have boundaries of safety and still forgive that person all at the same time. Forgiveness is about having peace in your heart.

The last key toward opening your heart for inspiration and guidance is to live and move forward in faith. So what does having faith look like? Sometimes it is easier for me to say what faith is not. Faith is not having a scarcity mindset that there won't be enough love, money, or jobs. Faith is acting on what you are inspired to do even when you don't know how you are going to do it. The more we act in faith upon the inspiration that is given to us, the more inspiration we receive.

I've also instituted what I call the five-minute prayer. I used to go through the motions of prayer because that's what I was supposed to do. I said my piece about being grateful and what I needed, got up from my knees and called it good. Well, what good is a one way conversation? In all honesty, we are talking about communicating with God here. He loves to hear from us, but I believe He is all-knowing. He knows the deepest desire of our hearts. He also knows how to helps us in the best way possible. It would do us good to spend more time listening than speaking. How are we supposed to follow the guidance we receive if we don't take enough time out of our day to listen to what that guidance is? To solve this problem for myself, I started challenging myself to pray longer. So I set the timer on my phone for five minutes and didn't get up until the timer went off. You'd be amazed at how much more meaningful your prayers become when you just take that little bit more time to think about what you are saying and then listen for the answers that He gives.

As Paul Harvey would say, here is "the rest of the story." Today I produce the "Joyful Living Women's Conference" where the hundreds of attendees are uplifted and inspired from the best speakers, authors, and coaches from across the country. I have had several attendees tell me how something they heard at one of our conferences changed their life. I think back to that moment when my friend was inspired to teach me about how to eat healthier and what has come from that moment. She never could have guessed that was the turning point to everything good that has come in my life since then. She was my light in the darkness. She was what I would now call a "shiny gal."

We never know when we are going to become that light for someone to follow and what impact that is going to have on the world. If we live in fear, blame, bitterness, and anger, the door of inspiration closes and we are left in the darkness. When we forgive, love, pray, and have faith, God's love can flow through us as a light for others to follow and we will really shine. Now imagine for yourself a world in which one person's light helps to light hundreds of other people's lights. Then each of those lights helps to light hundreds more. It would be an explosion of light across the world. Because, in truth, we don't just affect one person. We affect hundreds and thousands of people throughout our lifetime. What are you doing today to shine for someone else today?

About Julie May

Julie has been inspiring youth and adults as a teacher and mentor for over ten years. She is the President and Chief Habit Coach at Excel Your Habits which provides mentoring, coaching, events, and seminars specially designed to help individuals retrain their brain. Her Excellent Habits System is revolutionizing the world of self-help. She is a fiery speaker who excites individuals for change and provides the follow through to make it happen. Julie is the producer of the Joyful Living Women's Conference which is attended by women from all over the country. Also look for the Joyful Living Family Conference coming in April 2017.

Some of Julie's favorite things include: music, theater, teaching, and anything Disney. She is currently the music specialist at Naples Elementary school in Vernal, Utah where she teaches music to over 500 students.

Julie and her husband Joseph reside in Vernal, Utah and have 7 children together, two of which are currently serving LDS missions.

For information about Julie's events or the Excellent Habits System, please visit our website at www.excelyourhabits.com. To find out more about the upcoming Joyful Living Conference and purchase tickets, please go to www.joyfullivingconference.com.

"Every day is a new chance to create the life you really want to live. Take the chance!"

Chapter Fifteen
God Does Not Call the Qualified,
He Qualifies the Called
By Shantel McBride

Chapter Fifteen
God Does Not Call the Qualified, He Qualifies the Called
By Shantel McBride

"When we are no longer able to change a situation, we are challenged to change ourselves."

"Everything can be taken from a man but one thing: the last of the human freedoms—to choose one's attitude in any given set of circumstances."

~Viktor Frankl

One cold winter day in February as I was getting ready to take on the day, I had several places to go, things to do, and people to see. Suddenly my phone rang. I looked down to see the call was from one of my dearest friends, Heidi. My face automatically smiled wide in excitement to hear from her. Heidi and I had worked together at Nordstrom. You work very closely in retail, and we were just that, very close. For years we had lunch together every day and would laugh like there was no tomorrow. The first time I met Heidi, we went to lunch; she had a drink on her tray and managed to spill it all over—and I mean all over! I was a little embarrassed but Heidi was stunning and charismatic and people were drawn to her. Before I knew it, the whole restaurant was helping with "cleanup on aisle 4." There would be many more times like that. At the time of that phone call, our friendship had spanned 25 years.

"I need you to come over here and make me laugh," Heidi said. I could feel by the shakiness in her voice that she was scared about something. The tone in her normally jovial yet calm voice gave me chills.

My smile faded.

Feeling suddenly wary and cold, I glanced out the window at the huge Wasatch Mountains from my home in Utah. They were covered with snow and today seemed brutally icy and insurmountable. I found myself wondering what obstacle my gorgeous and funny Heidi could possibly be facing.

It would have been so easy for me to make an excuse—to run off to one of my myriad jobs and use "busy-ness" as an excuse not to connect. I had done it before. Heck, I had even run away from saying a prayer in church several weeks prior. However, I had attended a "Genius Bootcamp" just a month earlier that my friend Leslie Householder taught. As the author of the *Jackrabbit Factor, Portal to Genius,* and *Hidden Treasures*, Leslie had amazing wisdom to offer, and that boot camp had begun to powerfully awaken me spiritually. (It affected me so much that I later became a facilitator in the three-day training program, and am still doing so today). Tentatively, I had begun to learn how to listen to God and to my inner guidance.

I set aside my lengthy to-do list, and went straight to my friend's home.

When I got there, Heidi couldn't look me in the eye.

"I have been diagnosed with bone and lung cancer." Her words said that she was ready to fight, but her body language said otherwise. She was distraught, and regrets about her life started taking over immediately. I started thinking about all of mine as well. At the time, I helped people write their obituaries—not to die, but to live through a training I had written called "Live Like You're Dying." Heidi wanted me to help her write her obituary as well, and also write letters to her kids just in case she didn't make it. Many tears fell that day.

We ended up having a deep conversation about death. At that time, I had never really talked to someone about that on a deep level.

"How does it feel to be told you don't have much time left?" She could not explain the feeling, and just burst into tears.

"I've been given three weeks to live," she said tearfully, "but I'm going to fight. I feel like I can win."

Who was I to take that hope away? So, not really knowing what to do, I listened and even let her borrow some hope from me.

Heidi said she needed help processing some things, so I had us both take some deep breaths and then started to ask questions.

"What are you most scared of?" I asked her.

"I'm really scared about leaving my family." I wrote that down on a yellow pad of paper. Then she added, "I'm scared of the 'C' word," and I wrote down "Cancer." She said, "I'm scared of the 'D' word," and I wrote down "Dying."

She proceeded through a list and then asked me to read it back to her. I read back, "You're scared for your family," and she said "Yes."

"You're scared of the 'C' word, cancer," and she replied, "Yes."

"You're scared of the 'D' word, dying," and she said "No, diabetes!" and that started the laughing, but the laughing soon turned to crying in each other's arms. I was amazed at her bravery, and I hoped Heidi would live longer than three weeks.

On that drive home, I felt raw and empty. I felt I had nothing to offer my sweet friend. As the days passed and we began to spend more time together, I discovered that listening, and giving hope and my love, was *exactly* what she needed.

Knowing that Heidi would be facing enormous difficulties, I decided just to be there for her—to be a strength for her. What I didn't know is that I was going to be facing a mountainous obstacle that I had never before dreamed of or contemplated.

While Heidi was fighting for her life, I began to face sudden and severe loss of my own. No, I didn't have cancer, but I felt as though I must have some sort of disease. *Eight* of my friends and family members would die from various causes over the next three months. My husband and I were emotionally shattered as both of his parents died within just a few weeks of each other. As if that wasn't enough, another sweet friend tried to take his own life. Fortunately he was able to survive after enduring a two-week coma, but his lost desire for life in the midst of all of our loss was devastating.

Even as the weather warmed, our home and hearts felt permanently chilled. It got to the point that every time the phone rang, our hearts sank. What was going to happen next? Who would go next? Weekend after weekend, we attended one funeral after another, holding onto each other in our grief. We were in a war zone, and the casualties were adding up.

Unlike life in a war zone, however, for most people, life went on as usual. My coworkers at the high-end retail shops at the local malls kept gossiping about customers and other employees, with selling being the top priority. It was all about the almighty dollar, while my life was falling apart one seam at a time. My friends at church who were not affected by the losses kept up their daily routines. Logically, I knew life had to go on, but I couldn't fathom how life was not stopping for everyone else the way it felt it was for us.

I drove to my friend Heidi's almost every day. She talked about the things she didn't do. "I just want to finish so much," she cried. Alone here with the friend I had previously laughed with every day, it all felt so heavy. I started to feel the guilt and asked myself why I hadn't been there pushing her to fulfill her dreams. One of her biggest regrets was not finishing nursing school. She was fighting to be able to complete that before death could take her.

In the meantime, I kept my own grief and guilt from my friend. She had no idea that when I couldn't be there on certain days, it was because I was attending yet another funeral. Emotionally, I was drained. I was surrounded by this thing we call death, and the pain from it all consumed every thought.

Still, as the physical and emotional pain for Heidi worsened, I just sat through it with her. At first, I didn't realize as I was fighting the numbness that I had a gift for being able to sit with people in their pain. Most people have to hop off the phone, leave the room, or change the conversation to escape the horrible reality. I eventually realized that Heidi could be her raw and real self with me. She could express extreme tenderness, joy, or love, and I would not be embarrassed or uncomfortable. I celebrated those moments with her. Conversely, she could express pain, anger, fear, sadness, rage, and regret. I walked through the pain with her.

Each day as I drove home, however, I was facing my own darkness. My life was turning into three months of pure hell. In addition to losing several close friends, I was dealing with business issues that ended up shattering my world. While still working for Nordstrom, I had invested nearly all of my energy for more than two years in helping build a training program for improving personal, family, and business communications. I had worked like a slave helping others build their business and their dream. I had run networking, organized events and meetings, and conducted trainings. It had all been upon the promise from them that it *would* pay off...eventually.

I couldn't believe the words I heard: "YOU ARE FIRED!" This was the first time I had ever been fired from *any* job; through the work I had done, my resume was full of the relationships I had built that spanned decades. I was devastated, to say the least. This just didn't happen in my world.

What I didn't know at that time is that if you have never been fired, you are missing out on one of life's universal, defining moments. I know that sounds strange, but being fired creates the potential to set great transformation and growth into motion. All I knew was that it was a crushing blow—a dreaded, crippling punch slamming into me from my blind spot.

I was traumatized. I felt like the sucker in sucker-punch.

I spent the next three months fighting off fits of sobbing and depression. I was grieving deeply. Having never been fired and never having lost someone close to me before, I didn't even recognize grief for what it was. *I thought something was terribly wrong with me.*

In truth, I was beyond devastated. I really didn't want to live. I had been so invested in that job and absolutely loved the people there. I had honestly felt I was truly thriving in that position, and had convinced myself that I would do that work until my last breath. In losing what I had thought of as my home, I felt a darkness that was smothering me. And it wasn't over.

Despite everything we could do, I watched another one of my best friends slip right through my fingers. My dear friend Raegan lost her battle after facing five different cancers. She was one who had clung to life, and was committed to really live, especially for her young children. Her death was particularly hard, too. After Heidi and Raegan's funerals, I started studying death and near-death experiences. Death for the sake of death didn't make sense to me.

I wanted to learn more about heaven. I had so many questions as to why these things were happening, but felt I had no answers.

Why could God do this?

How could God do this?

I was a victim to my pain. Some days my heart was heavy. Other days it actually just felt empty. I began to think that maybe I had no heart left—that everyone that had passed had taken a piece and it was simply *gone*.

Becoming enveloped, surrounded, and nearly suffocated by this thing we call death, I almost let it take me. But I had two children I adored and a husband to support and love, so for the next two years, I just set out to save the world. I did everything I could to keep my mind *off* of what happened. My husband took a different turn, and went into a funk himself. He was diagnosed with depression and anxiety. His business went down the hole and he ended up not working at all. We ended up short-selling the dream home we had built from scratch and lived in for a decade. I felt guilty because I thought I was being materialistic and that grieving over an object was selfish. While we were handling things differently, my husband and I were both lost, and felt we had lost everything.

In the midst of all of that pain, I was on my way to Vegas with a carload of women for a seminar. The driver was a chaplain. She knew me fairly well, and had been following the thrashing I was experiencing in my life.

"Shantel," she said soberly, keeping one eye on me and one eye on the road as we traveled into Nevada. "Have you thought about becoming a chaplain? You're already helping people with grief! Maybe you should look at taking it a step further."

I glanced out the window at the dry and dusty desert whizzing by, knowing that we were headed to a beautiful oasis. Was it possible that from the desert of life, I could lead people to discover their own oasis?

I was very drawn to the idea. I pondered it while we were at the seminar, and I looked at every palm tree with new interest and new eyes. I felt a deep inner longing to be able to use what I had been through to help others. Most importantly, I felt a spiritual calling.

By the time I returned home, I had an unexplainable fire within me. I looked into chaplaincy immediately when I returned home. For the next eighteen months, I attended Clinical Pastoral Education, or CPE, which was essentially chaplain school. It didn't take me long to log in more than 2100 hours to become a professional Board Certified Chaplain. I set out to help others heal others from their losses. Little did I know this would be prove to be my own healing base.

I had never really known how to be guided spiritually. It wasn't until I learned how to listen to my own inner guidance and to God that my life unfolded before me in miracle after miracle. Before I had always been focused on the things of the world as my benchmarks for success. I traded in selling lip gloss for working for the "Big Boss" (God), and it was in Him that my heart and spirit thrived. I was led right to the doorstep of Good Shepherd Hospice, where I became the Hospice Chaplain—something that was never, ever in a million years on my radar. I hadn't even known what a hospice chaplain was. As a chaplain, my job is to hold space for people—to create a safe container where people can shed their tears and say everything they need to say. It's a place to grieve and allow pain a voice. It was pretty much what Heidi had taught me. I started to learn that in our own "woundedness," we can become a source of life and light for others. I had resisted so much of the spiritual aspect of life for so many years. I was always running the opposite direction, but now realized it had been calling my name.

And the miracles? They began to happen *when I answered back.*

In his book *The Wounded Healer*, Henri J. M. Nouwen says,

For people of prayer are, in the final analysis, people who are able to recognize in others the face of the Messiah. They are people who make visible what was hidden, who make touchable what was unreachable. People of prayer are leaders precisely because through their articulation of God's work within themselves they can lead others away from confusion and towards clarification; through their compassion they can guide others out of the closed circuits of in-groups and towards the wider world of humanity; and through their critical contemplation they can convert convulsive destructiveness into creative work for the new world to come.

Nouwen's quote is profound. In our lives, our "mess" can become our message, our test our testimony, and in our wounds we find the very thing that can not only make us stronger, it can become our creative, healing work for a better world.

What I discovered was that I needed to adjust, adapt, and overcome! I discovered that when I really take a look at myself and do some switching or tweaking, I become more finely sculpted, or even more finely attuned—like a radio frequency—moving past the noise and static to exquisite learning and attentiveness to be with others. I did not at first see that as my gift, and it took someone else with the eyes of God to point it out to me.

And that job I loved so much and was so devastated to lose? Being fired from it turned out to be one of my greatest blessings. Had I stayed I would have been working on someone else's dream, and someone else's calling, and not my own.

I loved the fact I could learn from my "failures" and actually make them my successes. I discovered that each thing we encounter in life can turn out to be a huge learning experience. With this perspective now I can light a candle in the darkness so that others can see their learning experiences as blessings and successes, and not failures.

Now my life is centered not just on comfort in the dying, but on the joy in living! I participate in celebrations, I facilitate weddings, I organize grief groups, but with living at the forefront. I love to teach people how to enjoy their lives and "kick some dash"—what we do with the time we have while we're here, from birth until the end of our glorious lives.

Just the other night as I was driving home from The Bradley Center, which offers support for grieving children and their families (where I'm now a facilitator), I was thinking about all of the blessings that have happened in my journey from grief. As I looked up, I couldn't see the mountains that normally guide my journey, because there were so many clouds with an impending snow storm.

"How weird it is to know something so big is there, but I can't see it!" I thought. As I drove a little further, I could finally see an outline of the mountains if I looked really hard. I laughed to myself, that this was how I had to learn to trust God. He is SO BIG, and if I really looked hard, I could see the outline of Him in my life. That was where faith came in. Through my loss, pain, and the whole chaplain experience, I have learned without a shadow of a doubt that God is there, even when I can't see Him.

So my prayer today is for you to feel God's comfort and grace—that you can know that He is there, even when you can't see Him. I promise, if you really look, you will be able to see the outline of His loving hand in your life.

And if you are a feeling a calling, but the fog of doubt feels deep and thick to you, please remember this: "God does not call the qualified, he qualifies the called." He sure did with me, and He will with you, too.

May God Bless You!

Shantel McBride, The Cheerful Chaplain

About Shantel McBride

Shantel McBride is a Certified Trainer, Mentor, Entrepreneur, Inspirational Speaker, Hospice Chaplain for Good Shepherd Home Care & Hospice, Grief Facilitator and is also the owner of her own company, focusing on assisting others with emotional and mental balance—the "Circle Of Life."

Over the past few years, Shantel's life has been touched by numerous passings—best friends, parents, relatives—and in true form, she's turned the pain, fear, and compassion into a training entitled "Live Like You're Dying." Shantel says, "The truth is that any day could be your last day on Earth, because the future is never guaranteed. I have learned to never take my continued existence for granted. I live mindfully, looking at life in a whole different light. This was actually the gift I received from having so much death of family and friends. I see life as so much more than the gift it is."

Shantel works with several different companies, learning and gaining new skills. She graduated from CPE (Clinical Pastoral Education) with The World Spiritual Health Organization as a Professional Clinical Board Certified

Chaplain and is now working on her Master Certification. She is a TedX speaker and also hosted a local radio show on K-talk called *Inspired Conversations* for two years. Shantel loves to serve others and her community. Her experiences have taken her to service projects with many charities. She was also on the HOA board in her community for 10 years and now sits on the Advisory Board as well as Director of Mentors for WOW Utah, a non-profit that helps women who have been in an abusive relationship, gone through a job loss, catastrophic illness, or abuse with alcohol or drugs.

Shantel has been married to Paul for 31 years. They have two children—a very cute girl named Tayler (19) and a handsome young man named Tanner (21).

Chapter Sixteen
My Passion is Paying It Forward
By Anita Mibey

Chapter Sixteen
My Passion is Paying It Forward
By Anita Mibey

My journey started when I was 12 years old growing up in Bomet, Kenya. Families in Bomet were deeply rooted with strong cultural beliefs that a girl child has to go through circumcision to be a woman. Girls are married off to men not of their choice, and who are aged like their fathers, in order for the girls' families to be paid a bride price. I had to fight against all odds to finish my secondary level and join the university to pursue my degree in Commerce. I am the second child born into a family of nine children, and the first born daughter. As a result, I had to fight big battles in my village and I received much peer pressure from my schoolmates about my trying to continue with school. Fortunately, I had strong support from my parents to finish school; many girls of my age were forced to drop from school after eighth grade. The social and cultural pressure was for a girl child to be married off and not advanced in school. This pressure did not deter me from achieving my dreams and changing the narrative of educating a girl to take leadership roles.

Despite the challenges I faced as a girl child, I managed to go through high school and joined college, which provided me with skills and landed me employment where I managed Kiva loans on the Kiva platform. Kiva is an online lending platform that has created opportunities for entrepreneurs who might not otherwise be able to pursue their dreams and improve their lives. My hard work did not go unnoticed. I successfully managed to climb the ladder within a few years and was promoted as Area Manager to manage clients and a loan portfolio of about 1,200 clients in the micro bank industry. My engagements prompted me to obtain more knowledge, and I started attending degree evening classes every night. This required a lot of sacrifice and time away from my newly married husband and my friends, while balancing between family, work and studies.

Then I got pregnant in November 2014, which was my happiest time. The glowing, radiating energy that comes with pregnancy followed me through the whole course of carrying my daughter—minus a mere month and a half of sickness. My blissful pregnancy seemed uncannily comfortable and easy despite my engagement in work and studies. Thank God for my understanding and supportive husband. As the final months approached on June 2015, I had to take a break from studies. I watched my belly grow but was I still energetic and reported to work without any challenge.

My baby was due in two days, and I was caught between anxiety knocking and the expected happiness of being a mother. About five days went by and I had no labor pains yet, which prompted me to visit my gynecologist to check on my baby. He reassured me that all was well and the baby was in good condition, so we added another week to wait on any signs of the baby coming. It took about five more days until I started feeling labor pains, and I rushed to the hospital without further delay. My eyes filled with tears—a combination of excitement and anxiety—as I managed to say to my husband beside me, "I am cannot wait to hold my daughter."

Labor was a whirlwind of surprise, fearful intensity, and pure joy, followed by induction in the evening to take me through the night and probably have my baby by midnight. The night was long as I labored through with no luck in delivering daughter. Early morning at around 3:00 am I had a normal checkup by the night shift nurses on my progress and my baby's heartbeat. The nurse said all was well and that I should keep on—I would deliver in a few hours.

The unexpected happened two hours later. When the nurse came checking on my progress and that of the baby, she seemed frightened and was trying hard to get my baby's heartbeat. This did not go well with me, and I was hoping my baby was alive and I would be going to hold her soon. The nurses made an emergency call to my gynecologist, who scheduled an emergency caesarean section to try to save the baby. It was all too late, and I had lost my baby girl through the rupture of my placenta. The moment felt surreal—madness whirling around my husband and me as we gripped each other's hand. This couldn't be happening, not to us.

It was only a few minutes later before a nurse wrapped my baby girl in a blanket and let me hold her. Her body felt so empty. But I cradled her close to my chest and she felt like my baby. My daughter appeared so peaceful and beautiful, like she was sleeping—a little angel in my arms.

A day at a time, a week at a time, I hoped and prayed I would survive this. The promises of eternal families never meant more to us as a family than it did when we were going through the loss, as we remembered with gratitude the blessings of our Heavenly father that we will be with our daughter again. My experiences in those early days testified to me that during our hardest times, the Lord does not leave us alone. During my darkest times, when I have felt utterly alone and consumed by torturous grief, I learned that spiritual experiences are always within our reach. The key, however, is that we do reach—that we actively seek out these pieces of heaven. The assurance of good things to come has encouraged my husband and me to walk forward from our daughter's death, one step at a time.

The experiences and the healing journey have continued to strengthen and shape me to be a person of much gratitude. I started working tirelessly to support women in achieving their dreams in life—to be the ones who can offer support and protection at all times to their own daughters. I reflected back to the women in the village of Bomet and the challenges they faced because of their lack of education. Because of their ignorance, they were not included in decision-making, which adversely affected their daughters in trying to pursue their educations. My own experiences gave me strength to find the best ways to support the women and give them skills so that they can regain their confidence and play an important role in their families. As Heavenly Father would direct, I connected on Facebook with a wonderful woman from Utah named Margaret Heighton, who has been a blessing in my life. I just recently got to meet her in person for the first time. One morning I received a message from Margaret's daughter Heather that they were considering bringing a group to my community to support and mentor families and establish sustainable projects and create a ripple effect as we learned from them. They asked me to organize and engage families that were to be given first priority for mentoring by the team coming from Utah under a families mentoring families program. The preparation went well under the guidance of an amazing lady named Heidi Totten, the founder of the organization 100 Humanitarians. When the team arrived in Kenya, our first meeting was totally emotional. I had a strong connection with Heidi and I felt like I already knew her before meeting her in person. I have shared a lot with her. She has helped me grow and changed my perception of things. As the journey to mentor families began, many miracles occurred, and lives have been transformed. I have witnessed a widow put a smile on her face as she sees light and hope for a bright future as she works towards financial freedom. She now has a cow, a goat, and vegetable garden that enables her get enough food for the family and sell the surplus to pay school fees for her children—all because of the support of 100 Humanitarians. My full potential was really tapped in here as I was part of stimulating the change and worked with these families to make the garden boxes and planted vegetables in their gardens, which all came out successfully. How fortunate we are to have so many avenues available to us when we are ready to move forward, changing lives of others in our service.

The mission of 100 Humanitarians is to mentor families globally through education and entrepreneurship in an effort to eliminate physical, mental, spiritual, and emotional poverty. The connection with the humanitarian team is a blessing to me as we work together to engage women and empower them in finding themselves and teach them how to play prominent roles in bringing up their daughters through school and other programs. We have had successful training workshops involving about 100 women and girls on the Days for Girls and 7 Pillars programs. These sessions were accompanied by heartfelt emotions as we shared our trials and achievements with trainers from across the world. As a result of the training we had about 30 women express interest in learning how to read and write. They want to learn various skills to establish businesses to support their families, as they were denied education in their early years, followed by forced female genital mutilation and early marriages. These women speak to my heart. Some are my own mother's age, and others are as young as 20 years, but they all have a quest to learn how to read and write, and foremost to read their bibles.

My dream of supporting these wonderful women—to help them go through adult education classes and learn various skills and attend vocational trainings to support their families—is still underway. Education of female children is also affected by lack of support with sanitary kits during their most important days of their menstruation. This has contributed to high school dropouts and early pregnancies. This issue was something most parents living within an African cultural norm did not dare talk about to their daughters. Education about menstruation and support for the girls was badly needed. Mothers rarely discussed with their daughters how menstruation days affected them, and due to poverty in most families, they could not afford to buy the daughters sanitary towels during their menstrual days. These challenges faced by our girl children always impelled me to look for opportunities to support women in my village, and their daughters in their education.

My engagements were challenging, trying to get people to support me in establishing adult education classes and have women learn how to read and write again. I will share with you how I changed my ways of doing things to be able to achieve my goals and set up classes for adult education. This was followed by my making numerous requests to potential individuals I thought were in a position to support me in my efforts to have adult classes and girl child education classes.

One morning as I was contemplating about it and asking Heavenly Father to reveal to me how this should happen, I had a strong feeling and guidance on how to approach the issue. Within a couple of days, I managed to talk to a government official, sharing my intentions to support adult education. To my surprise, he was ready to offer me support and have a teacher present adult education classes for the women. The classes kicked off and women start learning how to read and write. The classes bring so much joy to my life as I see the light in those families that these women are bringing to them, along with their learning various skills to be independent and support their husbands in bringing up their children. This was a major milestone that followed what had seemed like a dark, difficult trial, seeing women who have so much in their hands to accomplish, but whose lack of education have put them in bondage. After years of their feeling hopeless and lacking any freedom, they are learning to lead self-determined lives. An understanding of one's own strengths and limitations, together with a belief in oneself as capable and effective, are both essential to self-determination. When acting on the basis of these skills and attitudes, individuals have greater ability to take control of their lives and assume the role of successful women.

From time to time, I struggle with self-doubt. Sometimes I look at what I've done and I feel like I failed or at least didn't succeed as much as I wanted to. But I was not being true to myself. Actually, a great deal has happened in me and in my community through education offered to mothers. As I have worked with them I have both learned and taught that if you desire better results on a day-to-day basis, it is necessary to realize that you "create your own reality." On a subconscious level you create your own reality with your feelings and your thoughts regardless of when, where, or how they were established. I created in my mind that I will spearhead the support mechanism for the less fortunate families at some point, and that is the goal I am working towards. As this happened to me, it can happen to you.

Doing humanitarian work and being employed at the same has taught me to be very flexible and create a balance between my work, giving service to the needy and to my family. I am doing what I love the most every day, working with communities to improve their livelihoods and working towards eradication of poverty. My journey has created many mixed feelings and experiences for the last six years of my career, and at 28 years of age I can say now it has been quite a ride. But I have grown from each and every failure and success that I have experienced.

My accomplishments did not end with the women learning how to read and write. I continued to figure out how to bring the Days for Girls enterprise into my community that will help in making reusable menstruation kits for girls, to allow them to remain in school during their learning years. It also works towards my dream of having girls achieve their very best in their studies. Thanks to my new international network of friends, I engaged with people who have supported Days for Girls in the United States and managed to obtain guidelines on how to go about the enterprise and the cost implications involved in setting it up.

Not sure of where to get the funding to set up the enterprise, I started communicating for some time with a series of friends on the importance of the program. My lovely friend Kristi Corless organized a Halloween "Bootique" to raise funds to start a Days for Girls enterprise in my community. Kristi was guided by the spirit, and she could attract people who were willing to fund the DFG enterprise. Thanks to Kristi and the 100 Humanitarians team, and to Radha, who helped organize what needed to be done to set up Bomet DFG, the program is now fully set up and supporting hundreds of girls in the community to gain confidence in their menstrual days.

I currently work with an organization in Mombasa, Kenya, working with farmers who collaborate with Doterra in outsourcing essential oils. I also manage the Healing Hands Foundation grants for community developments in Kenya. Recently a large community development project was funded by the foundation. This was a big achievement in my career. Being able to implement the projects from the ground level until its completion has taken my capabilities to the next level. During the 2016 Doterra convention the project was highlighted, as this goes hand in hand with Doterra giving back to the community.

I would say this has been an amazing journey and I have enjoyed and cried through each and every step that I have taken to be who I am today. I consider myself a living example of a successful woman in my community, despite my personal hardships. They did not deter me from continuing to change the community approach to educating women and girl children. My passion is to see women step up and become self-reliant and be a voice for girl child education. I also want to continue to establish adult education classes where young women who were forced into marriage and did not get a chance to go through school are taught how to read and write and learn business skills, which in turn will provide freedom and independence to them. That is my happiness and success.

When people ask me how I did this, I respond: "Believing in my inner self and becoming accountable." It is definitely less painful and less threatening to think of someone or something out there to blame for our failures. Blaming protects our unconscious survival system. It allows us to stay in our comfort zone, where we are assuredly feel safer. We cannot grow from our experiences as intended when we blame others: we relinquish our agency, our will, our freedom of choice, and our personal power. And we allow someone else to be responsible for what is happening in our lives. Learning this has been an important tool in my achievements and success. By being aware that each challenge in our life is an experience to learn from, then determining to do our best to confront and overcome the obstacle, we can move out of our "no growth" comfortable ruts. Remember, staying within our comfort zone is equal to little or no growth. Happy is the day when we are willing to step outside that zone of comfort, evaluate our willingness to become accountable, and expand our horizons by risking a little effort, or a lot. When we are ready and willing to take risk, to step outside that comfort zone, our growth expansion begins. Yes, often it is uncomfortable and perhaps painful but it is necessary to acquire discomfort in order to grow. Allow yourself to make a mistake. Give yourself permission to be wrong. That's how we all learn.

About Anita Mibey

Anita is from Africa, Kenya. She comes from a community that strongly believes in Female Genital Mutilation (FGM) as a cultural practice, and where girls are known to be a source of wealth to the families. Once they reach the age of 12 years they are married off to men aged like their fathers, not of their choice, for the families to be paid a bride price.

Anita had to fight all odds to finish her secondary level and join university to achieve her degree in Commerce. Anita has worked with a microfinance institution in Kenya where she managed Kiva loans and ensured that loans are fully funded by lenders. She changed many lives of poor women who could not afford to get loans from the banks to improve their lives of poverty.

Anita currently works with a non-profit organization working with farmers in Kenya, which collaborates with doTERRA in outsourcing essential oils. She also manages Healing Hands Foundation grants for community developments in Kenya. Anita also works with 100 Humanitarians, a non-profit organization from USA. The mission of the humanitarian group is to mentor families globally through education and entrepreneurship in an effort to eliminate physical, mental, spiritual, and emotional poverty.

Anita is a living example of successful women in her community who have passed through challenges. She is passionate about helping women and a voice for girl-child education. She has established adult education classes in which young women who got married at the age of 12 and did not get a chance to go through school are taught how to read and write and offered business skills. This in turn gives freedom and independence to the women who will be in a position to start their own businesses and educate their daughters to become better people in the society.

Contact Anita directly at anichero@gmail.com.

Chapter Seventeen
Unexpected Success
By Ashlee Miller

Chapter Seventeen
Unexpected Success
By Ashlee Miller

I remember the day I turned in the keys to my fully loaded company car. My husband Justin waited for me outside my office building in our used Toyota Corolla. I had graduated from college and gone to work for a major auto manufacturer. Initially, I loved my experience, but the point finally came when my freedom mattered more than any paycheck. I had gone to college intending to graduate with a business degree so I could find an awesome corporate position and compete with any guy out there. I had achieved my goal, but found I really didn't love corporate life the way I had imagined.

I started out as a marketing assistant, responsible for lots of fun things working for a luxury brand. I was floored to think they were allowing someone with very little experience be in charge of moving prototypes of new cars around the country to various car shows. I sent promotional items to special corporate customers and dealership owners, and was also responsible for ordering all the "trinkets and trash" promotional items for our events. But my favorite part of the job was coordinating competitor trades. I would drive one of our high-end vehicle models up the Pacific coast and trade with a competitor for the week. I couldn't believe I was being paid to drive next to the ocean with palm trees dancing all around me. The executives in my department would occasionally drive the cars overnight, but most of the time I was the one given the keys to flashy top-of-the-line vehicles. It was just plain fun to drive a different brand new car every week.

I was proud of myself for having landed a fantastic corporate job and making a *real* salary. The Idaho farm girl in me knew how to work hard, and I was pretty focused and grounded for my young age. I was awarded with a couple of promotions and continued to surprise and delight my managers. My final promotion required me to travel to 25 dealerships in a Southern California region. I spent hours driving in the company car I had personally customized with every option available. I would sit in traffic and then go visit dealerships, to consult their parts and service departments. I offered value in the form of strategizing market growth, but my real task each day was selling aftermarket parts to dealers who couldn't afford my products but were obligated to buy whatever I was marketing. It was a challenging time in the auto industry, and both the manufacturer and dealers were under pressure to find profits.

My days were spent fighting traffic and dealers and every night ended with me falling asleep with my laptop. The intense stress was a new experience for me. Looking back I can see anxiety had become a way of life. My salary and the company car with free gas and insurance felt like golden handcuffs, and I began to lose the joy I had found in working. Finally, a moral dilemma led me to walk into my office to resign that day. I could no longer stand the pressurized environment I was in. I wanted happiness back. I didn't have a plan in mind for my future career; I just knew I was beyond burned out and wanted my integrity to stay intact.

Disillusioned by corporate jobs, I decided to become my own boss and started teaching piano lessons and selling on eBay. I have never been an outstanding pianist; truthfully, I have always struggled to keep time while playing! I didn't let my lack of experience stop me because the drive for a bit of income mattered more. My eBay business was exhilarating. I had found a sweet little niche selling one-of-a-kind scrapbook pages to crazy ladies who had more money than creativity. I would create little pieces of a kit and the buyer only had to add her own pictures in order to create a great scrapbook page. Little tiny paper pieces would sell for insane prices, and I never knew how much money each listing would produce. It was fun to see how much money the market was willing to pay for each theme. A baseball-themed kit I made once went for more than $200! I didn't need to make tons of money, but these two little side jobs kept me going. Unintentionally, I had become an entrepreneur.

Working from home allowed me to control my stress level and I was left to focus on other aspects of my life. Business ideas, as well as miscarriages, came and went for a few years. I was constantly exploring new business ventures with my husband while we waited for our family to begin. We moved out of state for his job and finances eased, which meant I no longer had to create tiny little scrapbook projects in order to survive. Fortunately, my career as a piano teacher also ended when we moved. With no babies and no job, I was officially a stay-at-home wife.

I continued exploring different business opportunities and made sure dinner was on the table every night. I hope my husband doesn't remember those fancy meals because I certainly don't cook like that anymore! I dabbled with a direct sales business, but despite spending hours each day, I couldn't figure out how to create a true income while working from home. Looking back, it was a peaceful time because my only stress was timing dinner just right; but it also was a season of floating along not knowing my true purpose.

Our first son Boston was born a year later and now I had a full-time job that was truly stretching me. I felt grateful that my husband could support me and I could focus on our sleep schedules, diaper changes, and feeding times. I threw myself into motherhood and left business interests aside. We hadn't forgotten our dream of creating a successful business, but babies have a way of changing absolutely everything. Five months into motherhood, I was surprised to find I was expecting baby number two and my husband was really starting to want his own business. While we had a great income, we didn't have freedom, and he was missing out on family time because his job was in charge of our schedule.

We analyzed idea after idea and even put money behind a few different ventures, each leading to an eventual dead end. The goal was always freedom and family time, but we didn't know how to create it quite yet. Shortly after Jackson was born, we found a property management franchise we believed could be successful in our area. We opened our own management company and had a fully operational business within three months. I would take our babies plus two Pack-'n-Plays to the office so that I could work. We spent every weekend working late into the night and would let the boys sleep until we could no longer keep our eyes open. We would load the boys into their car seats, drive home at 2:00 or 3:00 in the morning, put the boys in their cribs, and sleep for a few hours until it was time to do the baby and business things again. Both of us knew we were getting somewhere financially, but although we were now running a profitable business, life was extremely out of balance. We lived on Easy Mac and Cheese because it was just so easy to pop in the microwave.

Every entrepreneur has days like this. Days when the momentum is definitely moving in a positive direction, but days when balance is lost and survival mode has kicked in. We made expensive mistakes and dropped all kinds of balls. Properties were coming in faster than we could rent them. One can't anticipate the problems that happen at rental properties, and we were responsible for fixing whatever happened at more than 300 homes. Justin lived on his cell phone, addressing late rents, broken toilets, fires, noisy tenants, angry owners, and more. I lived in between business and babies, always feeling like I fell short of what was truly needed. We kept at it, figuring out how to manage taxes, vendors, employees, maintenance issues, and more. Our boys grew up at the office as we grew up as entrepreneurs.

Ninety percent of startups fail, but we were determined to be part of the rare ten percent. Even though on paper we were successful, we didn't just own a company. Our jobs owned us, and the freedom we wanted seemed out of reach. The lack of sleep, nutrition, and self-care was getting to me. I wasn't depressed, but I was disconnected and not truly living. I didn't feel like myself and I didn't know how to get myself back. I tried slowing down a bit and tried to create boundaries, but I still felt mixed up and off course, no matter what I tried.

Sometimes life creates circumstances so that we will listen and be open, and that is what was happening to me. It was at this time that I heard about "energy work." Energy work can be many things, but I was just wanting to feel like myself. I was out of balance and stuck. I debated whether there could be any truth to this method of finding balance, and wasn't certain my situation even qualified for energy work. I found a lady I trusted and had a phone call with her. I discovered there was truth to energy work and was amazed to feel so different after just one session.

Everything shifted because I had found a way to let go and was no longer holding onto the stress. We started to identify and recognize the routines in our business as well as our family activities which allowed us to create a life that was less chaotic and crazy. I pulled back from our property management business, hiring people to fill my roles. I started studying and learning more about energy work and found that I had talents in this area. I found that I could help many people who were struggling by simply helping them release the stress and connect to who they really are. My business background and intuition combined in a serendipitous way. I specialized in helping both women and entrepreneurs and started to create a coaching business simply by word of mouth.

My life was full between owning the property management business, working with energy clients during nap times, and raising my boys. I stopped short of cloth diapering, but I was open to anything natural and healing. I didn't grow up focused on natural solutions, but now I wanted what was best for my children. I was finding myself interested in healthy living and embraced juicing, herbs, and essential oils. I researched to find the "best of the best," and little by little, I felt empowered. I loved taking care of my family while my husband ran our business. We had not struck it rich, but we were happy and had found a balance as both entrepreneurs and parents.

Five years had passed like a dream when I learned I was pregnant again after multiple miscarriages. I was miserable, though excited to be expecting our first girl. Charlotte rushed into the world after two weeks of false labor. I had planned to deliver naturally but had not planned on a home birth in the middle of our hallway. I was preparing to leave for the hospital when I looked at my husband and told him we were not going to make it. He demanded I get in the car or else he was calling 911. I remember looking at him and saying, "Whatever." I dropped to my knees, he made the call, and Charlotte was born 26 seconds later into Justin's arms. Fire trucks and ambulances arrived ten minutes later and we were rushed to the hospital. We had a great morning, but Charlotte developed some complications and ended up in the prenatal ICU. We had great help and miracles and took our little girl home just a couple of days later. One would think that a home birth is cheaper than a hospital, but alas, it is not. It seemed every department in the hospital billed separately and we also had ambulance bills. I dreaded getting the mail because although we were insured, this baby girl was already an expensive venture!

Two months later, we were in a car accident and our only family car was totaled. Despite owning a successful company and doing all the right things to prepare our family, the combination of the endless baby bills and a ruined car was devastating financially. Remember how I said life circumstances often demand our attention until we listen? Those envelopes in the mail had my attention and I was being forced to listen. I understood that while we had created a successful life, we were on the brink of failure with three kids in tow.

I had two serendipitous visits from a couple of strangers that changed the course of my life forever. In my pursuit of the very best health options, I had started ordering essential oils from a network marketing company after discovering the essential oils at my health food store were not truly pure. Every month, my "upline" Brooke would call to educate me on my oils and to see if I wanted to learn more about "the opportunity." I would politely tell Brooke, "No, thank you, but we are focused on our property management company, my coaching business, and raising kids." I was not looking for any other opportunity and certainly did not want to become a network marketer. My short prior experience had me believing that nobody could make money in these kinds of things. Networking had never paid off and I had zero interest in selling to others.

Shortly after our car was destroyed, Brooke's sister-in-law Chelsea happened to be traveling to San Diego and wanted to meet me. Chelsea was as real as can be—just a stay-at-home mom like me. She asked if anyone had explained the business plan to me and casually mentioned to me that she was making TEN THOUSAND DOLLARS EVERY MONTH. FROM OILS. That $10,000 number caught my attention. After having to purchase a new car and dealing with all those hospital bills, I never wanted to feel so poor again. I trusted my husband and our little property management business to continue providing well for our family, but I wanted a residual income for those unpredictable expenses and maybe even some fun family experiences. I started asking questions about how Chelsea had created this financial freedom and what it would take for me to do the same. Brooke offered to fly in and come teach a class for me. I invited just a few people who were interested in natural solutions and watched Brooke teach simple tools that moms could use to help their families. Brooke didn't sell to my friends—she taught them how to take care of themselves using essential oils, and the people who bought had awesome results. I watched Brooke help my friends with everything from sleep and digestion issues to tantrums and emotional struggles.

Chelsea and Brooke were not tricky or desperate—they were confident and inviting. These two ladies were stay-at-home moms *and* successful businesswomen. Like me, they kept family and health a priority. It blew me away to see real women creating real incomes while making a real difference to real people everywhere.

And I knew the product worked from my own personal experiences. I had managed my entire pregnancy and delivery with these very same essential oils. I had experience after experience with the oils helping me with pregnancy-induced back pain, stress, focus, nausea, and insomnia. I determined that I would reach that same level of success. I didn't care how long it took me or how many failures I had along the way. If Chelsea and Brooke could do this, surely I could too. I had tried the corporate path and created my own businesses, but I had yet to reach the success I wanted for our family. Becoming a network marketer made sense. I had the right company, the right product, and the right compensation plan. I could do it with very little investment, while raising my kids, and I could create a residual pipeline of income. As an eBay seller, piano teacher, coach and company owner, I only made money when I was actively working, which wasn't so different from the corporate world and golden handcuffs I had left. I didn't want to haul bucket after bucket to create an income for my family. I wanted to be paid multiple times for work I did in the past.

I determined that I would not sell essential oils, but I would change the lives of people around me. I set my goal to be making $10,000 a month within four years. It wasn't about the dollars; it was about the financial and time freedom. I knew that level of income would open up what I wanted. I started offering in-home classes and samples when it was appropriate. I would take my crazy marketing ideas and run with them. Some ended up as home runs and sometimes I struck out. My goal didn't change, though my activities sometimes did. Two years later, I had achieved my goal in half the time I had planned.

Our property management company was successful, but it required much attention to keep it running right. Justin had missed out on raising our boys while they were little and wanted to be there for those moments that matter most. We sold the property management company in order to give our family more time. We could work our essential oil business together in little spurts of time and focus on teaching our kids things nobody else could teach them.

Failure wasn't an option because my vision was clear on what I wanted. It took twists and turns to get me to see that what I wanted most could be found in something I never wanted to do. Now I am a successful network marketer and proud of it. I teach other women and men how to strengthen their families and create residual incomes. Our financial freedom has created unique experiences for our children and given us the means to make a real difference in the world. We travel frequently, give back to charities we value, and help other entrepreneurs find their purpose and expand their incomes. We no longer trade our time for dollars and instead get to choose where our time goes.

Success comes line-upon-line and can often not be seen while in the journey. I couldn't see my success while I was in the midst of failing! I believe the most successful people are continually seeking success, celebrating wins along the way, and always seeking new paths of growth. The difference between successful people and others is the willingness to continue moving forward regardless of frustrations or setbacks.

Failure isn't failure to me, but simply learning experiences along the way. I have had many learning experiences in my journey—disappointments and flops of all kinds. Many people would say I am successful, and though I know that to be true, I am still growing, learning, and opening myself up to both more failures *and* successes. Failure to me would be not trying and not experiencing every opportunity.

I never wanted to be a network marketer but I am so glad I found myself on this journey. This unexpected career has made me "successful" by most people's standards, but more importantly, it has given me a chance to grow. I can practice failing every single day, yet I still find success that comes with persistence. When I stumble, negative self-talk naturally begins beating me down, but I have learned that I get to choose how to view those experiences. I would not know how to navigate the ups and downs in all aspects of my life without the mentoring and coaching experiences I have had in network marketing. I have learned how to have critical conversations, how to inspire and lead others, how to speak to large audiences, strategy and marketing, negotiation, presentation skills, and how to work with all kinds of people.

Success isn't just what is in your bank account or who you know—success is found in who you are becoming along the way. For me, success wouldn't be success if I was not personally growing and becoming the greatest version of myself possible. Success wouldn't be success if I wasn't making a difference to others. Success wouldn't be success if I sacrificed my family along the way in the pursuit of ranks and recognition. Success wouldn't be success if I plateaued right where I am today. I know that everything I want to become and experience is possible, but only if I am willing to risk potentially failing.

I am a successful network marketer, but more than that, I am a successful wife and mother. I am a successful business owner and friend. I am a successful coach and a woman of faith. I am a successful person who has learned to trust myself even when I fall.

About Ashlee Miller

Ashlee Miller is a happy mom of three children and is married to her favorite business partner! Ashlee is a talented teacher of faith-based results, natural healing, and prosperity. Ashlee is a student of the scriptures and discovered energy work when life had presented some overwhelming challenges. After working with thousands of clients, Ashlee has created her own energy modality to empower others and create immediate results. Purely Alive energy work is the easiest way to clear blocks, see truth, and create freedom.

Ashlee was raised to be an entrepreneur while growing up on an Idaho farm and has not stopped thinking business since. She has created a six-figure income in network marketing while maintaining her private coaching business. Ashlee trains individuals and companies how to create breakthroughs in their lives and business. Ashlee is passionate about using her knowledge and gifts to inspire other moms and business owners to discover their personal power.

www.ashleemiller.com

Chapter Eighteen
Failing, the Cornerstone to Real Changes
By Iraima Otteson

Chapter Eighteen
Failing, the Cornerstone to Real Changes
By Iraima Otteson

As we sat on the idling bus in Miami, I knew I was taking a big step in my life. I felt fear, but I didn't let it take the stage; I knew I had control of my outcomes. Shortly we would depart for Salt Lake City. I felt empowered in that moment because when God's love envelopes you, your strength like none other takes over. Following my heart, I was determined to turn an old page and write new lines for our chapter.

Being on a bus was not unfamiliar to me as this was my second time using Greyhound to cross the country. Our destination had been to reach Florida, headed for an overseas flight to Venezuela. This was one of the most adventurous trips I ever had taken. I am a really determined woman, which I attribute to my mother's remarkable example of bravery and faith. Everything she did was always preceded by deep thought and prayer, along with her great determination. I learned from her that God is always looking to unconditionally help his children.

So many changes were swirling! I had tried my best to hide from my son and family the painful and eminent reality of my divorce. One night after tucking my son in bed, I lay on my couch and cried my heart. I felt my world was crumbling; I felt like a total failure. The thought of how the unstoppable changes would affect my son and me spiraled me down to a dark place I never had been. I felt like the ground was breaking and swallowing me deep down into misery and desperation. After hours of crying, I was tired but relieved. Now everything was in my hands. I got up that day with a strong desire to open a new chapter in our lives. I was ready! I didn't want to feel that misery again! Deep inside, I knew there something greater was waiting for us.

The potential for failure was great, but I was motived to provide for our needs. Being a single mother required careful thought and planning. In Venezuela, child support laws are not enforced, and I knew that right after our divorce was finalized I would be on my own. I needed to find not just a good job, but a career we could invest in. I had only a few customers who purchased my services as a graphic designer, and my income was not even close to sufficient to provide for all our needs and sustain the style of life my son was used to.

The possibility for a sustainable career had come to me years before when I realized the need many companies had for website development, because the internet was starting to become a vital part of communication. Straight away I began looking for training in web development. Around this time, an opportunity was offered me to go to Idaho. There I could study English as a second language. My plan was to relocate yet again to Salt Lake City to attend an international students' college and join their multimedia program; this opportunity offered me everything I needed for a fresh new start and career.

We left behind the place that was our home. I had never realized before how every piece of furniture you intentionally collect becomes your home—not the walls that shelter you, but what is inside. After everything was gone, the feel of a home left that place, and there was just the echo of our voices moving through the air. We left our friends, family, the smell of culture based on food and traditions, all the places we routinely visited—everything I knew was left behind. My 24 years of life were packed in two suitcases, my four-year-old son, and my lifetime of memories.

Everything was going well: I was progressing on learning the language, and my son was going to school. We were in Idaho for nine months, but I needed to go back to Venezuela to comply with immigration policies and process a new visa. There was also the issue of finalizing the sale of an old property that was supposed to be sold before I left, but the sale had fallen through. The deal and monies made from the sale would be crucial in helping with our success. My not being able to work during all that time had consumed a great part of my savings. I often worried that I wouldn't have the resources to accomplish my goal or even provide for our basic needs through that period of time when I needed to invest in my education. There were nights that I was restless and unable to sleep, with those thoughts of uncertainty invading my mind. I found a great source of strength and peace in the scriptures, and the short passage that reads "Be still and know that I am God" became my favorite. Faith was definitely my rock.

In preparing my son for the long trip, I explained this would be a great adventure as we would be crossing the U.S. via bus and finally reaching Florida. To further push the adventure narrative to my son I added a perk—all our meals would be from McDonald's or Burger King. My grandmother would be turning in her grave if she knew. Rarely was fast food an option, as I was raised in a humble family with high standards for nutritious homemade foods. In his happy meal frenzy, before we even started out he counted how many toys he would be getting.

Just before we departed at the bus station our dear friend Nancy gave me a packet for our trip. Lovingly packed were my favorite homemade rolls, two paperback books for my son, snacks, and a cute note with a reminder of how much Heavenly Father loves us.

The trip did not start out as planned. After a few hours on the bus, my five-year-old developed a temperature. Since he was hardly ever sick, I did not bring proper medication. Having this happen made me question how wise it was to undertake this trip. As we rode on he barely ate. The first stop was only 30 minutes long. Not nearly enough time to find medicine. Fervently I prayed to stay under control, and I asked God to please keep watching over us.

In answer to my worried prayer, a gentleman seated next to us noticed my distress. He attempted to comfort me and offered to look for medicine at our next stop. In doing so, he generously walked two blocks from the bus station to find a store. This much-needed act of kindness was embraced with gratitude, as hope was now with me. That gentleman was definitely an angel sent by my Savior.

The next day he woke up feeling better and looking for the toys and Happy Meals he missed. In looking for activities to occupy us, I bought a map to learn about the states as we drove through them. As we passed through each state we crossed off all leading to Florida. The trip started to feel more like the adventure I planned. It was fascinating to see the diversity of people and their culture. How could there be so many differences in people from one state to the other? I had a strong impression of a deep love that my Savior also has for every one of them—the same love that he has for me and that carried me throughout my journey.

We stayed in Florida for one night and the next day boarded the plane to Venezuela. It was overwhelming to be returning after an eight-month absence. Everything felt so different, from the traffic to the people and the economy.

The political winds of change that originated a mere year ago had taken hold. The feeling in the air had moved from hopeful to agitated. I sensed division even among family members and friends. Venezuela was not the same as the last time I left; but neither was I the same. There was no longer a place for us there.

After we had spent almost two months in Venezuela, the property sale had not yet gone through. To add to our stress, the day of our return flight to the U.S. was rapidly approaching, and without a job I was worried about how I would sustain us. After almost a year without work, while waiting for my visa and learning English in Idaho, my funds were at a low ebb. Time and money were running out.

As I departed, I had only hope that someone would be interested in a great deal on a property, so my accounts could again flourish along with my dreams of tranquility and financial peace during our stay in the U.S. The reality of my circumstances would have scared anyone from leaving, but staying was not among my options. Deep in my heart I knew everything would work out.

As I traveled, I thought of how blessed I had been with great people along the way. People like the Thompsons in Idaho, who not only introduced me to the gospel but soon became like family. During that time, I learned about strong families. I was fascinated with how religious spouses dedicated themselves to building a healthy family. It was like a dream to me that someone would commit to a marriage and be willing to work out differences, with the goal of protecting the family unit as an eternal symbol of God.

Up until that point I had known a rocky relationship with men in families. I hadn't met my father until I was probably five years old. My dad left my mother when I was only one. And my ex-husband was completely out of the picture after our divorce was finalized. I was attracted to all these new gospel principles and values like a magnet.

As the bus unloaded in Salt Lake City, and I saw my dear friend Marah, her big smile made me feel like I was walking through the doors of heaven. We had arrived not only at our destination but also our future.

It felt like a victory and a glory, even though I knew there were many obstacles to overcome! My friend's home was always a peaceful place; there was so much love. They were a great example of what a family should be like. We stayed with the Ewells for one month until we found a cozy apartment for us. My son was so excited to have our place. I was able to find a job, which helped me provide for our needs.

A fast two weeks after my arrival in Salt Lake, I meet Rob, my sweet husband-to-be. From the start, he was attentive and willing to invite us to different activities. Soon he became a frequent visitor in our home and earned our hearts. The standards, goals, and values he displayed were everything I wanted in my future relationship. Our six-month courtship flew by and we were married in Salt Lake City. I could see Heavenly Father's plan and hand in my life.

At this point, looking back into my life a few years ago, I wouldn't have ever imagined that all of the circumstances I went through, when I felt lost and scared to be a single mom, that moment when I allowed the world to crumble and collapse in front of my feet—that was the very moment when I made the decision to made the sacrifices that led me to the blessings of a new family.

I didn't fulfill the goals as I originally planned for my education, but thanks to the decisions I made, I was presented with many more options. Among those I chose to be a mother and to build a new family for us.

With a new family I was finally living moments of success after my earlier failures. But my son, who was too young to understand, had lost his home, toys, friends, culture, family, and biological dad. Despite his apparently normal behavior and display of adjustment to all the changes, he was internally struggling. I failed again in recognizing his struggle. He was more sensitive than other kids when it came to his space and sharing with other children. He was the oldest of an inexperienced mom, who was also trying to adapt, learn a new language, and find her own space in a new culture. It was difficult for me to recognize my son's need and that most children struggle with sharing their possessions with other kids.

It was not until his teenage years that the dynamic of our interactions in our home changed. It became complicated, and as an artist, I describe it as really abstract! I thought learning English was difficult until I tried teaching teenagers.

I didn't understand anything! They become "individuals" with their opinions and free will. I went from being a mom at the center of their kind actions, to being the reason for their anger.

From this point, my struggles as a mother became more obvious. Now he had a voice, and it was loud. Sometimes he didn't have to speak to let us know he was rebelling; through his actions we got the memo. The cycle of unfulfilled expectations became the daily battle: instructions were given, and expectations were not met, leading to frustration anger and more imposed consequences.

I was in the habit of always finding solutions to my obstacles, but parenting to me was one of the most defeating experiences I ever had. It was a regressive process. There were skills I didn't have and behaviors I needed to get rid of. It takes a conscious and determined effort in every interaction with others to shift and mold new behaviors. Most important, I didn't understand the principles of free agency and allowing my son to learn from his failures and experiences.

I often felt alone and isolated in a battle that I was definitely losing. We were new in our neighborhood when our struggles became more apparent and out of hand. I felt I didn't have that tribe to raise my child, with no mother or sister near for guidance and support, or a good friend who could understand and offer a word of comfort at that moment when I felt so lost. My prayers were more intense, and so was my search for new ideas and solutions. I never lost my hope, despite the situation and the struggle.

In our search for help we visited different therapists. Our interactions would improve momentarily and then collapse again, and I decided to educate myself. I went through a large pile of books, connecting more with some than others. I learned about myself and the changes I needed to make to become a more influential mother to my children.

The sad reality is that often home is where we are loved the most but still act the worse. There was so much contention in our home, that the most basic interaction could be dominated by explosions of arguments. Any attempt to bring a good spirit was unsuccessful. I often would ask myself "When will I ever learn a new way to handle this?

I feared for my two younger children, who were witnessing their older sibling breaking the rules and disregarding any concern from us as parents. I was so desperate for answers, I prayed for peace, and mostly to have my kind and the sweet boy back. My traveling companion, that little boy who filled me with courage to move across the continent to a new country and face the most challenging obstacles—that boy was lost somewhere in that teenage body.

When I was alone, I would cry just from thinking of him and his struggle. One day I walked into my closet sobbing uncontrollably when I felt an excruciating pain as if a hole has torn through my heart. I kneeled down and pled to my Heavenly Father for help. He was his father, and I had tried everything I could to help him. I was immediately overcome with peace, and the pain decreased in scale as I was calming. I felt my Heavenly Father's love for his son and me. I knew that He, more than anyone, understood us and knew our suffering.

Our home was not a sanctuary of peace, and that fact was a sign of many other bad things that could have gone wrong if we had not fixed our situation. In my search for answers and guidance, I learned so much about myself, and that our reactions to situations are in significant part tied to behaviors we learned growing up and also to our personality types. I was trying to raise my family following a new set of beliefs and expectations, but my reaction to challenging situations took me back to my own ways. Growing up I only saw my mother making decisions and giving instructions, while some of her children followed and obeyed.

From the beginning of our family interactions I had remained as the disciplinary parent to our son, as I had been as a single parent. That also became a pattern with the rest of our children. But our family needed to be different— educating and disciplining our children needed to be not the role of one parent, but a balanced act of both parents. Our interactions became a model for teaching our children by example that adults also obey and surrender.

As adults we go about our days switching roles from "parents" (teachers) when one or both parents lead the family in learning, to "spouses and adults" (equals) when we relax and spend time together, and "children" (learners) when we allow the other spouse to lead us in a learning situation. Understanding our different roles as parents as well the forms of delivery are fundamental in keeping harmony and opening bridges of communication in our families.

I also learned that most children who rebel have been taught correct principles in the home, and that their rebellions are not a rejection of the values taught as much as they are a rejection of our approach and our authority. (*Parenting the Strong-Willed Child*, 78, 81)

Our power struggle lasted years. If only I had understood that the role of teaching as a parent should always be preceded with demonstrations of love and concern, instead of long lectures and lessons of disapproval. If I had realized that his mind and heart was probably much more fragile than those of other boys because of our journey, I could have replaced those teaching moments with more hugs and hopes, so that love would allow my son to soften his heart to learning and understanding. If only I had understood that my relationship with him was the foundation of my influence on him. If only I had understood that free agency allows natural learning from our own mistakes.

But how could I ever know! If it were not for this, my first time failing as a mother, I would not have learned all that I now know. Still to this day, when my memories take me back to those moments of struggle, full of anger, frustration and despair, I feel pain over that power struggle we both lost. In my attempt to break his will I broke mine too.

"I did then what I knew how to do. Now that I know better, I do better." <u>Maya Angelou.</u>

Now when I lovingly correct my daughters and I am even able to kiss and hug them tight after a disagreement, I know because of my experiences they would be able to be great mothers to their children, and that the cycle of control and use of force as a form of obedience was ended. As my children have their own children, I hope my experiences can spare them some dreadful and unnecessary moments. Now after my struggle I can appreciate those moments of failure, I know that failure does not define me; it is not part of mine or anyone's nature, but a transitional stage during which we recognize by the results of our actions the areas we want to improve in order to attain success. Failure is an important part of our eternal progress.

About Iraima Otteson

Iraima Otteson is an artist, entrepreneur, and leader with a passion for learning and self-improvement. Through her own trials Iraima discovered the healing effect of visual art. Later she learned how powerful and effective this tool can be when used as an instrument in helping children develop and grow. The creation of Hands on Art blossomed from her vison and passion in assisting others find their purpose. Fulfilling potential is what this studio located in Utah is all about. In the studio an atmosphere has been cultivated that is safe, dynamic, and inspiring. It's a place where children and adults are provided with the tools to explore art fully through various medium forms. As soon as you walk into this one-of-a-kind studio the colors and vibrant atmosphere invite you in, be it working on clay, screen printing, or painting, the imagination will soar as we create.

Iraima puts great focus and care in helping children, creating an art program that empowers children to tap into their "Inner Creator." They see themselves as powerful individuals who can accomplish anything. "If we can help young children understand their capacity to create anything they want, and make that concept applicable to all areas of their life, we are creating a generation of successful individuals."

A zeal for learning and remaining competitive in the marketing industry as a graphic designer led her to the United States. Arriving 17 years ago from Venezuela with her 4-year-old son, she fearlessly embraced a new country. New blessings awaited her. As she learned a new language she met her incredible husband, best friend, and cornerstone. Together with their three kids, Iraima has found her greatest joy.

Even when art seems to take center stage; behind the scenes, her family life and sacred duty as a parent has led her to the greatest teaching moments and life-changing experiences. Iraima describes family and parenting as the ultimate test to become something in life. Her real success has come after overcoming parenting pitfalls, through learning, forgiving, and understanding.

To learn more about Iraima Otteson and her program visit www.handsonart4everyone.com.

Chapter Nineteen
She Needed a Hero, So She Became One
By Jentrey Potter

Chapter Nineteen
She Needed a Hero, So She Became One
By Jentrey Potter

DARING GREATLY

The phone call came the afternoon of July 22nd, 2013. I didn't expect to hear from my older sister; I hadn't heard from her in more than a month. In fact, I hadn't heard from anyone in my family during that time. I felt anxious just seeing her number and name come across the screen. I answered hesitantly, "Hello?" I heard my sister's voice shaking on the other end: "Jentrey, it's me. I'm calling to tell you the news about Dad. Something happened. There was a four-wheeler accident. He's gone." Her voice choked on the last few sentences. My heart dropped into the pit of my stomach. "He's gone. There's a funeral this weekend. I would be nice if you could come home and be here."

My head was swimming. I didn't know what to think or feel. My world had just turned upside down. Could this really be happening? My adoptive father had caused me so much pain, and now he was gone without warning. Should I be relieved? Should I be heart-broken and mourning his loss? What would everyone think if I went home? What would they think if I didn't? Of course, I had to go home for the funeral! I didn't get to say goodbye!

I rarely went home—maybe every two years or so at most. But when my Grandpa passed, I felt I needed to reconnect and show my support. He was Dad's father, and I knew it would mean a lot to him. I had never had a close relationship with any of his side of the family. They were all so formal, and gatherings with them were rare. Who could blame them? Our household of 10 kids would overwhelm anybody. Little did I know that coming home for Grandpa's funeral would change everything. It wasn't the first time a report was made regarding the sexual abuse, but it definitely took a turn for the worse that no one could've planned if they tried. Secrets came to the surface that had seemed a thing of the past, but they were all too fresh. I had to do something. It was time to speak up. After coming back home and calling my therapist to get advice and clarity, I made a report to Idaho Social Services. Little did I know that the whole family would shut me out, and worse, send me regular hate texts accusing me of being evil and manipulative. When did I become the perpetrator? I was a victim too. Or didn't they remember?

The next few days were a blurring whirlwind. My husband and I and our five kids buckled into our SUV and made the 15-hour drive from Aurora, Colorado to Idaho. I had always hated that drive. I didn't mind the beautiful Rocky Mountains of Colorado, but once we hit Utah and Idaho with the miles of wide-open terrain, the two-lane highway seemed to last forever. I felt sick with the odor of cattle farms and factories. It was a crude reminder of what was coming. The crap was definitely about to hit—hardcore.

I saw his body lying in the coffin. He looked so peaceful with what appeared to be a strange curve of a smile at the corners of his mouth, as if he would wake any moment from a Sunday afternoon nap. Conflicting emotions coursed through me when I was coerced into singing his favorite song, "Wind Beneath my Wings." He had an irritating way of loving music that made me crazy. Or maybe it was just what happens to everyone who grows up in a torn home—developing a distaste for the music you grow up hearing. I was the last to leave the gravesite, sobbing and longing for understanding and forgiveness, and hoping he now knew that my intentions had been pure in wanting to protect my family.

When we got back to the house, we learned that Social Services had called and talked to the grandparents of the cousin on the 4-wheeler. Dad had been called a hero throughout the funeral service for having pushed her off and saving her life. But Idaho Social Services had made a call only hours later saying that they were conducting an investigation of the accident, suspecting that it might have been a planned suicide. This was the first time that distant cousins and Dad's siblings learned about the abuses and subsequent periods of probation. It was also the first time they learned that I had only recently reported him a second time.

A family feud quickly broke out and everyone was looking to me for answers. My husband took me and the kids back to the house I grew up in, seeking refuge from the madness. Instead I found immediate family and close family friends had gathered for a "council." I was up before a jury. I heard expressions of hate and confusion from my siblings and Mom. There were endless arguments, discussions, and questions: "Why would you ever call Social Services, Jentrey?" "What were you possibly thinking?" "How could you be so selfish?"

I couldn't take it anymore. I made one last stop before leaving town to place flowers and a teddy bear on his grave as one last goodbye; my one-year-old clutched the brown bear tightly one last time, as if it were "Grandpa." We packed up early and skipped town to leave the drama behind. We headed back home to Colorado without stopping to say goodbye to anyone. All I remember is wondering if I would ever wake up from the nightmare.

The drive back to Colorado was endless. Although I felt relief build with every mile that separated us from the chaos we had left, with every mile I also felt my heart breaking into a million pieces. Numbness overtook my body like a thick heavy black liquid more dense then tar. It consumed my entire being. I wasn't sure if I existed anymore. I was just ... there. What did I have to get out of bed for? Did I even thirst or hunger anymore? What did I have to live for? What did I have to die for? I hated my life. I hated my family. I hated my kids. I hated my husband. I hated people. I hated men. I hated mankind. I hated myself. I hated God. How could God allow the endless hell of my childhood to happen? And worse, what had I done to deserve being the family target? All those years in church were just a lie. No loving God would just leave me all alone like this. There was no one to talk to. No one to understand. People sent cards and their condolences for my Dad. They knew nothing. How could they know the raging torment that had me chained to my past? No one could possibly begin to know or understand.

I was completely and utterly alone.

FINDING BRAVE

"He was chosen to retain His scars, to remind us that we can be rid of ours."

Brad Wilcox, *The Continuous Atonement*

We had moved into a new home and neighborhood two months before the funeral. My kids wanted to go to the pool. I wanted to hide under my sheets and never come out. My husband wanted help with the kids every morning, and family dinners and together time at night. I wanted nothing more than to be alone. The more my family needed me, the deeper into the darkness I fell. It was safe there. I didn't have to feel, I didn't even have to exist. I just...was. A few weeks passed. School would start soon. I couldn't hide forever. I needed a distraction from the darkness and the pain. Something to make me feel "normal" again, whatever that meant. I had been introduced to essential oils the previous year. They gave me a glimmer of hope and empowerment for my family's health, but this time, a training opportunity. My team leader was putting on a 12-week online training. I wasn't interested in the business, but it was definitely something to distract me.

As the seminar progressed, I started to feel I had a grasp on my life, if ever so tiny. But as Christmas approached, something wasn't feeling right with my husband. I had nagging thoughts, but my heart couldn't go there. Not there. My husband's past pornography addiction had been unbearable as it yo-yoed throughout our marriage, and I couldn't stand the thought of it happening yet again. I didn't even dare to ask, but I could see the signs—sudden detachment, irritability, short-temper, lashing out at me and the kids, and an unexplainable distance I felt between us. After all that I had been through over the past few months, I despaired. Then just days before Christmas, he came to me and fell apart right before my eyes, confessing his latest fall to pornography. The heartbreak & distrust was more than I could stand. Once again, I began to question everything—my faith, my family, my marriage, my existence.

Months went by and our marriage and family were hanging by a thread. Summer had found its way back around again. I was volunteering with the youth at church and they were doing a scripture challenge for the summer. I was weeks behind. Maybe I could catch up. I didn't care how many hours it took; I was determined to finish the challenge with the rest of the group. I was desperate to know if God cared about me anymore. I poured myself into the stories of valiant and faithful saint warriors. Could I ever be like them? Hours passed while my kids played outside and I submersed myself into the scriptures. By the end of summer, I had finished the 535 pages in less than 45 days, and I felt a new hope for my faith and my future.

It's funny how life can test you and what you stand for, but ultimately bring perspective. I needed to draw closer to God and understand what he wanted for me and my family, and what he wanted me to do. In the midst of my desire for understanding and peace, God gave me the people and tools and experiences that allowed me to heal, and to love and forgive myself and others.

One night I turned to my preferred online hangout on Facebook. My newsfeed popped open to a friend's post: "I'm looking to start a Mastermind group. Who's interested?" My curiosity had the best of me. I scrolled through the comments: "Hey, we're starting a new group in a few days, you should check it out." Hmm. I didn't know this Jennifer Lamprey gal, but what was this new group? Hmm. She's a "Christ-centered Energy Healer." What did that mean? I scrolled through her page in hopes of catching a clue. A post from the day before: "It's my birthday! And for my birthday I want to give a gift to all my friends for a free body scan! Message me if you're interested." I was interested. I sent Jennifer a message and asked, "What do you do and what is a body scan? I don't know you, but I found you through a mutual friend. I don't know why or how, but I think you're supposed to help me. PS—tell me more about your mastermind."

My journey of self-discovery with Jennifer Lamprey began with one of the core principles I learned in her program. It was the analogy of the airplane and the oxygen mask—if I was going to be of any use to myself, my family, my friends, my church, or even my potential business, I needed to put the oxygen on MYSELF first and stand in value and choice, rather than the bonds of my past! What?! I actually have PERMISSION to do that? This is REQUISITE for me to thrive and succeed at having a fulfilling life, family, and business? This was all such foreign news to me.

The second thing I learned was that God has asked me to be a voice. I fought it in the beginning, until I realized that this is what God and even my Dad want. I have felt and heard his voice telling me he is sorry and he loves me. This has brought me great comfort and strength. Too many men in my life have struggled with the painful shame of pornography. I hated men for a long time, until God taught me that I need to be a vessel to free both men and women from this pain, and the associated pain of feeling unvalued. I have felt worthless and unworthy almost my entire life. But all the feelings of unworthiness, of feeling like a total failure financially, sometimes even feeling a failure as a parent and wife, are part of my journey. I have to know what all of these aspects of pain feel like so I can help others and lift them up. I know that my deepest pains and sufferings and heartache are a gift. Yes, a gift! If I did not have them I would not be able to help others, or even truly appreciate what I have in this life. I could not know joy without knowing the pain, and I couldn't bring others to joy.

Many of us are hurting and struggling to find our way and we often act out of those pains and unmet needs and sometimes our choices hurt others, but if we don't forgive and speak truth it only results in continuous pain and struggle for all of us. It continues the vicious cycle. I don't understand everything that God is asking of me, and many experiences and requests from God I would not choose for myself. But God is asking me to forgive and to stop the cycle. To be a voice for those who have none and are powerless as I once was. To stop the needless suffering and lessen the pain and burdens that many people carry in their hearts of shame. Shame is the culprit!!! It's Satan's greatest tool, and he uses it in every possible way. Shame for the porn addict, shame for the sex addict, shame for the abuser, shame for the abused, shame for the innocent children, shame for the victim, shame for the overweight, shame for the underweight, shame for the childless, shame for the poor, shame for the lonely, shame for the homeless .... Satan wants us to feel ashamed! But that's not God's way! How do we stop the endless cycle of shame? By being a voice for change!

I started by learning to love myself and the importance of self-care. Have you ever heard of "emotional eating" or "stress eating"? How about "retail therapy"? When your emotional or mental health is in disarray, it affects your physical and spiritual health. You can't ignore one without it affecting the other and ultimately affecting how you show up in life. I now coach women to take back their power through health and life transformation coaching, looking at all areas of their physical, mental, emotional, and spiritual health. I created a simple tool I call "The SHERO Rescue Method" that anyone of any age can use to go from stuck and powerless to moving forward & stepping into their super powers! This is a five-step process using the acronym S.H.E.R.O. to help you remember the pattern and order of the process. This process has helped many people in a time of anxiety and crisis to find peace, control, and calmness.

S- Stop and Self Evaluate. If you could view the situation with a video camera what would it capture? What would the simple truth of the situation be without judgment or your own perceptions? Where do you feel it in your body? What does it feel like? Just allow yourself to be aware and in tune with yourself, your surroundings, and your body.

H- Help. Enlist help from those around you! Enlist your kids and spouse to pitch in with the housework and responsibilities. Delegate areas of your business to others who have more time and skill sets. Hire a maid, cook, or babysitter when money is available to you. (By the way, if you're NOT getting help remember that you are responsible for teaching others how to treat you!)

E- Excuses. Stop making excuses and playing the blame game!! It's not your fault, your husband's or kids' fault, your dog's fault, your boss's fault, your parents' fault or anyone else's. Everything happens for a reason. Learn from it and move on. Stop being a victim in your life and start living and owning your life! Be responsible and take OWNERSHIP of your own life!!

R- Receive your value!! What do you need to receive from yourself and others? Are you putting up walls to protect yourself that are actually keeping others or your Higher Power (God) out? Are you not allowing yourself to receive peace, truth, or forgiveness in your life? Stop it!!

O- Okay!! It's going to be Okay!! Take a deep breath, be kind and gentle with yourself, and remember how far you have come and that tomorrow is a new day! Remember that the "O" is also a symbol of the continuous process. It's intended to be repeated as often as needed for your continual growth and experience. Embrace and find joy in your journey!

About Jentrey Potter

Jentrey a.k.a. "The Self Care SHERO" is a highly sought after Board Certified Health Coach and Incite Certified Life Coach, Presenter, Speaker, Author, Facebook Live Video Star of "The SHERO Show," Creator of "The S.H.E.R.O. Rescue Method," and a mom of five and wife of 15 years.

Jentrey is passionate about helping women through self-care, self-love, and self-empowerment. From personal experiences of overcoming childhood sexual abuse, depression, anxiety, chronic fatigue, and choosing to stay married to a recovering pornography addict, she takes a very personal approach to healing the whole person from the inside out and discovering the root causes and trapped emotions that are creating the mental, emotional, and even physical health issues of modern families.

Jentrey can be found at www.jentreypotter.com.

Chapter Twenty
Forgiveness is the Key to Freedom
By Sabrina Redmond

Chapter Twenty
Forgiveness is the Key to Freedom
By Sabrina Redmond

I've always heard from others that I am a leader—powerful, inspiring, creative, independent, forgiving, and honest. Others have said I am controlling, bossy, stubborn, spiteful, bitchy, intrusive, and clingy. So who am I really? At different times in my life, I may have been all of these. What I now know is that I am the one who decides who I am—every single day and minute of my life. No matter how positively or negatively someone else may view me, I know the truth. The lyrics of this song from the Disney movie *Moana* resonate with me:

"I have crossed the horizon to find you,

I know your name.

They have stolen the heart from inside you,

But this does not define you.

This is not who you are,

You know who you are."

I am a daughter of God, a faithful and committed wife of ten years, a nurturing mom of four, and blessed bonus mom of two. As a nurturing mom, I am also my children's student, while teaching and guiding them in ways to influence the world for good. I am a friend, offering loyalty, trust, and commitment. My desire is to help others find and create their own freedom from their self-imposed prisons.

Like many of you, I've had my fair share of trials and struggles. My greatest and most harrowing trials have become my best teachers and most valuable gifts. Without these difficulties, I would not be who I am today. Those who have "done me wrong" have added value and depth to my life story. I invite you to think of your own trials and "wrongdoers" as gifts. I invite you to see them as spirit beings, earth angels having a human experience, making their own mistakes and life stories.

I've been blessed with many opportunities to transform. My biggest transformation came from freeing myself from the effects of childhood sexual abuse, PTSD, and depression. In all my experiences, and as clichéd as it may sound, the power of forgiveness and reconnecting on a deeper level to my Heavenly Father have been the main keys to my own freedom.

My journey of forgiveness began when I least expected it, at the age of 19, when I grasped the gravity and depravity of the four different occurrences of sexual abuse that had marked my childhood. I mourned the loss of my innocence, my power to choose, and my self-worth. Why was I not worth saving? Why did no one care? Why did this happen to me? By the time I was 21, I had told almost everyone I knew about my childhood trauma, praying someone would do something to help me get out of the recycling hell played out in my mind. I desperately wanted the recordings to stop so I could be free from my self-imposed prison.

During those two years of speaking out and searching for help, I was a "rage monster." I was angry that no one seemed to care or have any answers to help me get out. Because I knew no differently, I continued to cling to a man who was abusive, because he was my fiancé at the time. Granted, I wasn't the easiest person to live with, and I was broken in ways that he couldn't have understood or helped me repair. But the choices he made for me were inexcusable, ones no one should ever put up with. But I did, for months, out of sheer desperation and fear.

I remember the first time Adam punched me in the head and kicked me in the stomach. I was four months pregnant with my first child, Landyn. The months that followed were an unchanging pattern. I knew I was in a cycle of abuse, wanted out, but didn't know how to get out. I felt that I couldn't tell anyone, because I was ashamed that I was "that girl"–the girl who had gotten herself into that mess, so she could find her own way out. My wakeup call came when Adam and I got into an argument and he threw me to the ground and strangled me to the point of blacking out. I knew then that if I didn't find a way out, I might very well die or lose the baby. It was either live with this man though dead inside, perhaps literally die, or escape the abuse and run as fast as I could.

Foolishly, one of my first failing moments came when I chose to elope with him out of fear that he'd abandon me with a child. I was terrified of being a mother, let alone a single mother. We eloped, and four hours later he left me. I haven't heard from him since. I was able to get the marriage annulled, and I gave birth to my firstborn son. I have since forgiven Adam for abusing and abandoning me. I found this forgiveness by looking at him with compassion, consciously choosing to see him as a confused and hurt man with no tools to deal with the weight of my burdens. What I learned to call "compassionate eyesight" is the ability to see the world through another person's eyes, while letting go of your own judgements.

What happened next was nothing short of a miracle. Someone had finally seen my pain and heard my cries, and led me to the light. When I was six months pregnant, three "angels" offered to pay for and take me to an experiential training, known as "Great Life" at the time. All they told me about it at the time was "It's where you'll really start to live and be free from everything in your childhood. You need help and this is the way." These were the exact words I'd been waiting for. The process involved freeing the spirit and inner child from the past history in order to let go and be an adult with a clearer purpose. My favorite and continually used tool was walking on fire. It taught me to face any "fire" in my life with courage, faith, truth, and wisdom—to seek the lesson in every situation. This was the point when I began to transform from victim to victor, from wounded child to child of God, and from scared little girl to free, inspiring woman. To this day, I hold that training and the people in it as my "first lighthouse"; a decade later I am still close friends with many of the people I connected with there.

During the period of falling in love with me again, I fell in love with my eternal companion. He was one of the three angels. Our love story was magical. We played, laughed, danced in the rain, jumped through sprinklers, watched the sunrises together, connected on a spiritual level, and fell in love. This gentle man of mine, Dustin, chose to be my son's father. Dustin adopted Landyn as his own and we have lived our lives blissfully and free ever since. Ok, not exactly . . . .

The "Lockdown" began in 2007 and dragged on until 2013. Dustin and Ashlynn, his former wife, began divorce proceedings in March 2006, but tried working it out in May of that year. Sadly, even though she became pregnant, they were unable to work it out, due to her infidelity and the uncertainty of the unborn child's biological father. Over the next year-and-a-half, Dustin was dragged in and out of court because of false accusations of abuse, in her effort to thwart the court's decision to grant custody of their son Kaden to Dustin. Fortunately, in every scenario the judge saw through the agenda in front of him and dismissed the case.

Despite the chaos from his still-pending divorce, Dustin and I had given birth to our first biological child together, a beautiful baby girl, in December 2007. We named her Axzona, which means eternal love. Exactly three days after I came home from the hospital, we were informed of the biology of the now ten-month old baby girl Kylie, whom Ashlynn had delivered in February 2007. Out of the three possible biological fathers, Dustin was the father; and yes, we did feel the "Jerry Springer" aspect of it at the time. Within nine days of receiving the results, the papers for their lengthy contentious divorce finally got signed! Unfortunately, none of their paperwork included a decision about their daughter Kylie, so the two of them made a decision to simply just share the children and get along for the sake of the two kids. For the next five months that followed, Dustin, Ashlynn, and I became close friends again and worked together effortlessly, like one big, odd, happy family.

Then it happened—the perfect links in our chain fell apart. Ashlynn had an opportunity to leave Utah to become a flight attendant in Arizona, but because there wasn't anything legally binding their daughter to either parent, Ashlynn placed one-year old Kylie with Dustin's ex-mother-in-law in Utah, instead of with him. Dustin agreed because he wanted to support Ashlynn in living her dreams, and not stress her about the possibility of losing her child in another custody battle.

While she was away, Dustin and I got married in May of 2008. We requested that both Kaden and Kylie be a part of the wedding, but Ashlynn's mother refused. Sadly, this one decision caused a series of events that led to the actual lockdown. Dustin no longer felt he could trust Ashlynn's decisions because of her mother's influence. Ashlynn chose to disappear with their daughter and cease all contact with Kaden for six months. During this time I became the only mom their son knew, transforming from stepmom to "bonus Mom," and he went from stepson to "bonus son."

In 2009, we reconnected with Ashlynn, sending Kaden for visits and requesting visits with Kylie, who had turned two by that point. Sadly, our efforts were not met in kind. Ashlynn told us she would not share her without paperwork to support their daughter's return. Naively, we opted to modify the decree and upon our attorney's advice filed for full custody. He said, "She disappeared with your daughter and abandoned your son, so if you want visits, go for the most, so you can at least get the minimum or maybe even custody so the kids can live together." Although this advice may have been well intended, we now know that ensured our own path into the "lockdown." Unintentionally, our act was construed as an attack upon Ashlynn, and thus the beginning of the "war." It was followed by a series of mediations, court meetings, attorneys and more.

In December of that year, three-year-old Kylie finally became reacquainted with her dad, me, and her siblings. A month later she came again for another visit, and even though we were enjoying our new life with our family being reunited, it would soon be torn apart. In February 2010, right before our first birthday visit with Kylie, Ashlynn and her therapist falsely accused me of sexually abusing the precious child I knew as my "bonus daughter." I can't fully explain or ever understand what would lead Ashlynn to do what she and her representatives did to me over the next three years, but I've come to accept that it's not mine to fully grasp. It was the only way I could move past the pain. I had to allow life to just be, let go of the control, and let go of the desire to fully grasp all aspects of the situation.

As to my personal trial, I've simply done my best to accept it and trust that this woman was in so much pain that she made a decision based on survival instincts alone, to do the only thing she knew would keep her from having to share her daughter again. Ashlynn had known about my childhood trauma and reported to the investigator that she believed I would do what her therapist was accusing me of, because I had been sexually abused as a child. My initial reaction was that of shock: "Are you kidding me?! I would never sexually abuse another human being, because I know the damage it causes, and I'd never want anyone to ever experience that pain." This accusation went against everything I stood for; it labeled me the very monster I had despised for so long. After the Utah investigator closed the case as unfounded, Ashlynn nevertheless filed a restraining order in Arizona against me with regard to their daughter, even though I lived in Utah.

This is when the physical "lockdown" began. I no longer answered my door, for fear of being served another paper. We stopped using the front door altogether. Whenever someone knocked on the door we would hide; the kids couldn't play in the front yard; and we kept our blinds closed at all times, especially when we thought she might be trying to "attack" us with litigation again. Years before, in the first phase of their custody battle over Kaden, Ashlynn had tried, to no avail, to take down Dustin through the court system. Because it failed with him, she knew the only way to cause the most damage was through me. For three years, we lived in turmoil and fear, with constant DCFS calls being made, accusations, restraining orders, and court hearings. She had a genius strategy and it worked to perfection. Granted, she didn't get custody of Kaden, but she also didn't lose custody of Kylie.

Blindly and naively, I continued to live my innocence and truth, right down to deciding not to get an attorney to represent me against the restraining order she requested in Arizona. I was so confident that "the truth shall set you free" and that "love would prevail," that I went into court on my own. The moment I stepped into that courtroom, I knew I had made the biggest mistake of my life. I felt like a lamb walking into the lion's den—she had not one attorney on her side, but two! The attorneys even used my own term "bonus Mom" against me, claiming I was "grooming" Kylie. The judge granted Ashlynn the one-year restraining order, as he said, "Even though I don't believe you did it, I have to err on the side of caution because there is a professional therapist involved." All I remember from that day was feeling as though God had abandoned me. I kept repeating, like a mentally-disturbed person in a psych ward, "But I didn't do it, I'm innocent." Even now as I look back on that moment in my life, I see my inner child being told again, "It's not safe; hide away all the good parts of you because the world will destroy you otherwise." I wish I could fully transcribe the depth of sorrow and hell I lived that day onto paper. All I can say is that it was one of the pivotal moments in causing me to feel like a complete failure. I had failed to do the very thing I had set out to do—win my freedom with the truth. But in this case, at this moment, the truth did not set me free. Instead, I locked away all of the good and alive parts of me.

For the next three years, I was a shell of a human being, living in cycles of PTSD as a result of my childhood abuse and the trauma of that day in court. Even though we had many angels helping us along the way—Dustin's attorney, friends, my therapist, my uncle, Dad, and church leaders—I still felt alone. I existed merely because I had to. I became consumed by the injustice of it all. How could I have overcome such grievous atrocities from my childhood, and now be dealing yet again with sexual abuse, but this time as the "villain"? I had begun giving up on God, because I believed He had given up on me.

After three years of this hell, in 2013, Dustin and Ashlynn sat down for their final mediation and came to a final resolution on all matters. At that point, the custody evaluator cleared my name of any accusations they'd made. She even shared with us that the accusations were used by Ashlynn as a ploy to keep from having to share Kylie. Sadly, because their daughter had never had sufficient time with us to form a bond, the court determined that it would not be in her best interest to be in Dustin's physical custody.

On Thursday, January 10th, 2013, the day after mediation, I finally gave up and gave in. Why, after all those years of choosing to survive did I just decide not to try anymore? I had finally lost all hope and faith in God and in people. I opted for suicide. After writing each of my five children and husband a final letter goodbye, I did the unthinkable. Anti-depressants I had previously taken in 2010-2011 were sitting uselessly in my medicine cabinet, and I didn't want to experience any more pain. I swallowed the bottle of pills.

I awoke in the hospital, not understanding why I was still alive. I stayed there for three days, receiving love and support from the hospital staff. On the last day, they came to me and said, "We found 0% trace of anything in your system. Are you sure you swallowed anything?" It was in that moment that I realized God was there, He hadn't forgotten me. I do believe in miracles and I've come to know I'm one of them. I got on my knees for the first time in years and begged for His forgiveness, thanking Him for my life and saving me. I knew right then Heavenly Father had a bigger purpose in store me, and that my life is a story to be shared and message delivered. I got up from that prayer and received a message as clear as day, "You were never alone, dear child. In your toughest times, I carried you and held you close, even when you couldn't see or feel me. It's not your time yet; you have a huge mission with the children of this world."

I had promised my husband that I would never tell anyone what I did that day. However, I know it's time to break the silence and not be ashamed, but be proud of my triumph over these trials. My strength came from reconnecting me to Heavenly Father. I chose to look at my past and those who affected me as my teachers. I learned to see through their eyes what I couldn't see with my own. And most importantly, I learned to forgive myself and the role I played. I look back at who I was then with compassion and forgiveness for giving up on my children, husband, and self. Forgiveness is never for the other person; it is only to free ourselves from the self-imposed prisons of our minds. True freedom comes when you can look at yourself and the other person, with compassion and say, as Christ once did, "Forgive them, for they know not what they do."

Through all of my failing, I've come out successfully as a committed and loving wife, present and nurturing Mom, peaceful co-parent, loving daughter, caring friend, grateful woman, and awakened daughter of God. I have gone on to owning a successful mentoring business, "Create Your Life," and "Red's Cleaning and Mentoring Services." I help women become free of their self-imposed prisons. As a home alignment specialist, I share tools on how to get their homes in alignment to better support all other aspects of their lives. I know from experience that when my mind was in turmoil, so was my home. I also support children with tools to help them cope with life's trials at a younger age with my P.O.S.I.T.I.V.E. Action class. As I continue on the path God has set before me, I know and accept that I may fail at times. That will be OK, because through all I have been through and all I will yet experience, I have learned to stay connected to my Father in Heaven.

So, if you're finding yourself in an endless cycle of abuse, repeating the same patterns and experiences again and again, you may have areas of forgiveness to work on. You simply have to decide, are you going to LIVE or just exist? If your decision is to live, then start with reconnecting to Heavenly Father, forgiving others and yourself, and find the lesson you need to learn, so you can be free. Don't wait until you're at your breaking point to choose to live. Save yourself the pain and choose the freedom now. I invite you to be the creator of your labels; be the decision maker of who you are. And if you can't remember, turn to the only one who will remember for you—Heavenly Father.

About Sabrina Redmond

Sabrina Redmond is a Freedom Mentor, Presenter, Speaker, Author, International Entrepreneur, Homeschooling Mom of six, and wife of 10 years.

She is the CEO of Create the Path, in which she empowers women and children in creating the life they truly desire and deserve to be living; with specific tools to be free and upgrade their lives, relationships, wealth, and health.

As a woman who has become free from childhood sexual abuse, PTSD, and depression, Sabrina she has a deep desire for others to have their own freedom. Sabrina teaches the power of forgiveness and reconnecting people to their higher source, so families and the world as a whole, can be free.

Contact Sabrina directly at Sabrina.Redmond1@gmail.com or find out more at http://www.createthepath.com/.

Chapter Twenty-One
The LIFEStory Story
By Becky Rogers

Chapter Twenty-One
The LIFEstory Story
By Becky Rogers

The LIFEstory Story

Have you ever had a slow motion moment during which you gave every ounce of your best effort to stop the unfolding calamity and to save yourself, but there was not a thing you could do? Picture arms flailing, muscles clenching, and a huge amount of adrenalin while subconsciously calculating which body part is most important to protect. Realizing it was too late and that I was about to go for a ride across the steep, icy parking lot, with lightning speed my mind reviewed the importance of my face, the possible ramifications of a head injury, the stitches that were still holding me together from a major abdominal surgery less than a week before, and the valuable fine instrument that was now sliding across the pavement in my violin case. Sometimes, when you are utterly helpless, it is better to roll with it than fight it. Ouch! I don't know what hurt worse—all the bruises that were starting to form, the abdominal wound I was nursing before it was re-traumatized, or my pride. By the following day, I could definitely tell what hurt worst. My whole body! The sudden response of my entire musculoskeletal system to an imminent disaster left me feeling so sore I could hardly move at all! It was the perfect metaphor for my life, actually.

I had just finished playing the violin in a performance of the *Nutcracker*, something I did every single year. Every Christmas, I traded my time with my loved ones for a pittance because I "needed" the money. This particular experience was especially painful because I was recovering from the birth of a child via cesarean section a few days earlier, and I should have been home taking it easy. But I could not afford the time off. Of course, I tried to be tough, but I resented not being free to live the life I wanted. I needed things to change desperately, but I did not know how to stop the train wreck sprawled across the treacherous black ice.

Everybody has their stuff, and that includes me! My stuff consisted of all the stories I told over and over, including all the reasons the sweet things I wanted in my life would never be achievable. It included all my beliefs about not being good enough or not being worthy. I was really good at talking about how my stuff was everyone else's fault and how my life would be perfect once "they" got *their* stuff together! I told that stupid story so many times I even had it memorized!! I filled in all the details about not having enough money, having to work five times harder than regular people, not having five extra minutes to take a shower, and having to do everything myself.

I told that story so well that before long, I was working a full-time job typing medical reports for doctors, I had a full violin teaching studio, and I was attempting to homeschool my children, which was actually my passion in life. As you can imagine, I didn't do any of those things very well because I never slept. My home life was a mess! I was angry at my husband because this was obviously all his fault! I was irritable with my kids because they kept asking for things like food, supplies for projects, basic clothing needs, and more gas in the car! I didn't understand how I could work so incredibly hard and have NOTHING to show for it. I still wasn't able to put food on the table or meet the basic needs of my family. Every day was overwhelming because I knew there was no hope for anything better. I was a success at one thing—failing. It was embarrassing. Eventually, I found myself in deep depression.

I wasn't always like this. In my youth I was quite the go-getter, and I was accustomed to winning. I studied music very seriously and participated in competition after competition. Through countless auditions for various programs and events, I regularly came out on top and came to respect myself. I knew what it was like to set my eye on a goal, go after it, and achieve it.

An early mentor taught me that I could produce whatever I wanted by putting up a picture to look at (before vision boards were cool). Through that process I managed to bring about a vacation to Mexico, a trip to Disneyland, and three cars. This demonstrated to me clearly that I had a power within me to create from my thoughts. But I had somehow forgotten to use that power intentionally. Somewhere, I switched from playing offense and creating on purpose what I wanted, to playing defense with my thoughts, just managing all the negativity in my life. I was so busy putting out fires and crises, one after another, that I completely forgot I could control what I was creating.

At this very low point of my life, I knew something had to change! Things could not continue in this path of mediocrity and failure. I knew I was destined for great things! I knew I had a message to share, but I had no idea what it was. Worse yet, I no longer felt liked myself, and I wondered where the old me had gone, the "me" who was used to rocking the world. When I did not know where to turn or what to do, when I no longer recognized myself in the mirror, a miracle happened! My husband had the crazy notion (or pure inspiration) to return to school to finish his degree in exercise science.

At first we thought it would be impossible. He had tried on several other occasions to go back and finish but, for whatever reason, it never worked out. This time was different. He applied, and within two weeks, he was admitted and began classes in earnest. It was difficult. He attended classes full time while still working his full-time job. At the time, we had received our second or third foreclosure notice, and I was working endless hours so we could keep our house while still trying to meet the needs of the children. My own self-care was in the toilet, and I was my own last priority. Needless to say, the stress in our home was off the charts, but we had taken on this project of my husband's education as a family, which helped us to grow closer in the long run. By the time he finished, we all felt we had accomplished something monumental. I even attended classes for my husband when he could not due to conflicting schedules.

One of the classes I attended in his place was called "Mind, Body, Spirit Wellness." In this class, we discussed scalar energy (energy of the universe that is not moving), its place in science, and its effects on the body. This class literally changed my life as I began to study and remember things I had known before but had somehow forgotten. I learned about frequency and vibration from the quantum consciousness perspective. This sent me on an incredible journey of exploration and shifting of my old belief systems and habits which, in turn, enabled me to completely alter the course I was on and to achieve very different results.

I made a string of discoveries, the first of which came as I enthusiastically shared with a friend all the amazing things I had been learning. She nonchalantly said, "You should talk to my sister. She does BodyTalk." Little did I know how much this collision with destiny would transform everything about my existence! BodyTalk is described as "whole healthcare," taking into account the effect of psychology on the body and addressing the energetic blockages that keep full communication from happening, consequently interfering with the body's ability to heal itself. (For more information, visit bodytalksystem.com)

At the time, I had some health challenges (including 18 years of fertility issues, low thyroid function, weight problems, and high cholesterol), and I saw this "BodyTalk thing" as a way to explore what was needed to improve my overall health, as well as those specific concerns. I had no way to know what a profound impact BodyTalk would have on my life.

I began to see a BodyTalk practitioner on a regular basis, and I immediately began to feel different. I felt lighter, and the stress I was under began to diminish. I was less angry at the world. Right away, I got little glimpses of the real me. I was so relieved to find me again that I was not eternally lost to the deep abyss of darkness of my life! I once again had hope of a better future. Was my life perfect? Absolutely not! I still experienced failure, but I now had more compassion for myself as I began to learn many new life lessons!

As my understanding of the energy of the body and the energy of the universe grew, so did my understanding of the nature and goodness of God. I saw immediately that I was going back to school myself, only there wasn't a man-made degree to be earned, but rather an intense education in things of a spiritual nature, and I was determined to be the best apprentice I could be! I even became a BodyTalk practitioner myself so I could go deeply into what I was learning. As I studied, I gained glimpses of immense powers of creation, three in particular.

First, I gained an understanding of vibration, which to most people feels like emotion or mood. As I worked with clients and heard their stories, I witnessed the healing of the mind and body that happens through shifting the vibration of their body by cleaning up the emotional baggage. I began asking, "What else is possible?" I saw countless instances when people would experience an energetic vibration in their body and would then attract experiences that were completely in alignment with what they were vibrating. Clients who were afraid (merely an energetic frequency) would attract over and over the exact thing they were afraid of. I observed that people who spent most of their time in a low vibration of anger, depression, or negativity had a difficult time creating any experiences in their life other than negative ones. In my own life, I recognized how much it cost me (in dollars and happiness) when I allowed myself to stay in that negative vibration. I began to practice managing my mood so I could actually create my life in the upper vibrations of love and gratitude.

The second power lesson was about the profound impact that our language—our word choice— has on the world we create. In listening to the words I was previously using, I could see that I experienced EXACTLY what I was talking about. In my daily casual conversation, I constantly talked about what I lacked and about problems, which, not surprisingly, automatically put me in a low vibration. I learned that words are symbols of energy, and as such, are basically just instructions to the universe of what you expect it to deliver to you. It was no surprise at all that I was experiencing the results I got. I was my own self-fulfilling prophecy based on the words I was speaking. Again, as I observed clients and how they would talk about their health, I determined to NEVER let any words come out of my mouth that would contribute more to what I did NOT want. Instead, I committed to be hyper-vigilant and guard my language as if my life depended on it—because it does!

Third, I discovered the capacity of the mind, through imagination, to tell a story and actually grow it. It turns out the mind has many filters that run conscious and subconscious belief programs that affect behavior. Even with all these filters in place, the mind does not know the difference between what you want and what you don't, so it will actively create all the time based on the thoughts and emotions you feed it. Like a computer, it will create garbage if that is how you live. Low frequency energy creates low vibration experiences. Conversely, high vibration creates exciting and fantastic reality. If you want a different outcome, you must imagine that desired result with as much high-frequency emotion as possible. Picture that new story, seeing with an eye of faith, believing in something you cannot physically appreciate yet. As you hold those images in your imagination and feel the finished product, the subconscious mind will go to work to bring you the opportunities necessary to form the exact reality of what you visualize.

There was one key piece to this brain puzzle, however. As long as I believed that the solutions to my problems were outside me, I was power*less* to change anything in my reality. The more energy I wasted blaming other people for my circumstances, the less ability I had to create anything different. In other words, *as long as I was blaming other people for my stuff, I had no way to shift it*. It was not until I completely owned my own story and took responsibility for what *I* had created in my life that I could re-write that story. As painful as it was, I had to fully acknowledge that my handiwork was just that—mine! As soon as I became aware of that responsibility, the next big miracle happened I woke up from the stupor in which I had been living, completely unaware of what I was doing, thinking, and creating. I decided it was time for a momentum swing back to playing offense. Since my mind was busy designing my physical world anyway, I gave it instructions as to what I actually wanted it to look like. There was only one problem. I could not concentrate hard or long enough to shift my focus from what I didn't want to what I did want. No matter how hard I tried, I was easily distracted, and my thought patterns would go straight back to the habits I had created over many, many years. My emotional state would often default to past feelings and stories.

To help train my wandering mind, I began to write down on paper, with a specific strong intention, the things I wanted to have happen. I began to physically re-write the story I had been telling about my life and, sure enough, new opportunities began to show up. Many things started going better. I wrote into my story some help with my house, and the perfect person came into my life within two weeks. I re-worded what I had been saying about not being able to go anywhere because we didn't have time or money. I wrote down a simple desire to take my kids on a tour of historical sites, a trip which actually happened by accident. I changed my story about my 11-year-old who could not read, and one day about six weeks later, he could read. I hadn't realized that it was my own fear that was keeping him from outgrowing his situation. After several obvious miracles, I asked myself, "What else is possible?" What *could* happen if I just wrote the story I actually wanted. I wrote down a new office, which seemed like a long shot, and it appeared. Large things and small things— washers, dryers, and cars—you name it! When I wrote it in my LIFEstory, it somehow showed up. Sometimes it was immediate, but sometimes it took a little more time.

While all the re-storying was going on, my clients and friends were noticing the huge transformation that was taking place in my life. Many of them asked me to show them what I was doing and asked for help in shifting their vibrations and telling different stories just as I was learning to do. From this completely unexpected yet wonderful place, LIFEstory Transformation was born. LIFEstory Transformation is a simple yet very effective system to teach the power of vibration, the power of words, and the power of the mind to imagine a different story and create a completely new result. It is a lifestyle of miracles and possibilities.

I experimented with writing my LIFEstory just to see what would happen. Since I was just playing around, the more impossible the request, the better! I wrote down "going to Africa to do humanitarian service." I had no idea how to do it, how to pay for it, or how to take time off, and I did not know anyone else who knew either. I thought perhaps in time (years) I could figure out some way to do that, but it ended up only taking 10 months to come to pass. I tried it again…and again…and again. I wrote down all kinds of things, especially things I could not get by just setting a goal, and I watched them shift, from my relationship with my husband and kids, to a complete change in the types of clients I was attracting, to multiple trips to Hawaii, Disneyland, Ghana, and Kenya.

Once I figured out what LIFEstory would do, I decided I wanted to really LIVE my life! It was a complete game-changer! Instead of seeing all the reasons I could not do what I wanted, all sorts of new opportunities opened up. Pulling out all the stops on living made an enormous impact on my family. I had spent many years teaching my children lack and limitation. Now, whenever they want to do something, they know to write it in their own LIFEstories, and they own their own creation. They know that no one is responsible for their happiness but themselves. They understand that anything is possible if they are willing to manage their mood, engage the power of their words, and utilize the power of their minds to tell a truer story. Now, as a family, we all practice holding images in our imaginations of what we want and see with an eye of faith, believing in something we cannot see long enough for it to be created spiritually, so it can come into the plane of physical existence.

Since the birth of LIFEstory Transformation, the power of LIFEstory continues to work its magic in my life, as well as in the lives of many, many others! I actively use it to work on relationships with my loved ones, explore my spiritual life, build my business, bring audacious goals forward, learn new things, and maintain my health, as well as strengthen my physical body. Sometimes I still wish I could blame other people for my challenges, but I now know the truth! More than blame, I love the power that comes from owning my own creation.

Because I am in so much awe of what LIFEstory Transformation has done for me and my ability to produce results in my daily life, it has been my dream to share it with as many people as possible, especially as a humanitarian give-back. I have been so blessed to observe the impact of this knowledge in many places on the African continent, and LIFEstory is quickly spreading across the globe! It is so exciting to receive testimonials from other people about things that were impossible but now are reality. I am humbled to realize that whatever struggle I have experienced in my life has all served to bless many, many lives, uplift and strengthen humanity, and alleviate suffering. I am blessed beyond measure by the relationships around the world I have developed through LIFEstory Transformation. Looking back those few short years, I would have never imagined the wonder I have been privileged to witness. Again, my understanding of the nature and goodness of God is deepened. I am indeed grateful!

About Becky Rogers

Becky Rogers is the founder of LIFEstory Transformation, homeschool mother of 10, BodyTalk practitioner, and manifestation specialist who is excited about living life ON purpose WITH purpose.

Besides spending time with her family, her favorite thing is helping people break free of seemingly impossible challenges that keep them from becoming who they truly are meant to be. She is also the creator of Families Mentoring Families, a nonprofit humanitarian organization that connects families all over the world for strength and support.

It's all about MIRACLES and TRANSFORMATION!! She can be reached at Becky@LIFEstoryTransformation.com, LIFEstorytransformation.com, and FamiliesMentoringFamilies.com.

Chapter Twenty-Two
Embracing Obstacles as the Way
By Amber Smithson

Chapter Twenty-Two
Embracing Obstacles as the Way
By Amber Smithson

Six figures in debt.

It's 2008. How did I get here? From a few thousand in student loans to THIS?! I had always seen myself as somebody who was an overachiever—who was successful, who got straight As, and was always striving for unattainable perfection. Typically, when people are in debt they know about it. They can say, "Yep, I bought that," and "Yep, I was not very responsible there." But that isn't what happened to my husband Jared and me. We were victimized in the worst of ways—by people we trusted and loved.

A scarcity mindset can bring stress—when you don't have enough money to buy groceries, or you don't know how you're going make your house payment. Your kids come home from school and say, "I need $20 for school supplies," and you think, "I don't even know how I'm going to come up with that." It affects all areas of your life, including your health. You feel as though you can't afford healthy food or afford to work out. Mentally, you wonder if you can provide for your family, whether you are doing a good job as a parent, whether you are giving your family the opportunities that they need or want or deserve.

Both my husband and I have always been entrepreneurs. We love to work for ourselves—the flexibility, the control, the feeling that you can create something great. 2008 was a period of transition for us. Since 1998, we had both owned our own companies. My husband had been working in insurance and financial services, and I had been in Web development. My husband's business had gone downhill with new government regulations, so I was providing for the family with my part-time 25-30 hours a week of work with Web development. We were busy looking for something new.

The day we found out.

I logged into our personal bank account to double check the balance before my husband stopped at the grocery store on his way home. Zero. Zero?! Overdraft fees? I balanced the checkbook every month when the statement arrived! What's going on? I saw that a transfer had been made and every penny was taken from us. I realized that many more overdraft charges were about to happen in the coming days. My cell phone rang and I heard a voice on the other line from an insurance company representative telling me they had seized part of what we owed them, but we'd have to pay the rest. I was so confused—where did this debt come from?

It turns out that my husband's business partners had written insurance policies in his name without our knowledge, gotten paid on the policies, then had the client cancel it and start a policy again. This resulted in a double payment to the partners, and the debt left to us to pay the insurance company back. Every time we learned about a new debt, we were reliving the pain and humiliation. It was as though someone was stabbing us, and every time we learned more it was another stab. As time went on, we learned our identities had been stolen. Business partners we had trusted completely had taken out credit cards in our names, and then maxed out the cards. They had cleaned out the business bank account. We had calls telling us that we owed insurance companies $20,000, $30,000, $50,000.... Finding out about these things made us feel like victims. We were in fact victims of a crime, but you can be a victim of a crime and not necessarily have a victim mentality. At this point we definitely were holding that victim mentality.

The business partners were my husband's brothers. These were people who were supposed to love us. We trusted them.

Each month, we were trying to pay back the debts. Thousands of dollars were going to debt. We barely had money to buy groceries, so we asked our church for help with food. After six months of not being able to make our house payment, we were scared that we'd be out on the street soon. It was a low point, and we knew something had to give. We were talking to a friend who was a lawyer and he said, "Amber, this is what bankruptcy is for. It's for people like you that didn't get into the situation yourself."

Bankruptcy?!

That was incredibly hard for us, because bankruptcy made us feel like such failures. We borrowed the money from my parents and decided to do it even though it went against how we believed you ought to run your life. The phone calls stopped. Thank you, Lord! I couldn't handle it any longer.

What now?

My mom had become a health coach and was finding success with her health and her finances. We were resistant because we thought it was "just another network marketing thing."

Lying in bed at three o'clock in the morning I said, "Jared, are you awake?"

"Yup."

"We need to become health coaches with my Mom."

"No." (Sigh.)

"Yes," I said.

"No way, c'mon."

"Yes."

"Ok," he said.

The next day, we started our new business as certified health coaches. We dove in head first! Our first full month of coaching, we made enough money (almost to the penny) to pay our house payment! The phone calls I received were very different, "I lost four pounds this week!" And, "I got on a bicycle with my grandson. I haven't done that in 20 years!" I could feel that our life was making a shift. The next month, we made more than two thousand dollars. People were improving their health, and I was curious about the company's motto of "Healthy Body, Healthy Mind, Healthy Finances." We were ready for this.

This might be the time in the story when you as the reader think, "And they lived happily ever after!" but there were still many years of struggle. We continued to relive our bankruptcy for years. We couldn't get a credit card, which reminded us all the time about what "terrible people" we were, having this bankruptcy on our record. We had to deal with that continually. It was definitely hard on our marriage. We still struggled financially for several years making a new business work (although we never made less than two thousand a month). We were slowly and surely building a long-term equity business. There were nights when I was running a meeting in one town, and my husband Jared in another at the same time.

The blessing that we had was our coaching family—a company of great integrity, and they helped us with personal development and support. Fast forward to 2016: Our business, HealthCanBeSimple.com, was named the sixth fastest-growing company in Utah County by *BusinessQ Magazine* (Utah Valley magazine). One of our mentors said that anything—all the crap that ever happens to you in your life—just makes for a good story later when you've overcome it.

We have a saying in our company: "We seek growth. We embrace obstacles as the way." A favorite scripture of mine says, "Seek and ye shall find." How do we grow? We must seek it! Some may view an obstacle or a trial in their life as something to avoid. But I see now that the obstacles are the WAY to that growth. The "failures" in life are blessings given to us. What if my brothers-in-law had never been in a state of desperation? What if they had not stolen from us? What if we had never overcome our judgements of network marketing and had not become health coaches?

Today, we have a thriving business. We GET to help others create healthy bodies, healthy minds, and healthy finances. We found someone who would give us a loan, and we are building our dream home—a million-dollar house! But it's not about that. It's not about driving fancy cars or having expensive stuff. It's about those we can bring to our house, those we can bring into our world and share our abundance with. We built our home so we can have retreats. We want to bring people to our house to play volleyball and to be active, and just to find a place that brings them joy. We want them to know that even though they're going through hard things, that there is always a way out.

We got a credit card last year—just a normal everyday thing for most Americans, but to us it felt as though we were really coming out the other side of this, and it's even better.

I have pondered many times about those really low times when I was so vulnerable and heart-broken that I cried myself to sleep and thought I didn't want to get out of bed. I had nightmares for years. Instead of letting them get me down, I realize instead that they gave me incentive and inspiration to work hard. I was going through a bankruptcy and feeling like people were thinking I was a failure. But it gave me inspiration to prove them wrong. I wanted to say, "No, that's not us; that doesn't define me; that doesn't define my success in life. Just because I'm a financial failure on paper doesn't mean that is who I am."

I admit that I could have just gone out and gotten a nine-to-five job and made some money that way, with a regular paycheck. It certainly crossed my mind. But I saw the opportunity to inspire other people and to help others who were going through similar hardships. I saw being a health coach as a vehicle in which I could say "I've been through something like that, and I came out the other end and look at me now." I wanted other people to know that they could do that, too.

Success is abundance—in your mindset, in your finances, in your health, in your time. It's a feeling of abundance that makes you feel that there's so much to give, so much out there, that you don't even know where to start. I go to sleep feeling good about myself and what I've accomplished that day. Each day I get up and I'm excited to start living—that's success for me.

Although we've come a long way from our low point, that doesn't mean there won't be more obstacles, that there aren't going to be more hard things. A year ago I found out that I had a brain tumor. I can't tell you how much the experience of going through bankruptcy and the accompanying lows in my life prepared me for being able to handle the health problems I was having. Even though I was healthy, even though I eat right and exercise, and I'm a health coach for heaven's sake, sometimes things happen over which you have no control. That was once again a difficult time. I had the surgery, and I don't even remember January 2016. It's not in my memory at all. My husband was a rock. I was able to go through that experience and see the blessings even **as I was going through it;** even as I was lying in bed, on drugs, people helped me with everything. They helped drive my kids around, helped me clean my house, and helped me walk. Through all that I was able to see the blessings. It didn't take me years to realize them.

Now it's October 2016, and I feel and look as vibrant and healthy as ever. It can still impact me if I push myself too hard too fast, but most people can't believe I had a brain tumor removed last January. The greatest blessing from all the "negative" experiences of the previous years is the knowledge that if I hadn't gone through them, it would had been devastating to find out about my brain tumor. I simply couldn't have endured it. Now I realize it's all about the dramatic reframing of my mindset, and of increasing my ability and skills to handle whatever happens. Many people wish they could have an easy life. They just want less stress. But that just isn't the way life works. It's essential to increase your emotional, mental, and physical skills, and the only way to do that is to have challenges. The process of overcoming them increases your skills, but also brings more abundance and more flow into your life.

It's interesting, but now that my husband and I are financially successful, money just doesn't seem to be that important. Success to me now is about what kind of relationships I have, both with others and with myself. What kind of relationship do I have with myself? How do I feel about myself? What kinds of thoughts am I allowing into my mind? What kinds of relationships do I allow? Success is more centered on relationships and balance in my life. I wouldn't go so far as to say I'm the poster child for balance every day. Is there even such a thing as "real balance" every day? Success is accepting what my situation is, and not forming judgment around it. Success is intentionally creating good things in my life. Success is centering my life on what matters most!

We have even made peace with our brothers. One day my husband said, "OK, I'm going to call my brothers." And I asked, "What are you going to say?" He said, "I don't know." He picked up the phone and got voicemail (honest internal sigh of relief). He left a quick message and hung up. But when they called back—some people might think that he would have said "I forgive you"—what he said was "thank you." We had realized that if all the trials we had gone through had not happened to us, we would not have had the success and the joy we feel now. The obstacle is the way. Every. Single. Time.

About Amber Smithson

Amber Smithson is a certified health coach and business coach. With her husband Jared, she owns HealthCanBeSimple, Inc recently honored by Utah Valley Business Q magazine as the 6th- fastest growing company in Utah Valley with 462% growth and $7.8 million in annual revenue.

Amber has personally worked with thousands of people to reach their healthy body, healthy mind, and healthy finance goals since 2009. Having been overweight herself in the past, Amber has a passion and gift for helping show the simple, FUN way to loving yourself healthy.

You can find out more about Amber at www.HealthCanBeSimple.com.

Chapter Twenty-Three
3 Pivotal Points: Turn Everyday Fails into Meaningful Metamorphosis
By Connie Sokol

Chapter Twenty-Three
3 Pivotal Points: Turn Everyday Fails into Meaningful Metamorphosis
By Connie Sokol

Have you ever noticed that women are harder on themselves, and on each other, than our male counterparts? This trait is not is not a figment of my overactive imagination—it's an actual societal pressure. For example, when a child shows up at school with unkempt hair or forgotten homework, which parent do we typically think should have been on it? Which parent feels the need to apologize if the house is messy when guests arrive?

I call these experiences "everyday fails"—the normal activities of life that we turn into failures, perceived or real. And they can take their toll. Whether it's burning the lasagna, running late for a sports carpool, or forgetting immunizations (for five years!), women have plenty of opportunities to feel less—less capable, less valued, or less visionary than we are.

When these everyday fails are perceived as personal fails, we begin to distort reality. This distortion can lead us into a "Perception/Expectation Cycle." We believe and hold onto a perception of how things "should" be at a certain age, stage, or situation in life. This creates an expectation, which in turn creates a success/fail outcome. It's not okay that the cupcakes turned out 80-percent great or that your children got As and Bs on their report cards. Not when the neighbor's child pulled straight As, a scholarship, and an Extra Miler Award at the school assembly.

Not that I've had such an experience.

At my daughter's sixth-grade graduation ceremony where they announced awards for afterschool pursuits such as running, artwork, and chess, my daughter's highest achievement had been to stop sassing the teacher or kicking the mean boys.

I listened, but didn't hear the award for that one.

What I did notice was that my daughter's friend received an award for uber-achievement in a random sixth-grade area. I smiled, I clapped, I nodded—fabulous, my daughter was keeping good company. Maybe this friend's overzealous ways would rub off on my daughter. And then, the girl's name was called again. And again. And yet again. In fact, I suspected she might have mafia ties with the PTA for all the awards she collected in that one hour. I'm sad to say that my smile turned to a courtesy clap which turned to outright confusion—some of these awards I hadn't even heard of. My first thought was, "Wait. Was this in the newsletter? Did they even announce that competition?"

Thankfully, I caught myself before going too much further with my woe-is-mom wails and returned to feeling great (ish) joy for this girl. And gratitude that my daughter had no idea about these awards. Her doing so would have meant endless organized carpools and afterschool errands to find perfect supplies for said achievements. I ultimately breathed a sigh of relief.

But this is what can happen to us as women, wives, and particularly mothers. We set ourselves up for a Pass/Fail system. And that's a no-win. I've learned a good deal about how to navigate the daily less-thans and turn them into positive more-thans. Thankfully, this process that I have termed "layered learning" has prepared me for the Big Fails. Without that everyday learning forged in the growth cycle of life, I might never have taken such meaningful emotional flight.

Pivotal Point #1: Emerging from the Cocoon—The Mother Fail

My first of our seven children was a golden-haired boy who seemed to be healthy and normal in every way. Until he hit two. Like an alien abduction, our charming little Ben disappeared and was replaced by a socially adverse, high intensity, obsessive-compulsive version. Unbeknownst to us at the time, that began our journey with Asperger's Syndrome. At Ben's young age, Asperger's was hardly on the radar. Instead, he was diagnosed with the then-popular Attention Deficit Disorder. But my mother gut knew that wasn't the full story. After several doctors and my firm belief that a missing link remained in his diagnosis, we found Dr. Sam Coates, a specialist who within a half-hour correctly diagnosed him. That began the longer journey of finding solutions that worked for this wonderful, complex young boy.

But, oh, the fallout. Ben was bullied, neglected, and mocked. One parent pointedly told me that my son would be a future serial killer—at the time Ben was a preschooler. Though I am the first in line (and pushing people out of the way) to admit that raising Ben was painfully difficult, the lack of understanding and compassion from others was more so.

After several years, my mother sense of failure became acute. When I couldn't find the right solution, or didn't have the right snack/toy/book that was his favorite, or understand his subtle signals of "winding" behavior that led to an all-out meltdown, I felt the fail.

But one experience put it in clear perspective. On the recommendation of a good friend I took Ben, then five, and his two-year-old brother to a music learning class. It was active, it was educational, it was "good parenting." Within five minutes I knew I was in trouble. I'll share this detailed excerpt from my *The Life is Too Short Collection*:

While the other moms sat quietly, I bobbed up and down like a kangaroo, not to the music but in chasing after my children. Others languidly watched their children clap, hop, dig, and even lunge in time to the music. I felt as if I wore a neon sticker saying, "Major Mother Loser who can't get her kids to dance on cue because she gave them cereal for dinner during one entire summer."

As I sat there, confidently smiling, then stone-faced, as I fought urges to duct-tape my child to the piano, I felt my mom self-esteem start to shake, then rattle, and finally roll over and play dead. Thankfully, a bludgeon to the head from a flying xylophone mallet brought me to my senses. I thanked the talented teacher, swept up my kids and said, "Park!" Off we went to a nearby park with blazing sun, blue sky, and wide-open running spaces.

From this Mother Fail I learned to go with my gut. To listen to my soul, to look squarely into my children's eyes, and to do what was best because of love, not fear of peer opinion.

That layered learning served us both well. I chose to homeschool him for a period of time, and we both survived. He went on to graduate from high school, with honors, and then to attend college. He served a service mission for The Church of Jesus Christ of Latter-day Saints and returned to attend more schooling, work a retail job, and start his own business for small engine tool repair. He does his own laundry, knows how to cook his own meals, and is a kind, helpful, and good-hearted young man.

Mother Success.

Pivotal Point #2: Wriggling in the Pupa—The Body Fail

Aging is a blessing. At least, I used to say that before menopause, but that's another chapter. The blessings, alas, can be hidden (covertly, masterfully, repeatedly hidden...I digress).

I moved through my uber-twenties into my overzealous thirties right into my more thoughtful but still way-too-wound forties, and landed currently in my "be more-do less" fifties. It is a wonderful place.

But it wasn't always.

The day it became truly wonderful was the day I couldn't move. My body-stop had begun as a slow tiredness that morphed into subtle but notable changes in my normal activities, such as dropping a Zumba class I loved. It was letting go of enrichment classes and enjoyable walks, and developing a loss of excitement about my favorite things, such as writing or speaking. Finally, it led to an unhealthy focus on my bed—how soon could I be in it and why did I need to get out of it? For someone who had demonstrated the lifelong zeal of an Energizer bunny this was devastating.

So I needed to deal with it. At first came awareness, followed by acceptance, although I avoided the latter because it really wasn't that appealing. But life slaps you like producing a newborn baby and I allowed myself this layered learning, namely, to prioritize three kinds of health—emotional, spiritual, and physical.

First, I acknowledged that I couldn't do what I used to do. Period. I tacked a sign on my bedroom door from 4 to 5 p.m. that said something helpful like, "You open this door, you die." I gave myself permission to rest before starting Phase 2 of dinner, homework, and activities. To myself, I repeated the mantra, "This too shall pass," and "Do half of what you think you can," and "Where is my chocolate stash?" Through prayer, scripture reading, and intentional pondering time, I gave myself hall passes to do less than I had before, shoving away the attending guilt. Over time, I felt my soul begin to heal.

Second, I verbalized to a medical person three words: "I'm not well." That was transforming. That was also the start of a joyful journey discovering what those words meant, and to listen to my woman-gut who knoweth many things not taught in medical school. As I added natural supplements, massage, acupuncture, and bioidentical hormones, my body responded like a starved teenager at a pizza party. My body almost hummed with happiness—I was paying attention, listening to my soul, and responding to its loving communication.

Last, I set boundaries in the three kinds of health to avoid a repeat experience. Although my official time-out sign was removed, my down-time remained. To this day, kids know not to mess with mom after 9:30 p.m., or it is not pretty. When I'm in a community, church, or school meeting that involves volunteer assignments, I choose which will actually work for me and my family, and keep my mouth shut for the rest. I consider it a gift to allow someone else the "opportunity for service." When I feel the burn-out begin, I read a book, take a walk, or binge-watch episodes of BBC's Agatha Christie's *Poirot*. And even when my health is strong, I continue to make supplements and good eating a priority, preventing some negative what-ifs.

Such layered learning is not new. It's not even earth-shattering, but it is lovely. Listening to our body and soul, partnering with the divine, and speaking truthfully, create what is powerful.

Pivotal Point #3: Taking Flight—My Purpose-driven Life Fail

For as long as I can remember, I've had a life message to share. And I talk fast. Put the two together and you get someone excited about helping women and families live purposeful, organized, and joyful lives. And you get a dilemma. Exactly how do I do that while raising seven children over a 20-plus year period?

At one point in life, I had produced four children in eight years and felt the aftermath. While in survival mode, I put my writing and speaking largely aside and gave over to the new breast-feeding, sleep-deprived haze. I love my children fiercely but those years are mostly a blur. And yet, those were also formative days when I was mostly unaware of the basic blocks being built in their minds and souls.

As they began to grow, I slowly re-emerged. Like the spring clearing after a numbing winter, my soul began to unfold and tentatively bloom. My dream of being a speaker and a writer returned with a deeper force. I dabbled with some church speaking assignments, wrote a few articles, and sketched a great many incoherent ideas. Meanwhile, after women heard or read my messages they expressed an interest in more—more talk, more content, more connection.

On the high of those early successes I gave in to a sudden surge of excitement. I contacted my city's university, then their community education director, and talked her into giving me a shot at teaching a community class. Within weeks my name was boldly on the schedule, in print and "out there." Then came the incredible good news—six people had signed up for the class. I was elated! For two hours I would be teaching six real people my favorite life principles and they would pay for the experience.

It was official. I was a speaker.

On the evening of my first class scheduled at 7:30 p.m., I arrived on campus an hour early. I toted about half my house furnishings to transform the cinderblock classroom (the lamps really did add that soft glow). My visual aids—including an overhead projector and plastic sheaths—were prepared, in order, and almost pulsed with energy from the vital information contained therein.

No one showed.

At 7:40, I smiled bravely—it was good to be fashionably late, right? By 7:50 p.m. I was taking it personally. When the clock struck 8:00 p.m., I was devastated. Gathering and stuffing and packing my belongings, I trudged out to the car and drove. But not home. The insidious thought came to mind, "If you go home now, everyone in the neighborhood will know you failed." Because this was The Age Before Cell Phones, I drove to a quiet park and bawled my eyes out. My only true victory was that I passed several Baskin-Robbins without succumbing.

When I finally arrived home, my husband opened the door and said, "Where were you? The university called and said there were six people there to take your class." Apparently, the department had given out the wrong class time.

That experience of perceived failure taught me a pivotal lesson. This was definitely a case of perception, and the beginning of my looking through the Lord's Lens (or, a Truth Lens). Had I not seen through cloudy, tainted glasses, I would have seen a better reality—an extra two hours, all to myself, with kids taken care of. I could have pulled out a good book and read. I could have laughed. I could have written the experience for a column and become a newspaper columnist (which I later did).

I could brand these experiences as a Loser Woman Moment. Or, I could embrace it as part of the progression path, of the growth and learning that every single person goes through. We don't get to skip steps. We don't leapfrog to triumph. We have to know where we want to go, and by painful, joyful process, know what it means to arrive. As author Brene Brown shares in her book, *Rising Strong*:

Whatever the experience, failure feels like a lost opportunity, like something that can't be redone or undone. Regardless of the context or magnitude, failure brings with it the sense that we've lost some of our personal power...[but] embracing failure without acknowledging the real hurt and fear that it can cause, or the complex journey that underlies rising strong, is gold-plating grit. To strip failure of its real emotional consequences is to scrub the concepts of grit and resilience of the very qualities that make them both so important—toughness, doggedness, and perseverance.

With failure we often ask ourselves, "What did I do wrong?" "Why can't I be successful/have it turn out like so-and-so?" "Why did I even try?" What we don't understand is that the problem *is* the path. The future success *is* part of the current fail.

Instead, we can look through a new lens and ask better questions:

What important life lesson did I learn?

How has it strengthened me and my core being?

What have I learned that I haven't learned before/couldn't have learned without it?

What pivotal purpose can I take from this learning? How can I use this learning in the future?

What purpose-driven fail have you experienced? Now look at it with that new lens and ask yourself: Was that experience for a good cause, a community event or function, a school fundraiser, a small business venture when your family needed the financial help?

Every experience matters. Every bit of learning builds and strengthens and defines our future success and fulfillment. When we stay focused on where we ultimately want to be, that Pike's Peak of life's mountains, we can find deeper purpose in our momentary vistas and rest areas during the climb. I remember reading years ago about a celebrity who had scheduled an ambitious hike up a mountain in Hawaii. She began the day with clear time goals—where she needed to be on the mountain at such-and-such a time to make it to the top. About a third of the way up she turned around and saw the breathtaking views. That's when it hit her—why am I hurrying? Why am I rushing this beautiful experience? Taking that rest can shift and renew our senses.

Failure does that, too. It gives us moments to pause, evaluate, and re-direct our course if needed. A few years after closing down a few business aspects of my life due to raising children, I felt compelled to return to providing a program called "Back to Basics." In this two-hour monthly meeting, women focus on a life area, learn simple tools to create change, and receive support to make it happen. But my soul felt tired before even beginning. I knew the energy it would take to start this flywheel again.

However, the feeling persisted. Out of the blue I met another like-minded woman who wanted to help the process, and we got to work. Boy, did we! The vision was tremendous, beyond far-reaching. We would train leaders and program hosts, we would offer classes of different varieties, we would create training conferences, and more. In short, we alone would solve the world's problems.

To start, we held an introductory class. Although my soul cringed at my prior community education class experience, we forged on. Initially, we had hoped for a modest 15 to 20 women. In an improvement on history, we were shocked to find that night more than 75 women attending—the chairs spilled into the hall. We rejoiced—success! This must be the answer!

We moved forward with our bold, global vision but suddenly, and oddly, just as suddenly the response dried up. In subsequent classes, we had only 20 to 30 women at most. Our first women's retreat, based on helping women through deep challenges, was ultimately cancelled. Even though our evaluations said the women loved the concepts, our model wasn't working. And the time and energy for set-up, promotion, and more for the initial ventures exhausted my soul, and forced me to re-consider the remaining arms of this newly created octopus.

What a gift. Because of that early, confusing failure, I took time to sit and ponder what it was telling me. And I realized the failure was a blessing. The pause allowed me to weigh our far-reaching plan to change the world, and to acknowledge the attending thick weight that had softly settled over me. With a sureness I can't describe, I knew at that time I was not to foray into those kinds of events, women's retreats, or a host of the other "really great and amazing ideas" that we had brainstormed. No more wondering—it was utterly and completely clear.

That clarity rings true in what J.K. Rowling shared in her Harvard Commencement speech, "The Fringe Benefits of Failure":

So why do I talk about the benefits of failure? Simply because failure meant a stripping away of the inessential. I stopped pretending to myself that I was anything other than what I was, and began to direct all my energy into finishing the only work that mattered to me. Had I really succeeded at anything else, I might never have found the determination to succeed in the one arena I believed I truly belonged. I was set free, because my greatest fear had been realized, and I was still alive, and I still had a daughter whom I adored, and I had an old typewriter and a big idea. And so rock bottom became the solid foundation on which I rebuilt my life.

That failure shift led me to better ways and means. I went from doing all classes in a primitive model to offering a high-tech method allowing me to connect in communities, in- person, and better than I could have done through the old ways.

Flying High

As have other women, through each of my Everyday Fails as well as Big Fails I've engaged in beautiful layered learning. The gifts of failure include wisdom and insight that cannot be obtained any other way. We emerge from the cocoon knowing what we want, wriggle in the pupa to recapture the vision of what can and needs to be, and take flight by becoming open to people and possibilities to make it happen.

And when we see failure as such, we rejoice in its surefire companion of success.

About Connie Sokol

Connie Sokol is a mother of seven, bestselling author, and national and local speaker for more than 15 years. She is a TV core contributor on *Studio 5 with Brooke Walker* and a national blogger for www.ksl.com. Mrs. Sokol is represented by Fuse Literary and has written 16 books, including *Faithful, Fit & Fabulous, Create a Powerful Life Plan, Motherhood Matters,* and *40 Days with the Savior.*

Connie's passion is helping women and families live purposeful, organized, and joyful lives! Often called a woman's cheerleader, she founded the Back to Basics program to teach women simple principles in eight life areas that get results, such as organization, weight loss, and healthy relationships. She resonates with and uplifts everyday women through her TV, podcasts, ecourses, and programs. Mrs. Sokol marinates in time spent with her family and eating decadent treats. For her newsletter, blog, TV segments, and more, visit www.conniesokol.com and all social media.

Readers: Want to find out how to make changes in your life? Connie has generously allowed us to share her wise words in, "3 Keys to Make a Life Change." If you would like to access a copy of this visit http://successthroughfailing.com/downloads.

Chapter Twenty-Four
The Call to Kenya
By Heidi Totten

Chapter Twenty-Four
The Call to Kenya
By Heidi Totten

"Go start a group on Facebook called 100 Humanitarians. I'll let you know why." – God

This wasn't the first time I had heard a voice in my head guiding me to do something that I didn't understand, but it was certainly the most clear and unwavering instruction I had ever received. I was standing in the bathroom in a towel after taking a shower one Sunday morning in June 2015, but that didn't stop me from obeying immediately. I grabbed my cell phone and the group was launched.

Three months earlier, I had returned from a humanitarian trip to Kenya with my DNA rearranged and no idea how that would radically change my life. There was not a cell in my body that hadn't been altered by the experience. When people ask me today why I went to Kenya, my response is "peer pressure." It's true. I had at least 50 other countries on my list to visit before ever setting foot on the continent of Africa, but two of my closest friends at the time convinced me to go with them.

I was terrified, to say the least. Up until that point, the only locations outside of the U.S. that I had visited were Mexico and London. I live with a condition called lymphedema that makes me highly susceptible to cellulitis, a deep tissue infection that I have contracted many times in the past 15 years. When it happens, I usually end up in the hospital with an IV drip of antibiotics in my arm. Committing to two weeks in rural Kenya with no access to medical care in a malaria ridden country didn't sound appealing.

So why did I feel so pulled to go?

Almost two years later I am only beginning to understand the answer to that question. It has been a faith walk every step of the way, with unbelievable miracles and gut-wrenching heartache on a daily basis. It all began in a church in a village called Butere in Western Kenya.

Butere, Kenya - March 8, 2015 – Today we woke up to monkeys, birds, and a rooster that sounded like it was right outside my window. I looked out the window through the mosquito netting surrounding my extremely uncomfortable twin bed and scratched the three new bites on my arm. "I'm in Africa!" was my first thought. I got out of bed, got ready, and went down to breakfast, which was being served in a grass pavilion outside of our guest house. "Jambo!" I think I cheerfully said to anyone who would listen. After eating fruit and scones and something that looked a little like sausage, I joined the seven other women and four Kenyans in our group heading to the Anglican church service in the compound. I could hear music coming from the doorway. The air was humid and warm, but not yet hot. The benches were wooden and hard, and the big open chapel was draped in purple and gold satin. We sat waiting. And waiting. And waiting. My new friend Moses, a Maasai warrior, was sitting next to me, so I grabbed my phone and said, "Smile!" and took a picture.

It was at that moment that something inside of me shifted. I had a flood of information downloaded into my brain, and suddenly I knew that I knew him.

"Do I know him?" I asked myself. "You do," I answered back. Then church started.

That same experience happened a few more times over the following two weeks as I connected with people. David. Christine. Dominic. Kaelo. Edith. Everyone seemed familiar, especially the Maasai people. My brain and my heart could not make sense of the feeling that I had been there before, that I had known them, and that this was a reunion, not a first-time meeting. I knew that I wasn't the only one having this experience. Several of the women in our group were having the same reaction. It felt as though we were called there. Twenty months later, I know this to be true. Friends all over the world who have traveled to developing countries have been called there by the people, and by God, both to be His hands to serve, and to learn and be served.

When I talk about Kenya and my faith walk, I tell people, "I have always believed in God, but I met him in Kenya." This is true. I have spent more time praying, crying, weeping, wailing, begging, pleading, and accepting His will during this time, than at any time in my life, and that is saying something. He has sometimes been vocal, and sometimes silent, just letting me go through the refiner's fire as He molds me into the person He needs me to be.

The Preceding Failures

"Gentlemen, I'm done." I pushed my chair back from the table and felt a huge wave of relief wash over me. It had been 18 months, and for at least six months I had been kicking against the pricks, so to speak, about what I wanted my future to look like. I had no idea what I would do next, but whatever it was, it would require extensive education on how to actually run a business.

It was late 2010 when I lit my hair on fire and started a business with two partners. Between us we had more than 30 years of experience in technical recruiting, surviving the dot com bust and the 2008 bust and whatever busts had happened in between. Shortly before we launched, we collectively closed $300k in business at our previous company, so we had every reason to believe that we were going to rock this whole thing and come out zillionaires. We met on a weekly basis, building out a comprehensive business plan, discussing the clients we would go after ad nauseum, and picking titles. I was the COO, which in retrospect should have been the writing on the wall. Just what is a Chief Operations Officer, anyway? What operations was I the chief of? I digress.

I really had no idea what I was doing.

That being said, I was determined to have my own business and try my hand at entrepreneurship, so I jumped in with both feet. I quickly closed $30k in business to get us started and we were on our way.

The problem with being an optimist and starting a business is that I forgot that in order to have a business I needed to know how to run a business. I also neglected to ask my partners if they knew how to run a business. Turns out, not so much. Or maybe our diverse personalities just didn't know how to run a business together. Whatever the reason, it wasn't working. Perhaps it was because I couldn't find a clear job description for a COO on the internet, and therefore wasn't entirely sure what I was supposed to be doing.

I remember one particular workshop I attended called "The Prosperity Summit." It was a three-day event, and I suckered one of my partners into going with me. It was held at a local hotel, and there were about 150 in attendance. It involved at least eight different speakers, and while it was mostly a pitch fest with stuff for sale at the back of the room, there was sharing of great content, and I came away from it with some amazing friends, who are still in my life four years later.

My partner, on the other hand, was totally checked out. In fact, he said, "I already know this stuff," when I wanted to discuss it with him. He left after four hours on the first day. That should have been my warning, but it wasn't. I'm not great with warning signs. I choose to believe in people long past their expiration date. That has both helped me and hurt me, as you will come to find out.

So there I was, in November of 2011, with no job and no business, and I had just walked away from about $20k that was owed to me in back salary. In fact, one of my partners had said, "I don't think you should be taking a draw, because you aren't supporting a family."

Ouch.

Double ouch that I believed him. And so began my journey to discover my own value in the business world.

I've always been the "wind beneath your wings" sort of person. I'm the mastermind behind the guru, the support team, and the connector. In 2012, about a year after I walked away from the recruiting company, I got involved in an organization in which I was the right hand woman for the CEO. I did the marketing, sales, website, helped run events, and was pretty much at her beck and call for seven months. I thought I was finally learning what a COO does. I was sure it was what I would do for the rest of my life! I loved the vision of the organization, the people I met and worked with, and I especially loved the CEO. She promised that we would travel the world, serving women and families. She promised me a trip to Africa to meet the native women who would meet under the Wisdom Tree. My friend Becky Mackintosh, who also worked for the organization, and I would talk about sitting with African women together under that tree.

In 2013 when I finally realized that the organization was a house of cards ready to fall because of the lies, I was devastated. And the worst part? I hadn't been paid. We were always waiting for the "investment money" to come in so that we could all get salaries, a promise that never materialized. I filed with the Department of Labor against the organization, and was eventually awarded $10,000 in the fall of 2014, a fraction of the payment for the work I had done. However, it was enough to pay for my first trip to Kenya, so I guess in a way she fulfilled her promise to me about going to Africa, just in a very unusual way.

Unfortunately, I didn't learn the lesson in that experience, and jumped right in to work with another organization led by another guru. Another epic fail, although I gained more experience in marketing and technology. What God has taught me from those experiences is that my worth is not determined by my ability to build other people's dreams. Funny, right? Why would I tie my worth to that? Validation? Acceptance in the "inner circle"?

Recently I attended a four-day training put on by the Arbinger Institute. The focus was on helping non-profit organizations, but we spent two days learning about The Outward Mindset. I have gone to workshops like this for years, but none of it compared to this eye-opening experience. I was able to look at all of those previous situations, in which I seemed to attract people who failed me in some way, and understand that I was the common denominator.

Ouch. Again.

I knew that I needed to forgive the people I was blaming, and then forgive myself for seeing those people as vehicles to what I wanted, obstacles preventing me from success, or irrelevant to my goals in general, and therefore irrelevant in my life.

How do you even begin to apologize to almost everyone you know? I spent a couple of weeks feeling ashamed of the role I played in every drama in my life. I sent apology emails to people I really wanted and needed to apologize to, and I forgave myself for not choosing better. Some beautiful healing has come from those emails, but that's another story for another book.

That's really the amazing thing about the self-discovery journey. It gives you the opportunity to make better choices next time.

The Successes

"I want you to figure out what you want to do, so that you can do it for me!" my friend said.

"I have no idea what that means," I responded.

"You have spent HOURS being mentored and trained by some of the best coaches in the world. I want you to figure out what you are going to do with all of that knowledge. In fact, next Thursday I am coming over. Charge me whatever you want. I want you to apply all of it to my business and tell me what I need to fix."

She came over and we spent three hours going over her business plan in detail. We mapped out a plan that she later expanded on and turned into more than $100,000 in six months. All of that time spent in business and marketing training and personal development workshops was coming together into something I could do to help people!

I remember the day I thought, "Maybe other people would want me to do the same thing for their business." Since then, because of all the things I have learned from going through all of those business "failures," I have helped hundreds of people build out different aspects of their businesses. I've worked with very famous people, as well as people who were just starting out and had an idea they wanted to chase. I have conducted workshops, alone and in partnership with others, and I have mentored people one-on-one in their businesses and projects.

If I hadn't had the failures, I wouldn't have had the opportunity to support so many other people, because it never would have occurred to me that I had the skills to do it. I will never regret my experiences, even the hard ones, because they all lead to the path that ultimately brings you the biggest reward, which is knowing why you are here on this earth, and who you are meant to serve.

Nkoilale Village, Maasai Mara, Kenya – November 7, 2015 – I'm back in Kenya! Today we went to David's village for a baby naming ceremony. On the way there, Moses asked me what Maasai name I was choosing for David's baby. I was so humbled. Since David always tells me he is "Happy and Smiling" when I ask him how he is doing, I asked what the Maasai word is for Happy and Smiling. Oloshipa. I gave the baby the name Oloshipa. His English name is Benjamin, which is what my parents planned to name me had I been a boy, but David and his wife didn't know that when they chose it.

After the naming ceremony, we went to Edith's house for her housewarming party with the women. We were sitting outside under a large tree. I looked up at the tree, and then at the hundreds of Maasai women next to me. I smiled when I realized I was in Africa, sitting under the Wisdom Tree with women.

Narok, Kenya - November 16, 2015 – Today Moses and I walked down to Naivas, a grocery store in Narok. I taught him the 7 Pillars program, and then we ate chips (French fries) and drew out on a piece of paper plans for a cultural center to be built on his family's land in Nkoilale on the Maasai Mara. It will have a kitchen and training center for classes. We planned out 10 guest houses. I wonder what this is really for. There is opposition to what I am being asked to do here. It will not deter me.

December 9, 2015 – Last night in my dream I was visited by my cousin, Camie, and an old Maasai elder. Camie passed away a couple of years ago at the age of 37, after a battle with breast cancer. At her funeral I learned that she had visited 91 countries during her life while doing humanitarian work. I felt she had a message for me, and asked her what I needed to do. She said, "I went wide. You are going deep. This is your tribe." The Maasai elder didn't say anything. Finally I asked him who he was. He said, "I'm Moses' paternal grandfather."

The shockwaves that went through me were tangible. I didn't know what to think or how to act. I didn't know what to say to Moses about it. The Maasai traditionally do not talk about their ancestors once they are gone. Finally I asked him about his paternal grandfather and shared with him my dream. I remember him being surprised, but supportive. A few days later he joked, "Say hi to grandpa for me," when I messaged him to say goodnight. That night I had another dream, and this time his grandfather had a message for me.

"I need you to teach my grandson how to do genealogy," he said.

When I woke up, I told Moses my experience. He said, "I wonder why no one has done it." I had to laugh. I live in Utah where entire companies are dedicated to finding ancestors. Suddenly, the real purpose for the cultural center became clear. We are to preserve the oral histories and stories of the Maasai. We are to teach families self-reliance and sustainability. We are to bring mentors and teachers to train skills to provide educational opportunities. The big picture became much bigger.

One year later...

Salt Lake City, Utah - November 24, 2016 – I just returned from Kenya, wrapping up leading my fourth expedition team. 50 people have come with me to Kenya in just one year, and I knew only six of them prior to starting 100 Humanitarians. How is this possible? We have supported 10 families with starting business boxes that include a cow, a goat, five chickens, three garden boxes or a corrugated tin roof for water conservation, and ten trees. We weren't able to plant because of the severe drought that the Maasai Mara is experiencing right now, so our next step is to drill a well to get water to the cultural center.

We held a big concert with several hundred people in attendance at the cultural center site for the groundbreaking ceremony. A few of the biggest performers in Kenya came and sang, including Lemarti and Stephen Leken, two of my favorites. They stayed for several days after the concert, going on safari with us, and performing at David's housewarming party. We now have plans to visit both of their homes on future expeditions. They are highly supportive of 100 Humanitarians and want to be involved.

The past nine weeks have produced a series of miracles and challenges. Moses came to the U.S. for five weeks as a part of our cultural exchange program. David was supposed to come as well, but his visa was denied. We held fundraisers and humanitarian workshops for kids, and met with organizations like Navanas Institute and Family Search about putting their programs into the cultural center. Two videos were made with Alex Boye!

Then I spent four weeks in Kenya with two back-to-back expeditions. A total of 28 people. We are already getting deposits for the 2017 expeditions. We have set up a business entity in Kenya to run the cultural center and expeditions. More than ever, I feel accepted by the Maasai. I feel supported and loved. I told Moses that I feel like I am just going back and forth between two cultures, trying to understand how I fit in with both of them now.

What I do know is that I am the one called to lead this, but I wouldn't have known how to lead it without all of the times I was in the shadow, content to hang out behind the scenes. All of the experiences that I saw as failures at the time were perfectly designed to prepare me for what I am doing now. It was my training ground, and the lessons will keep coming, because that is part of my human experience.

A few months ago Moses said, "It's time for us to step up as leaders." He is right. It's time. And we haven't seen anything, yet.

About Heidi Totten

Heidi Totten is a wife, mother of two children, runs a business consulting company, and 100 Humanitarians, an organization that focuses on projects in Kenya, Africa. Sometimes she sleeps. She is a best-selling author, speaker, coach, trainer, and loves helping people discover the mentoring, tools, and resources they need to achieve their dreams.

In 2015, Heidi went to Kenya on a humanitarian expedition and her life changed forever. One day she heard a voice say, "Go start a group on Facebook called 100 Humanitarians. I'll let you know why." Since then, life has been a faith walk for her, and every day is a new adventure! As of the end of 2016, she has taken more than 50 people to Kenya to implement for families programs and projects that are her passion and calling in life.

Heidi has helped hundreds of entrepreneurs over the past three years build their online programs, social media strategy, and sales scripts. She also teaches people how to manifest miracles in their lives and business.

She homeschools her two children, or as she puts it, "Facilitates their education and mentors them whenever they will listen." She loves people and loves life!

www.heiditotten.com and www.100humanitarians.com

Chapter Twenty-Five
My Messy Magical Adventure
By Kirsten Tyrrel

Chapter Twenty-Five
My Messy Magical Adventure
By Kirsten Tyrrel

I'm a Disneyland fanatic. It's important to put that out there right away so you know where I'm coming from. I'm in love with the nostalgia, the rides, the smells, the food—all of it. And my favorite rides? The big ones—the free-falling, heart stopping rides that give you a racing heart and serious case of the giggles. One of the best rides in the park is Tower of Terror—it's by far my favorite. You know right away that this is going to be an intense experience, full of free falls and uncertainty, yet you still get on and tightly cling to the handles at your sides, waiting for the thrill that will inevitably come. When I look at my past, my present and my future it is so easily compared to that ride—the scariest most exhilarating experience in the park. I've had a slew of failures and even more successes. The biggest wins have come as a result of the most painful losses.

I feel a little weird admitting this, but when I look back at the life I've lived so far, I don't for an instant feel like a failure. I feel pretty successful knowing the hardships I've overcome, and proud of how I've never let any of my failures keep me down for long. Think of me as a parade character at Disneyland, constantly smiling, even when my costume is itching, when it's 100 degrees outside, or when I feel anything less than magical. I still show up, I smile, I wave, and I keep bringing magic to others. It's a life skill that I think partially came with me at birth, and one that I have nurtured and strengthened, because I see the power in it. Even in the moments when the floor has literally shaken under my feet in anticipation of a stomach dropping plummet to the bottom of an elevator shaft.

On that note, back to that Tower of Terror analogy—I've ridden that ride more times than I can count. And some people might say, "Why? What's the fun in it when you know exactly what will happen and you've done it dozens of times before?" In reply, I ask this question: "Even if you knew how many ups and downs would be associated with your choice, would you still begin the journey?" Don't we all keep showing up to life, even though we know there will be dramatic falls and earth shattering excitements? Sadly, not all of us do. We get trapped in the monotony of life, we stop taking control of our own destiny and just wait out our time here on earth until we can finally rest from all the tiresome, mundane work. As a dreamer and a go-getter, it's really hard to stand by and watch all the people on the sidewalk, looking up at the ride in confusion, wondering why anyone would choose such a fate. I want to grab them by the shoulders and tell them what they are missing out on, how exhilarating it is to take a chance, to let yourself fall and to watch yourself rise!

I'm not a patient person by nature; are any of us really? I am the person who gets fast passes for all the rides at Disneyland because who has time for long lines? Who has the patience to wait their turn when they know the ride is going to be so incredibly fun? I love to find shortcuts to success, and really thought 2016 would be a year of total success. I thought if I believed hard enough, that the failures couldn't touch me, that I would somehow be immune to disappointment. At the beginning of the year my husband and I set a goal to become millionaires by the end of 2016. I believed fully that we would do it— that we deserved it and had everything we needed to make it a reality. We were fearless in sharing that dream with the world. I didn't for a moment think that it wouldn't happen. It was our time. As you can guess, it turns out we were *not* immune to failure. As I share bits and pieces of this story, just remember what I wrote above: through it all, I don't consider myself a failure, but rather a constantly evolving success story.

I'm going to let you in on a not-so-big secret—when you are on the fast track for success, you are also on the fast track for failure. Obstacles you didn't even know existed will pop up at every single turn. Lessons you didn't know you needed to learn will show up in your inbox every day.

In fewer than ten years of marriage, my husband and I have endured many years of unemployment, bad jobs, low income, and perpetual failure. He has been the one taking the jobs or not getting the jobs, but I have been right there alongside him with each disappointment. Those have been long hard years, but they pale in comparison to the tornado this year has been. There have been so many times when I've felt forgotten by God, tossed to the wayside, watching as everyone else's dreams came true but my own. In the last year as we've embarked on an intense entrepreneurial life, there have been far more failures than successes. There have been hundreds of moments when we wanted to give up.

The main thing we have focused on over the past year is e-commerce, specifically making money doing Amazon FBA. The FBA stands for "Fulfilled By Amazon," meaning they take our inventory and fulfill all the orders. It's the most passive income stream we have, but that doesn't mean it didn't take a lot of work to get it where it is now. We struggled with selling our own items and finding the balance between doing that and also creating online education to help others learn this amazing and powerful income opportunity. We also split our attention between a few other businesses, like the Disneyland Adventure guide I wrote, our DoTERRA business, and our photography business. We were desperate to make things work. We did as much as we were able to do, while trying to give ourselves a break and the gift of time and patience as everything clicked into place.

Halfway through the year we were uprooted and had to move out of our little two-bedroom apartment. We had to decide whether to stay in California, or move back to Utah to enjoy a cheaper cost of living and all the benefits of living near family members eager to help. We gave up Disneyland, beach days, and the most amazing set of friends to move back to a place where we had repeatedly failed. Southern Utah is where we had lived before as we struggled to find jobs and make life as awesome as we wanted for half of our married life together. For that reason it wasn't at the top of my list of desirable places to live, but we did it because it felt like the right move.

Post-traumatic stress is real and can arise in a wide array of experiences. Coming back to a place where we failed so many times caused us to feel like failures the moment we moved back. We had said we wanted to stay in California forever, and yet here we were. We had a nice house, sure. But we didn't believe we could succeed within the walls of this home the way we had succeeded in California. I was full of self-doubt, fear, and panic. I had no idea how we'd achieve millionaire status now that our lives had changed course, which was silly because our businesses, my podcast included, could happen literally anywhere in the world. We were totally untethered and that was a good thing. But it felt so wrong, so daunting. It was the first time we felt full responsibility for our future, for making a life we were proud to live. We went back into scarcity mode for a few months, worried only about how we were going to pay the monthly bills, rather than how we would reach a million dollars.

My husband sat me down one day and brought it all into perspective. I had been working so hard to make money and had made being a millionaire my goal, but had completely disregarded the journey necessary to get us there. I had forgotten that to achieve that level of success, I would have to serve many people, to work my way up. It wasn't enough to want to be a millionaire, I had to enjoy the journey that would get me there.

Less than a year ago from the time I am writing this, I started a podcast called Marvelous Moms Club. I had undergone some big transformations in my mindset, my life, and my level of happiness, and I was itching to share that with others. I wanted to bring positivity to the internet, to remind women, mostly mothers, that they were truly extraordinary. I wanted to share everything I had learned in a few short months, to inspire women to dream, to realize it was OK to want more and to work hard to have whatever it is they wanted. I had so many messages, all of them positive, that I knew they needed to be shared. I had learned so much through the audio medium, via audiobooks and podcasts, I knew I had to share the methods myself. So with no prior experience, I started my own podcast.

The first time I sat down at the microphone I just stared. I went cross eyed looking at the microphone, this big intimidating object that was waiting to claim my deepest, most profound thoughts. This device that would somehow project my words to people all over the world. And I froze. I think somewhere in the abyss of my computer files, that episode recording is still sitting, waiting to be shared. It probably never will be. All the insecurities I had ever known came rushing to me in that moment. I wasn't smart enough, interesting enough, or awesome enough to do this. I had nothing to offer. What if nobody listened? Even worse—what if everyone listened and looked at me as a fraud? "Hello Imposter, nice to meet you!"

So I did what any self-respecting, smart, fearless person would do. I called on the powers of my alter ego—"Vera"—to bring magic to the microphone. If she could do it, I was sure I could, too. After all, she was part of me. The part of me that didn't care what anyone else thought, the one who could say what was in her heart and make people feel something. So I shifted into Vera mode, and sat down and just talked. I talked for five minutes straight without taking a breath. And at the end I realized if Vera had this much to say, imagine what I— Kirsten Tyrrel—had to say. I also realized how boring it was for me as a social creature to sit at a microphone alone. I needed to talk to other women, to share their victories and failures with the world. So that's what I did.

I've been a pretty fearless person my whole life when it comes to social situations. Sure, I've been the quiet person in the room when I don't know anyone, and I like to play it safe in high risk moments. I wasn't the most popular girl in school, but I valued friendships and people. My report cards always said something to the tune of "talks too much" or "chatty Kathy." I can look back and honestly say I don't think my parents ever got mad at me for those comments. I think they knew back then that I was a social butterfly and that was nothing to be ashamed of. Fast forward 20 years and, "Guess what, elementary school teachers? It's my J.O.B. to talk to people!"

I'm getting ahead of myself. The point I wanted to make is that people have asked me many times how I got started, how I got people to agree to be on my podcast. And the answer is simple—I asked. It started as: "Could you maybe, I don't know, if you have time, and it wouldn't be too hard, be a guest on my podcast?" to: "I have this amazing podcast and it's important, do you want to be a part of it?" I wasn't completely fearless in the beginning. I was fully expecting people to say no to me. And when not a single person said no, I was pretty blown away. I realized that more than my own intentions, this was something special and important that was beginning, and I could never, ever give up on it. And that was before I even started interviewing and hearing the incredible stories from these women who agreed to talk to me.

I have interviewed more than 100 women, each of them with a different story to share, a life experience from which to learn. I have grown exponentially by hearing their accounts. I began this journey knowing that if I could help even one woman, I would be a success. I had no idea that I would be the one person who would ultimately change the most. I benefited far more than anyone else from each call. I gained dozens of new friends, all of whom I loved deeply and respected for their courage and spirit. They have all made me a more marvelous mom to my own children and have changed my life. These moments have been the part of the ride when the doors open to allow you to see outside the park and people below. The rush of excitement when you have finally made it to the top.

The podcast itself has been a monumental success—something I've been told dozens of times I was born to do—my purpose, the perfect fit for my life. It seems crazy to even admit this, and it will be one of the first times I've done so, but it is also something I consider a big failure. Not because it isn't amazing, powerful and important, but because I haven't yet pushed myself to make it as wonderful as I know it can be. For many people, the very act of interviewing people and putting their voice out there would be the scariest thing they had ever done. But as my track record proves, talking is not something that scares me. Socializing is my love language and I can't get enough social interaction in my life.

In the past year I have neglected to do one of the most important things I set out to do with the podcast—make money. Having grown up in a culture that views money as the root of all evil, my relationship with and understanding of money has been a huge obstacle. I have come very close to fully grasping the potential I have to make serious amounts of money, but have still felt blocked. It's felt morally wrong to get paid for something I also love doing. I haven't treated my podcast like a business, and yet I spend more hours of my week working on it than any other venture. That is something I plan to turn around in the second year of Marvelous Moms Club, because I know that the money is the vehicle by which I can take the messages shared to even more people who need to hear them!

I can look back at my past self from years ago when I was a full time photographer and give myself a lecture about not charging enough, and not valuing my work and believing in my abilities to capture beautiful photos. Hindsight is a magical thing—we always see things for what they are after we're done making our way through the weeds that get in our way. The other day I gave myself a pep talk from the future me. This future version of me understands success in a way that I have not even come close to glimpsing. This future me already has millions of dollars in the bank. She knows that while it took a lot of work to get there, it wasn't an impossible or foolish journey. She knows fully what it means to have faith and to keep putting one foot in front of the other. She also knows that the accomplishment of one dream means the beginning of another. I know that the future me who has achieved all the things I'm working on now will not feel that she's finished or that she's done making an extraordinary life. Because the person I am now does not feel that way, and I've come so far. I can look back, or almost down, because it's been an uphill journey that I've had to dig my feet into every step of the way. I've started to slide down the hill, and doubted there was even an end in sight, but I've kept going. The future Kirsten won't stop going either.

I started out at the beginning of the year with all the zest, hope, and fearlessness I thought existed in this life. Along the way, I have fallen down in a heap of tears in my closet, on the bathroom floor, and anywhere else I found myself unable to catch my breath. Not long ago, in September of 2016, I hit bottom. I was on a trip in Salt Lake City with a friend, for a work convention. I didn't want to be there, not even a little. I had so many businesses in the works and felt powerless being at a convention that focused on only one of those businesses. I knew it wasn't my purpose and wanted to be living my purpose more fully—- Marvelous Moms Club. I had some pretty ugly conversations with my friend about how faithless I felt, how forgotten I felt, and how sick I was of not having the answer I wanted to my prayers.

Something that I've realized only recently is that there will *never* be a way to calculate how much money I've made as a result of my podcast. And here's why. The moment that started this whole journey for my husband and me was the result of a seemingly unanswered prayer. We had prayed for him to get a job with more pay, and which would fulfill him much more. But it didn't happen. And if it had, I wouldn't be sitting here, writing these words I am writing now. I was blind to the things that were happening right in front of me to make it possible for the very near successes to happen. I didn't see at the time, how the people I was meeting and the relationships that were growing would lead to rapid growth in our business.

Life has such amazing little moments that help you comprehend a much bigger plan is happening around you. I got on Periscope one day, where a friend was talking about writing down prayers. I was intrigued by this concept, so I did it. I wrote much more than I thought I even had within me. I asked for things far beyond my reach. I thanked God for the blessings I already had, and with spiritual guidance made a plan for success. Within three days some things happened in our business that made it literally impossible for my plan to happen. I was out of tears and found it downright comical at that point. This has happened so many times before.

But two weeks later, we finally realized the reason for that moment of failure. It catapulted us into what is now the most successful aspect of our business. We are at a point where without question 2017 will be the year we make a million, if not multiple millions of dollars. Marvelous Moms Club has played a *huge* role in making our other dreams a reality. Little turning wheels and parts of a larger machine we didn't even understand are now integral parts of our story. God never forgot us—He just wanted us to trust Him and keep working. He was making little miracles happen along the way, and shaping my heart and soul into something much more than it was when I began.

If I hadn't been doing the podcast, I never would have met the people I know now who have not only helped me to realize the potential of what we were doing, but realize how powerful it can be for so many others. We really niched down and rather than promoting our knowledge to everyone in the whole world, we are now using the power of Amazon to help online influencers and people who have already worked very hard establishing their brand to add another income stream. The people I connected with on a personal level are now clients of ours who are benefiting from our extensive knowledge with Amazon FBA. We have a full service concierge program for a limited number of people, so rather than trying to save the world, we are working with people who understand the power of what we know and are willing to invest in that knowledge to add to their success! I think it was a willingness to serve from the very beginning that brought this opportunity into our lives.

My dream of becoming a millionaire hasn't been reached yet, but I have no doubt that I will keep getting on the ride of life, anticipating the steep drops and unexpected highs with open arms. I look forward to moments of failure because I know that they are shortly accompanied by overwhelming success.

About Kirsten Tyrrel

Kirsten is the mother of three children and host of the *Marvelous Moms Club* podcast during which she shares stories of inspiration from women all over the world to uplift and inspire women to break out of mediocrity and become the mothers they dream of being. Upon realizing she was in a very dark and stressful place with motherhood, she made significant changes that helped her realize how truly amazing a blessing it is to be a mother, and how capable she was of being a marvelous mom as well as a successful woman. She created her podcast to share that message with others who might be feeling alone, exhausted, and incapable of pushing themselves toward a higher level of joy. Now in its second season, *Marvelous Moms Club* has more than 100 episodes with stories from more than 80 women worldwide!

Kirsten and her husband are serial entrepreneurs and manage six different businesses from their home in beautiful southern Utah. When she's not working or interviewing amazing mothers, she loves reading to her kids, taking frequent trips to Disneyland and making every day an adventure!

You can find Kirsten's podcast at www.marvelousmomsclub.com!

www.ingramcontent.com/pod-product-compliance
Lightning Source LLC
Chambersburg PA
CBHW071954040426
42447CB00009B/1332